God's Awesome Plan

Editor: Doug Dohne

Layout: Timothy Lee

Front Cover design: Elena Lee

Cover layout and formatting: Treyton Zimmerman

ISBN:: 978-1-947837-10-2:

DEDICATION

This book is dedicated to all believers and those to come.

Format and Abbreviations

Quotations from the Amplified Study Bible (AMPSB) include abbreviations and several types of brackets, parentheses, and italicized conjunctions to amplify the text.

Parentheses in regular type ( ) supply the definition in context of the preceding name, place or word; not included when read aloud.

Parentheses in **bold** type **( )** indicate a parenthetical phrase that is part of the original language and included when read aloud.

Brackets in regular type [ ] contain justified words, phrases, or brief commentary not fully expressed in the preceding English text, but that are validated by meaning in the original Scripture.

Italicized conjunctions *and, or, nor*—-absent in the original text—were inserted to connect additional English words indicated by the original Hebrew, Aramaic or Greek.

Italicized words are not found in the original language but implied by it.

Brackets { } are used to add my comments or remarks.

Abbreviations for biblical texts appear with the copyright listings.

EDITOR'S NOTE: Language is cast not in stone but into the great cauldron of usage, there to simmer endlessly. Careful readers of this book will notice a pattern of inconsistency re: capitalization of the pronouns he, him and his (as well as the adjectival form of the latter) in references to God and Jesus Christ. While the practice of capping there three words is common (though not universal) in modern usage, it decidedly was not the rule in the early days of the church. In deference to the many fine thinker/writers quoted herein, their words appear-capitalized or lower case- just as written. There is a fourth and equally perplexing H-word in the text. Just about everyone agrees it is The Place to go someday, but we are divided over whether the destination is heaven or Heaven. Dictionary notations that it's "often capitalized" offer less than divine guidance. So you'll find that, too, in both forms, again in salute to our authors. In an effort to preserve the original flavor, we've taken a generally light hand in editing. Thus you might spot the 10 Commandments rather that much preferred Ten Commandments, four hundred in place of 400, etc.

Scripture quotations are noted by abbreviations.

Acknowledgments

My wife is a saint to have put up with the many hours I spent to prepare this book. What started out as a paper turned into a book before I realized all the hours it would take me away from her. Thank you, sweetheart, for your patience, your support, your faith and help in writing this manuscript. I could not have done it without you.

The support received from my family has been phenomenal,. especially my two grandchildren, Timothy, 19, and Elena, 17, each of whom prepared a portion of the book—Timothy the format and Elena the covers.

A thank-you to my son, Jonathan, is appropriate for his guidance and suggestions to improve the text from his knowledge of religious studies.

A great thank-you to Pastors Aaron Davis, Phil Mason and Travis Zimmerman for allowing use of material from their books which were the catalyst leading to my decision to produce this one. Thank you, thank you, thank you!!

A thank-you to the various publishers who are identified in the copyright listings for working with me to provide permission to use material from other books they published.

A thank-you also to Pastor Zimmerman for taking time from his family and busy schedule of ministry to the Faithful Dad program he established, to read the text as a trained pastor and born again Christian. It is easy to see the Holy Spirit at work in his life. Travis is the model of true Christianity.

A big thank-you to the pastors, teachers, friends, encouragers and all those who spread the gospel through the generations who have influenced my life and made the journey with God so meaningful.

Finally, but not the least, a super thank-you to my editor, Doug Dohne, for his patience and coaching to transform a grammar and spelling mess into a readable text. Doug took numerous hours from his retirement to wade through several drafts and indicated corrections with suggestions to improve the work. He deserves a medal, and I thank him x10.

Of course, a thank-you to our Savior for His sacrifice for mankind and to the Holy Spirit for guiding my thoughts and writing. It is not our work that does God's will, but the Holy Spirit that guides and lives in us.

A Personal Note

Why write a book that purports to tell God's plan? Is it my personal hubris? Who am I to think I know God's plan?

To date, no one knows the mind of God or His plan definitively. The Bible, however, gives us a history of God's creation and His people, and the hope that God has a plan for each of us and for His universe. The most difficult challenge, and unknown, is trying to understand and describe the infinite (God's plan) vs. the finite (mankind's understanding of His plan). What appears here is my interpretation of what I believe the Bible records and what has been found to date in the geologic history of the universe, and what other more scholarly individuals believe.

I am not a writer by profession. In fact, my worst subject in high school and college was English, especially spelling, grammar and composition. Most of my career involved writing technical letters and manuals. I thank God every day for spellcheck and a fantastic editor. Hopefully the reader will concentrate on the content of the message and not the quality of writing.

I was educated as a naval officer and civil engineer with geological training. I wrote this book because what I learned in college was different than what many Christians believe about how and when the earth and mankind were formed. I grew up in the Lutheran faith. Because of the significant differences in Science's theory and the literal Christian interpretations of the Bible as to how the earth and mankind were formed by God, I felt compelled to study Scripture and scientific findings.

I am not a theologian. I am a believer, with Jesus Christ my personal savior, a Christian, who has read and studied geologic history and the Bible. I think the outline of a plan that first appears in the Old Testament is developed in the New Testament, then finalized by the apostle John in Revelation.

As a Christian, I believe in God as revealed in the Bible and a God who has a plan. I believe in life beyond death because Jesus (God on earth) died on a cross to atone for our sins and rose from the dead, as witnessed by His apostles and many others. I believe in the word of those who came later and had profound experiences with the risen Christ.

I have read Aaron Davis' book, "Quantum Christianity," and Phil Mason's "Quantum Glory" and have incorporated much of what these two pastors have written as I believe they have a much greater understanding than I. The books "Seeking Islam and Finding Jesus" and "No God But One" by Nabeel Qureshi provided a greater grasp of the differences between Christianity and Islam. Many of his ideas were incorporated in the text.

Author Stephen Miller's "The complete Guide to the Bible" provided a wealth of detailed biblical information to help explain God's plan.

I also used excerpts from Erin and Jill Kelly's book "Kelly Tough," because of their example of courageous living in difficult times as a Christian family. I also incorporated passages from Pastor Travis Zimmerman's book, "A Family Guide to Joy," because it expresses the bliss of living in Christ. All of the thoughts and statements taken from other authors I quoted are backed by Scripture in their works and properly referenced in this book.

Pastor Davis writes, "I wonder if perhaps we find ourselves assuming that we know more information than we are privy to and try to comprehend things about God by placing Him within the box of our current understanding, while alienating ourselves from the benefit of what we could experience because of a failure to simply move forward doing what He told us to do." (As written in Matthew 6:33 AMP) "But seek (aim at and strive after) first of all His kingdom and His righteousness (His way of doing and being right), and then all these things taken together will be given you besides…" 1

This writing is my own understanding of the Scriptures and the history of world events to date. Hopefully the Holy Spirit has led me to prepare this text. I believe the Bible reveals God's battle plan for fighting sin from creation to a time in the future when He will destroy evil and build a new Heaven and a new earth. All that has occurred since creation is part of His plan; and all that will occur later is part of His plan. This book begins with God's creation and ends with the spread of the gospel..

Our Lord and Savior tasked believers to share the Word so that all can be saved. I hope believers will read this text and dig deeper into the Bible and thus strengthen their faith.

For those who have doubts or don't yet believe, may they be drawn to learn more about God's plan and His saving grace through our Lord and Savior Jesus Christ. I believe every person should know that God has a plan to save and include him or her in His kingdom. It starts with believing with your mind in Jesus and the Holy Trinity, then asking the Holy Spirit to enter your life and become your guiding light. God will then be in your heart.

CONTENTS

Part 2

Introduction

God exists. He is alive and has a plan. Some believe but don't know His plan or doubt He has one. While God's plan for each of us appears to be a mystery, He has revealed His overall plan for mankind in the Holy Bible.

Considering the state of the world, many doubt God is alive, or at least feel He is not caring enough about us or is no longer in control of His earthly kingdom. Many believe that we don't need God because we have conquered much of the sciences and the electronic world. We often forget that God set the rules of science when He created the universe. True, we have learned a lot of the rules and theories of the sciences that control earth, but we fail to recognize and give credit to Him who made them and why we are here in the first place.

We also forget there are two competing spirit realms, one of good, the other of evil—and we are part of a battle between them that has been underway for thousands of years. We must recognize there is a spiritual world as well as an earthly one, and both are controlled on earth by God. We also need to understand that Satan is part of the spiritual world and evil exists because of his actions.

My purpose for writing this book is to learn God's plan as revealed in the Bible, and to try to understand how science fits into it. To fully understand the plan, we first have to believe there is a God and that the Bible is the true word of God.

The method chosen to discern the plan has been to review what various biblical scholars and practicing Christians have written based on the Bible. Much of their work is incorporated in this book to substantiate my findings and belief as to what God's word means for us today. Bible commentaries and the books by Pastor Aaron D. Davis, "Quantum Christianity," Pastor Phil Mason, "Quantum Glory," Nabeel Qureshi, "No God But One," Pastor Jeff Kinley, "Wake the Bride," Rabbi Hayin Halevy Donin, "To Be A Jew," Erin with Jill Kelly, "Kelly Tough," Pastor Travis Zimmerman, "A Family Guide to Joy," and Pastor Adam Hamilton, "Creed" and "Half Truths," and many others have greatly influenced this writing.

Many words in this book are not mine, and those quoted are credited in the notes. Much of my research focused on books that I read. There is a rich literature from which to adapt a Christian perspective. I tried to include various interpretations of Scripture. While many of the biblical passages addressed specific groups or individuals long ago—and even though the circumstances and political and socio-economic systems have changed—God's word still applies to us today. I recommend the books referenced here for your reading; all have been very enlightening for me.

Hopefully the work will inform believers unfamiliar with God's plan—and most importantly, cause nonbelievers to embrace Jesus the Christ.

God is alive and in control. His plan has been and is ongoing, and we are part of it. Understand that God created the earth, has made a plan for its future, and is still active in making that plan succeed.

Many biblical scholars believe that Chapter 1 of Genesis was written primarily to establish the origin of God and His ability to create the universe. They recommend that not much else should be determined to be the point of that chapter. While I agree that the primary reason for Chapter 1 of Genesis is to establish God's existence and His awesome power, I also believe that He is telling us that He created life before Adam, as evidenced by scientific findings. While my belief cannot be proved by anything in the Bible, I believe that what I have written *is possibly* what may have happened on earth before Adam was created in Chapter 2. I believe the Bible is the written word of God's relationship with the human-spirits of His creation, and not a history of the earth.

Biblical scholars have long questioned the length of the time periods of each of the *days* of creations in the verses of Genesis 1. At least six theories have suggested the meaning of *days* as used for each verse.[1]

There is the *gap theory* which suggests there was an undetermined but large lapse between the creations in Genesis 1 and Genesis 2.

There is an *indefinite age theory* which supposes that the term covers each of the geologic eras. This theory also holds that the *day* in which man appeared has not yet ended.

A *creation as written theory* suggests the entire creation was accomplished in six 24-hour periods.

The fourth theory is labeled a *revelatory theory,* suggesting God revealed the creation story to Moses, the author of Genesis, in seven literal days.

Another idea called the *literary device theory* suggests the authors simply used the term *day* to organize the verses, meaning the details were true, but not the material organization (framework).

And of course a *myth theory* suggests the passages are symbolic, not historical.

This book supports the gap and indefinite age theories based on geological evidence and the apparent differences in the biblical text of Genesis 1 and 2. While theories are man's attempts to explain God's meanings, the heart of the matter is believing what He revealed of His plan as recorded in the Bible.

Part 1
CHAPTER ONE

"I AM WHO I AM."
Exodus 3:14 AMPSB

God's Existence [1]

Most cultures throughout history have included a belief in the existence of a superior spirit-being who controlled their destiny. These spirit-beings had many different names, but all were considered superhuman and worthy of worship.

Since the beginning of recorded history (Old Testament), Jews and later Christians (New Testament) believed in a spirit-being called "Yahweh, I Am," Jehovah and God, as recorded in the Holy Bible. The Bible is considered the Word of God (by Jewish and Christian believers, and many nonbelievers), given to mankind to explain that a superior spirit (God) exists and the earth and the Heavens He created are His domain. Agnostics believe it impossible to know if God exists, but leave open whether they would worship Him if He does. Atheists say they don't believe there is a God, but their disbelief leaves the alternative possible—they are kidding themselves because God wrote the truth in their hearts.

Rabbi Hayim Halevy Donin in his book "To Be a Jew" writes:

"Hear O Israel, the Lord is our God, the Lord is One. (Deut 6:4) (Old Testament) "These words express the underlying faith of Israel that there exists a one, indivisible God by whose will the universe and all that is in it was created." [2]

Christians believe in a triune God: Father (like the Jews), Son, and Holy Spirit as revealed in the New Testament of the Holy Bible.

Pastor Jeff Kinley in his book "Wake the Bride" summarizes the descriptions of God as holy:

"Holiness is the sum total of all God's attributes. His love is holy.

"His grace is holy. His justice is holy. This fact about God is so distant, so beyond our mortal comprehension that it eventually leads us to only one logical conclusion.

"This God is not like us. He is beyond. Infinite. Great. Separate. Different, Unrivaled, Unequaled, Without any peers.

"And when this realization re-enters the atmosphere of our minds, crashing into our heart-soul, there is only one thing left for us to do.

"Worship." ₃

A Holman Old Testament Commentary says it plainly and succinctly:

"The words 'In the beginning God created the heavens and the earth' show that the existence of God is assumed right from the start. There are no arguments or evidence given since creation itself will declare the truth of the existence of God." (Ps 19:1-4) ₄

The qualities of God the Father are written in the Old and New Testaments of the Bible. After His Son's (Jesus) death, His disciples wrote the New Testament over the next 90 years, filling it with descriptions of the triune God and the loving relationship with followers and the desire to spread the gospel (good news of saving mankind through the sacrifice of His Son) to bring all into His kingdom.

The Beginning

According to the first book (Genesis) of the Old Testament, the spirit-being called God created the earth and the heavens, and everything in them, with a plan for His creation. The plan starts with creation of the earth and mankind. Pastor Kinley explains:

"Biblical revelation begins with a simple, strong and sublime affirmation. Instead of arguing the existence of God, it declares that the very existence of the universe depends on the creative power of God.

"The world we live in was created by God and belongs to Him. His absolute ownership requires our faithful stewardship of all things." ₅

In the beginning, according to the Holy Bible's Book of Isaiah, God spoke, creating the heavens and the earth.

"For Jehovah created the heavens and earth and put everything in place, and He made the world to be lived in, not to be an empty chaos." (45:18 TLB)

Is there a God, and is the Bible the true word of God? The Bible was written throughout the ages by members of the Jewish nation, giving a firsthand account of what that nation experienced in their relationship with a spirit (God) from beyond the bounds of earth.

The Bible records many instances wherein God spoke straight to humans, directing their lives and their ancestors. Without God there is nothing; nothing would exist as God created everything.

God's creation of and interaction with human life has been recorded in the Bible since the existence of the first human-spirit, Adam. The Bible records more than 6,000 years of history of the descendants of Adam, whom God chose as His people. The Bible identifies His people as Jewish and credits them as forming the nation Israel. Thus the Bible is a true historical record of the Jewish people and their interaction with God (a spiritual being).

Pastor Phil Mason in "Quantum Glory" addresses the belief of God as spirit:

> "The traditional biblical idea of 'spirit' is something which is both *supernatural* and outside of space and time ....an omnipotent an omniscient being....a personal Creator; having all knowledge ....with nothing in the heavens and earth that He does not know." 6

The Holman Old Testament Commentary explains disbelief:

> "An atheist once complained to a friend because Christians and Jews had their special holidays. 'But we atheists,' he said, 'have no special day, no recognized national holiday. It's just not fair.' His friend replied, 'Why don't you celebrate April first?'
>
> "No one wants to be known as a fool. But a person is a fool if he doesn't acknowledge God. The Lord has not left us without evidence of His existence. Romans 1:20 explains that 'since the creation of the world God's invisible qualities—his eternal power and divine nature—have been clearly seen, being understood from what has been made, so that men are without excuse.' Creation gives evidence in its order, design and harmony that there is some cause for all this. And mankind must recognize that all creation points to the Creator. All of creation shouts that God exists and that He is a God of power and glory—a being worthy of worship. The fool may talk of 'Mother Nature,' but nature itself is powerless to produce life of any kind without the processes put into place by God himself. To substitute 'Mother Nature' for 'God' is to confuse the creature or creation with the Creator." 7

Geological Evidence

While the Bible is the first written record of man's relationship with a spiritual being, geological evidence shows there was animal life and prehistoric people [before Adam] who also believed in a higher spirit. These people (Homo erectus) would have been created by God on the sixth day of creation, long before Adam.8 These prehistoric people did not leave a written record but provided pictographic evidence that a spiritual being (God) played an important part in their existence. Aztec civilizations in Mexico and native American Indians are two such groups. These prehistoric people could have only existed as part of God's creation in Chapter 1 of Genesis.

Franciscan Priest Richard Rohr writes in his book "The universal Christ":

> "As St. Augustine would courageously put it in his *Retractions*: 'For what is now called the Christian religion existed even among the ancients and was not lacking from the beginning of the human race.'
> "Think about that: Were Neanderthals and Cro-Magnons, Mayans and Babylonians, African and Asian civilizations, and the endless Native peoples on all continents and isolated islands for millennia just throwaways for dress rehearsals for "us"?
> "Is God really that ineffective, boring and stingy? Does the Almighty One operate from a scarcity model of love and forgiveness? Did the Divinity need to wait for Ethnic Orthodox, Roman Catholics, European Protestants and American Evangelicals to appear before the divine love affair could begin? You might wonder how, exactly, primitive peoples and pre-Christian civilizations could've had access to God.
> I believe it was through the universal and normal transformative journeys of *great love and great suffering*, which all individuals have undergone from the beginning of the human race." 9

Believers

According to Adherents, an independent, nonreligious affiliated organization that monitors the number and size of the world's religions:

> "There are some 4,300 religions of the world. There are 19 of the world's religions with over a million believers, with the top three, Christianity, Islam and unaffiliated each having over 1 billion believers. Nearly 75 percent of the world's population practices one of the

five most influential religions: Buddhism, Christianity, Hinduism, Islam and Judaism. Christianity and Islam are the two religions most widely spread across the world. These two religions together cover the religious affiliation of more than half of the world's population. Christianity alone has over 2 billion believers." [10]

In his book, "Creed: What Christians Believe and Why," Pastor Adam Hamilton writes:

"Many physicists accept and occasionally use the term 'God' as shorthand for describing the mysterious, invisible forces that govern the universe, but Christianity doesn't stop there. Christians also see God as a being, an entity with all the attributes of personhood: intelligence, emotion, reason, logic and will. God knows, feels, loves, thinks, wills, acts and creates. "Christians (and other theists) believe in God. But is there any evidence that God exists? Is there good reason to believe? Throughout most of human history, the argument for God's existence, the case for God, started with the fact that the universe exists and that we exist. It seems unthinkable to most human beings that the beauty and majesty of creation should either (a) have always existed without a beginning or (b) have spontaneously generated out of nothing with no One to create it." [11]

Obviously you don't have to take my word there is a God. Besides millions of clergy, theologians, biblical scholars and common believers there are many well-known figures who believe in God.

In "Quantum Christianity," author/Pastor Aaron D. Davis identifies at least 16 famous scientists who believe in God including William D. Phillips, winner of the 1997 Nobel Prize in Physics for development of methods to cool and trap atoms with laser light, who confesses:

"I believe in God. In fact I believe in a personal God who acts in and interacts with the creation. I believe that the observation about the orderliness of the physical universe, and the apparently exceptional fine-tuning of the conditions of the universe for the development of life, suggests that an intelligent creator is responsible. I believe an ordinary scientist and an ordinary Christian seems perfectly natural to me. It is also perfectly natural for the many scientists I know who are also people of deep religious faith. " 12

Wernher Von Braun (1912-77), German-American rocket scientist, professed:

"I find it as difficult to understand a scientist who does not acknowledge the presence of a superior rationality behind the existence of the universe as it is to comprehend a theologian who would deny the advances of science." 13

The apostle Paul wrote in Romans that we have no excuse (but to believe) because of the evidence all around us:

"For ever since the world was created, people have seen the earth and sky. Through everything God made, they can clearly see His invisible qualities—His eternal power and divine nature... They know the truth about God because He has made it obvious to them." (1:19, 20)

Stephen M. Miller in his book "The Complete Guide to the Bible," referring to Paul's writings, states:

"Even if creation began with a Big Bang, Paul might argue today, someone had to load the universe and pull the trigger. In a physical universe, it's impossible for something to come from nothing. So there's more than a physical dimension at work in creating and sustaining the universe." 14

Paul's Gospel says that even gentiles who were never taught religious laws such as the Ten Commandments

"show that they know His law when they instinctively obey it, even without having heard it. They demonstrated that God's law is written in their hearts, for their own conscience and thoughts either accuse them or tell them they are doing right." (Romans 2:14 15

NIV)

In "Quantum Glory," Pastor Mason includes a statement from Jean Staune, a French professor of philosophy who wrote: "I firmly believe in a personal God." In his essay, "On the Edge of Physics," he explained:

> "The central idea of all monotheistic religions is that the world in which we live—the world of time, space, energy and matter—cannot be its own cause because it has been created by a transcendent principle: God. The science of the 19th century seemed very close to demonstrating that the world caused itself. Science not only failed in this demonstration, however; it has *actually demonstrated the opposite*. Science has suggested through quantum physics that it alone cannot provide a complete picture of reality. It has provided the basis for a credible way to understand the existence of God, because the world no longer limits itself to our level of reality. Quantum physics does not prove the existence of God. It nonetheless takes us through a giant step from a scientific materialism that ruled out the existence of God, to a position where, on the scientific basis, we can start to understand the concept of God's existence. A belief in materialism is still possible under quantum physics, of course, but only if it is transformed into a kind of 'science fiction' materialism, somehow able to integrate the 'de-materialization for matter.' New experiments show that matter itself does not have strictly material reality." [15]

George Washington, Abraham Lincoln, Frederick Douglass, Fyodor Dostoyevsky, Joseph Lister, Louis Pasteur and Charles Dickens were Christians.[16]

Many other famous individuals believe in God, too numerous to list here. There are many additional books more compelling than this one to prove the existence of God. Read Lee Strobels' book, "The Case for God," or works by C.S. Lewis to learn more about God's existence. But, for the time being, if you don't believe or are unsure, or even if you are sure, read on. Everyone should know God's plan.

CHAPTER TWO

"By the word of the Lord were the heavens made, and all their host by
the breath of His mouth."
Psalm 33:6 AMP

God and His Word

The Bible is viewed [understood] by believers as the true word of God given by Him to humans. The Bible contains 39 books in the Old Testament and 27 in the New Testament. Biblical scholars credit Moses as the author of the first five books of the Old Testament (the Hebrew Torah). 1 In the sixth book of the Old Testament, God chose Joshua to lead the Jewish people after the death of Moses, and told him the Torah was the "Book of the Law" and was to be enforced in all the lands he conquered. The Torah has remained the law of the Jewish people's faith since biblical time. Portions of the Torah form the basis for orderly societies worldwide.

Hebrews and Christians agree (AMPSB, pg 1) that Moses, with God's guidance, must have written the book of Genesis using 300-year-old ancient records. Those records have been entitled the Book of Generations of the Jewish People from Adam to Jacob, a period exceeding 2,000 years, together giving the framework for the book of Genesis.1 (Note, Moses was writing only the history of Adam and his bloodline, not necessarily of mankind as created on the sixth day.)

Stephen Miller writes in his short history of how and when the Old Testament was recorded:

> "Many of the oldest and most memorable stories—like those about Moses and Abraham—were passed along by word of mouth from one generation to the next. At least that's what Bible experts guess. The Hebrews didn't develop an alphabet until later, when they settled in Israel after Moses led them out of Egypt.
>
> "In King David's day, about a thousand years before Jesus, Jewish writers and editors started compiling the stories. They did it to preserve a record of their people and the new nation they started.
>
> "In time, Jews began to cherish certain books—treating them as sacred. First, the laws and stories of Moses in the first five books of the Bible. Then the books of the prophets. And finally the rest of the books in the Old Testament—a diverse assortment of writings such as Psalms, Proverbs and Job.

23

"It's unclear when the Jews settled on the 39 books we now have. But many guess that Jewish leaders finalized their Bible shortly after Romans destroyed the last Jewish temple in A.D. 70." [2]

God Reveals His Plan

Why, according to Jewish history, did God guide Moses to record the Torah approximately 4,000 years ago? Why was it necessary for God to have Moses write the Bible? Through these writings, God provided a plan and rules for mankind to live in an orderly society by giving Moses the early history of His creation and the ancestral bloodline from Adam, as well as the Ten Commandments.

The Bible provides the means by which God can communicate His plan for salvation from sin. Through the Bible, mankind could learn of God's rules for guiding life in His Kingdom on earth, and life in a hereafter. As biblical scholars studied the Bible over the centuries they came to realize that it reveals God's plan for His creation and for mankind to live eternally in a parallel universe after death, made possible by the death and Resurrection of His Son Jesus Christ. The facts that the universe exists, and earth was created, indicate that a spiritual realm must exist. The Bible states that the spiritual being responsible for earth's creation is called God.

Pastor Mason explains in his book "Quantum Glory":

"The Bible is a revelation of God to humanity and it takes the form of prophetic utterances through God-inspired prophets who heard the voice of the Lord and recorded what they heard. There is an underlying presupposition that the entire Bible is founded upon. (The Premise) This presupposition is that there is a personal God who seeks to communicate His heart and mind to humanity through His word." [3]

When our life's experiences don't match what the Bible tells us, we tend not to believe that the Bible is God's truth, or that God exists at all. Essentially, though, God is the reason for life. Anyone who reads the Bible thoughtfully and looks at God's creation will come to understand there is a God and know that He is alive and has a plan for mankind.

Biblical Prophecies

The Bible is the only book that has been available for every generation since it was first written during a period from 4,000 to

2,000 years ago. It and it alone contains prophecies made thousands of years before being fulfilled. Only God could have known and given those prophecies to the writers.

Isn't the Bible just a story about the Jews and Christianity? Doesn't science explain many of the events attributed to God? How do we know it is God's word? After all, human beings wrote the Bible.

William H. Bragg (1862-1942), British physicist, chemist and mathematician, awarded the Nobel Prize in 1915, wrote:

> "From religion comes a man's purpose; from science, his power to achieve it. Sometimes people ask if religion and science are not opposed to one another. They are: in the sense that the thumb and fingers of my hand are opposed to one another. It is an opposition by means of which anything can be grasped." [4]

Science began only *after* God created the universe. Lacking understanding of God, mankind has questioned His existence throughout history and turned to science for answers. In "Quantum Christianity" Pastor Davis writes:

> "God has been on trial since day one for His participation, or lack thereof, in their (man's) pain." [5]

The Bible was written to record God's existence and His relationship with the Jewish people and the State of Israel. The Old Testament is a history of the Jewish nation, God's chosen people.

The New Testament details the existence of God's Son, Jesus, and His relationship with the Son's generation and all future generations until the end of time. It also records God's interaction with His creation through His Word. Since all humans are part of His creation, He is showing us how we should live to be part of that creation. It is telling us God's plan from the beginning to the end of time.

Sir Nevill Mott, recipient of the 1997 Nobel Prize in Physics for his research on the magnetic and electrical properties of non-crystalline semiconductors, writes:

> "I believe in God, who can respond to prayers, to whom
> we can give trust and without whom life on earth would
> be without meaning (a tale told by an idiot). I believe that
> God has revealed Himself to us in many ways and through
> many men and women, and that for us here in the West
> the clearest revelation is through Jesus and those that have
> followed Him." [6]

The Bible reveals God's plan for His creation as recorded by the biblical writers and as interpreted for generations. Satan's introduction of sin caused God to provide His plan in written form so that generation after generation would have a guide to resist evil. The very existence of the Bible, and the God who directed its writing, reveals Him as a spirit-being from another realm. All of God's predictions have come true. That fact alone proves the Word of God is truth and the Word is from Him. 7

Pastor J. Vincent Nordgren, in "The Heart of the Bible," writes that Christians cherish the Bible because it is the only book that describes how God wants us to live and worship Him. The Bible shows us God's plan and the way to eternal life. 8

In a PBS documentary entitled, "Fires of Faith: The Coming Forth of the King James Bible," one of the narrators, Professor Richard Mouw, president of the Fuller Theological Seminary, considered the Bible as "God's manufacturer's instructions," somewhat like those included with the purchase of a new car (Operators Instruction Manual; the OIM) 9 A perfect analogy!

Many don't read the OIM (instructions) for their car unless they have a problem they can't solve. Many probably skim through the contents just in case they need to find something in a hurry. Others may read them and use them when there is a problem.

But God's OIM includes instructions to read and follow to avoid problems and to help others. I would add that not only does the Bible contain the manufacturer's instructions or OIM, but it also comes with a lifetime warranty. If the instructions are followed as the maker planned, when the current model stops running, you can receive a new improved one that works forever.

CHAPTER THREE

"God is spirit [the source of life, yet invisible to mankind], and those who worship Him must worship in spirit and truth (reality)."
John 4:24 AMP

The Spiritual Realm

If God exists, where was He before the earth was formed? God is spirit, unconfined by the forces of this universe. Since He created the universe and made the laws that control and govern the forces of the universe, God can be anywhere and everywhere. Pastor Davis includes an explanation by Dr. Dave Martin in "Quantum Christianity":

> "God is the Creator of both the physical world and the spiritual world. He is the architect of both the visible world and the invisible world. So the same principles apply in both domains, because the same mastermind designed both. So Jesus was the world's greatest at helping people visualize the tangible in order to grasp the certainty of the intangible. He was the world's greatest at equipping people to believe." [1]

Pastor Mason in "Quantum Glory" writes:

> "His (God's) knowledge is absolute and unlimited. That is because He is an omnipresent being who sees everything and who subsequently knows everything." [2]

Mason cites numerous biblical passages leading readers to conclude there is more than one world.

> "Jesus said: 'My kingdom is not of this world!' (John 18:36 NIV) The writer to the Hebrews indicates that Christ is the one through whom God 'made **the worlds.**' (Hebrew 1:2) Note that the term 'worlds' is plural, not singular. We see this same term in a later chapter of Hebrews. By faith we understand that **the worlds** {during the successive ages} were framed {fashioned, put in order, and equipped for their intended purpose} by the word

of God so that what we see was not made out of things which are visible." {added from AMPSB for understanding}

Mason concludes:

"There are two worlds revealed in the Bible. ... There is this material world and there is another world that is above and beyond this physical universe because it exists in another spiritual dimension." [3]

Two Realms

Thus Heaven is where God is, not necessarily a physical place. The Bible refers to the existence of angels (spiritual beings) created by God. The Bible makes more than 76 references to angels interacting with mankind or other spiritual beings (Satan). There are also 18 references citing the angel of the Lord appearing to the prophets and the Israelites to influence their actions, as well as 11 instances where God's Son identifies Himself as an angel of the Lord. [4]

These spiritual beings work for God and assist in carrying out His plans. Pastor Davis believes many Christians see God and angels "as distant and removed from us, where Jews see God as being with them everywhere all the time." [5]

Twelve times during Jesus' earthly life angels appeared to tell mankind of His importance.. Even Lucifer (Satan), an evil angel, appeared to Jesus.

We can't see these spiritual beings, nor can we prove they exist other than believing the Bible and knowing evil exists. However, we do know the truth of the Bible, and therefore, enough to grasp that the universe is larger than we can fathom, so that when earth was formed billions of years ago, God and the angels were in a spiritual realm and thus could be anywhere and everywhere in or out of the universe. [6]

Mankind has tried throughout the ages to determine just how God formed the heavens and the earth. Quantum physicists have discovered many of the laws that govern the way the earth was formed, and are certain there is at least one parallel universe from which the spirit realm exists. The physicists believe the Bible reveals that two worlds exist.

As Pastor Mason noted in both passages of John and Hebrews above, the writers make reference to the term *worlds* plural, indicating at least two worlds exist. We see this same term later in Hebrews.

"By faith we understand that *the worlds* were framed by the word of God, so that the things which are seen were not made of things which are visible." (11:3)

Pastor Mason expands:

"Jesus frequently talked about this world and the world above. He said to those who opposed Him, 'You are from beneath: I am from above. You are of this world; I am not of this world.' (John 8:23) On another occasion He said, 'I came forth from the Father and have come into the world. Again, I leave the world and go to the Father.' (John 16: 28) Clearly Jesus revealed there are two worlds. There is this material world and there is another world that is above and beyond this physical universe because it exists in another spiritual dimension. [7]

"Both God and His eternal kingdom exist in a dimension outside of space and time. God is an infinitely transcendent Being! His kingdom exists in an eternal, extra-dimensional realm that is not subject in any way to the constraints and limitations of either space or time. God inhabits eternity. He created time because He is the Alpha and the Omega, the Beginning and the End! He is the 'Eternal God,' the great 'I AM,' and His kingdom is described as an 'Eternal Kingdom.' "[8]

For a spiritual-God to exist and create a physical realm (earth), there must be a spiritual realm, a different dimension that coexists with earth. Further, if spiritual beings (us) live the human experience, then it may be reasonable to believe there is a spiritual realm (heaven) into which the spirit can return. Jesus, the Christ, is proof a spiritual world exists.

"He (Jesus) is the exact living image [the essential manifestation] of the unseen God [the visible representation of the invisible], the firstborn [the preeminent one, the sovereign, and the originator] of all creation. For by Him all things were created in heaven and on earth, [things] visible and invisible, whether thrones or dominions or rulers or authorities; all things were created and exist through Him [that is, by His activity] and for Him."
(Colossians 1:15-16 AMPSB)

After Jesus died, then rose, He appeared to Peter, the apostles, and more that 500 followers. Father Rohr explains:

"The risen Christ transcended doors, walls, spaces, ethnicities, religions, water, air and times, eating food and sometimes even bifurcating, but always interacting with matter. While all of these accounts ascribe a kind of physical presence to Christ, it always seems to be a different kind of embodiment [a spiritual one]." [9]

29

The risen Christ could only do those things as a spirit, not as some altered human.

Need for God

Why do we care there is a spiritual world, and why do we need a God? God is the source of all that exists on earth, and He provides the very forces (laws of nature) so that mankind can exist. God gave the world light on the first day of creation, and He gave Christ as the light to the people of the world. 10

With His light, we can see the wonders of the universe and know that a superior being [Christ] created it. Father Rohr believes that the light [Christ] was not a one-time incarnation but:

> "an ongoing, progressive movement continuing in the ever-unfolding creation. It has been working throughout the entire arc of time, and will continue. This is expressed in the common phrase the 'Second Coming of Christ,' which was unfortunately read as a threat ('Wait till your Dad gets home!'), whereas it should more accurately be spoken of as the 'Forever Coming of Christ,' which is anything but a threat. In fact, '*it is the ongoing promise of eternal resurrection.*' Christ is the light that allows people to see things in their fullness. The precise and intended effect of such a light is to see Christ everywhere else. In fact, that is my only definition of a true Christian: *A mature Christian sees Christ in everything and everyone else.*" 11

Furthermore, as His creation, we have a spiritual component in our makeup that will enable us to enjoy life eternal through belief in God. Without God, the earth would not have been formed, the laws of physics that keep the earth in orbit and things on the earth would not exist, mankind could not live in harmony with one another and manage life under the forces that control the universe. God gave us the Bible as a plan and a guide to live by. Throughout the Bible God has instructed mankind to ask and seek answers to understand His creation.

The Letter of James states:

> "If any of you lacks wisdom, he should ask God, who gives generously to all and without finding fault, and it will be given to him." (1:5 NIV)

Revelation states that all will be judged in the end.12 Hopefully, Father Rohr is correct that Christ gave us all a saving grace—if we accept it.

CHAPTER FOUR

"For I know the plans and thoughts that I have for you," says the Lord, "plans for peace and well-being and not for disaster to give you a future and hope."
Jeremiah 29:11 AMPSB

A Plan and God's Prophecies

From the beginning (Genesis), God spoke to Adam about what would happen to his life, [1] and later He spoke to Noah, Abraham, Moses, the prophets and many others, providing to them predictions of the future (prophecies) to prepare them for things to come.

The prophecies that God revealed to them all came true, some almost immediately and others hundreds of years later. God told Noah there would be a flood covering the whole world. [2] Some biblical scholars believe the flood occurred 120 years later to give Noah time to build the ark. Genesis 5:32 establishes Noah as 500 years old when his sons were born, and Genesis 7:6 records the flood starting when Noah was 600, leading to the conclusion it took almost 100 years to construct the ark.

God predicted Abraham's descendants would become as numerous as the dust of the earth. [3] And they did.

God told Isaiah, and later Micah [4] that His Son would be born of a virgin and his name would be Immanuel (God with us) more than 725 years before Jesus' birth. [5]

God told Jeremiah that the Jewish exile in Babylon would end in 70 years according to His plans.

> "For I know the plans and thoughts that I have for you," says the Lord, "plans for peace and will-being not for disaster to give you a future and hope." [6]

God also told Jeremiah more than 600 years before it would occur that He would make a new covenant with Israel through the birth of His Son. [7]

God's servant Daniel had a vision so bewildering that the angel Gabriel had to interpret. The vision contained the prophecy that the nations of Babylon, the Medo-Persian Empire, the Greek and the Roman empires would one day rule the land of Israel. The vision further prophesied the birth of the Messiah, Jesus. [8]

All these prophecies came true.

In Daniel 11:40, there is a prophecy as yet unfulfilled. The prediction is that a final form of the Roman Empire will emerge in the end times. Since the apostle John (writer of Revelation, including the end times) did not know of many other empires that would rise before the end times, the Roman Empire may symbolize some future empire that will arise.

Throughout the rest of the Old Testament each book contains prophecies describing God's plan for the future.

Prophecies and Us

For us today, the apostle John recorded God's word in Revelation (last book of the Bible) almost 2,000 years ago. John's vision included a prophecy predicting what will come in the end times. Life Application Bible Commentary explains:

> "Revelation is a book of *prophecy* that is both prediction (foretelling events) and proclamation (preaching about who God is and what He will do). Prophecy is more than telling the future. Behind the predictions are important principles about God's character and promises."9

Pastor Kinley in his book, "Wake the Bride," writes:

> "A few hundred years ago, virtually no one could have envisioned the rebirth of Israel and the return of Jews worldwide to the land God previously gave them. But this happened in 1948, giving us fresh insight into Scriptures that for centuries were mysterious in their potential fulfillment. The existence and rebirth of Israel is considered an undeniable affirmation of biblical prophecy." 10

Nave's Topical Bible and others list more than 100 biblical passages that predict events concerning the Messiah and the fulfillment of God's prophecies. 11 Kinley continues:

> "It's been calculated that 28 percent of Scripture was prophecy at the time it was written. That's over a fourth of the Bible. With over 1,800 prophecies in Scripture taking up over 8,300 verses, including 1,239 prophecies in the Old Testament and 578 in the New Testament, that's a lot of verses! Only four of the 66 books of the Bible. are without prophecy—Ruth, the Song of Solomon, Philemon and 3 John. Even the shortest book of the Bible mentions prophecy. (2 John) From the first book (Genesis) to the last (Revelation), Scripture's pages are filled with truth about

the future. God even chose to complete His Word to humanity with an entire book devoted to prophecy. (Revelation)

"Apparently revealing truth about future events is something God likes to do. He actually wants His people to know what's going to happen in the days ahead and what's in store for us and our world." [12]

God wants us to be ready when His prophecies impact us. God's prophecies all (except the one for us in Revelation) have come true, showing us His plan as laid out in the Bible. Kinley puts it this way:

"Prophecy tells us what's going to happen before it happens. Some people in God's long story have been privileged to see prophecy fulfilled in their lifetime, while others have had to believe by faith that certain things would one day come to pass. Others have even suffered for those beliefs, considered fools for believing what many labeled as ridiculous fantasies.

"These prophecies also give us great comfort and peace in uncertain times. Knowing that God Himself is orchestrating history brings calm in the midst of a gathering global storm.

"Perhaps best of all, prophecy also inspires us toward a different kind of life." [13]

The prophecies form the backbone of God's plan for mankind. Why does God need a plan? Pastor Davis answers that with a quotation in his book from the winner of the 1927 Nobel Prize in Physics, Arthur Compton:

"For myself, faith begins with a realization that a supreme intelligence brought the universe into being and created man. It is not difficult for me to have this faith, for it is incontrovertible that where there is a plan there is intelligence—an orderly, unfolding universe testifies to the truth of the most majestic statement ever uttered—'In the beginning God.'" [14]

If God is omniscient, didn't He know that His creation was not going to become as He envisioned? Pastor Mason observes:

"The biblical revelation of the 'omniscience' of God would incline us to believe that nothing is hidden from the observation of God, whether macroscopic or microscopic or even sub-atomic. The Bible teaches that 'Nothing in all creation is hidden from God's sight. Everything is uncovered and laid bare before the eyes of Him to whom we must give account.' " (Hebrews 4:13 NIV)

"If God is indeed omniscient, then we could also safely assume that God knows the entire number of atoms in the entire universe. That is a staggering thought to meditate upon, but this seems to be the implication of the words of logical Jesus who said that 'The very hairs of your head are all numbered.' (Mathew 10:30) The psalmist declared that God 'counts the number of the stars: He calls them all by name. Great is our Lord, and mighty in power; His understanding is infinite.' "(Psalm 147:4-5) 15

Think about that. God who created and named the stars also knows your name and the very hairs on your head. Awesome!

A Plan of Salvation

As an omnipotent, omnipresent and omniscient God, He undoubtedly knew His universe would be hijacked by Satan. There is nothing in Heaven and earth that God does not know. There were problems in Heaven with the fallen angels, especially Satan, before Adam was created. It must have been heartbreaking for God to know that His creation would be attacked by Satan, but His desire to create this universe must have been very important to Him.

Although Satan stole God's intended plan (at the Garden of Eden) for man to establish His kingdom on earth, God had a backup plan to include mankind in His spiritual kingdom.

Pastor Davis believes God's plan was always redemption:

"Because of God's love for mankind (His creation) and His desire to have a relationship with we who were created in His image and likeness, God integrated a sin-contingency plan into our existence that would restore our relationship and authority back to a place where we could directly communicate with Him and live in the authority that He created for us to live in, free from the dominion of sin in our lives. In essence, giving us the opportunity to choose for ourselves what kingdom we would want to participate in establishing and ultimately be ruled by and freeing us from the default bondage that would otherwise be our reality. According to the Bible, this sin-contingency plan for redeeming man was established in the very beginning of Creation. Revelation 3:18 refers to Jesus as 'the lamb (the intended sacrifice for sin) slain from the foundation of the world.' 16

:

"The great thing about God is that if we ask Him for clarity, He will give us insight {about what we are to do with our life}. So often we quit asking and just assume everything is on track because we compare ourselves to a standard of other people, rather than His standard for us individually. The problem with that is we all have a different purpose in the body of Christ, and God may have a different plan for us than the guy we are comparing ourselves to. As a result there may be something He would reveal to us that is much different from what He would reveal to someone else, if we just sought direction from Him." [17]

Why God Tells Us of His Plan

Why a plan and why has God been telling mankind about it? Pastor Kinley believes God has been doing that:

"so we can have *hope* in the midst of uncertain times"... gives us "*faith* and assurance in God Himself"... to "instill us with confidence in God's Word"... and so we can prepare ourselves (for what is to come)." [18]

Believers know that mankind is both human and spiritual as God created them; that He loves and sustains His creation according to Scripture. [19] He wants us to survive life's trials and eventually the judgment that all will face in the next (eternal) life.

The Bible tells us that is what He wants, and He has a plan, as contained in Revelation, to save His creation. [20]

Kinley explains:

"The entire book of Revelation is a vision given *by* Jesus Christ to John *through* an angel for the church. Most of Revelation's chapters are prophetic, or simply 'history written in advance.' " [21]

The apostle John wrote what was revealed in a vision, telling what God has planned for the future, our future. God's plan was revealed to the prophet Jeremiah when the Israelites were in captivity in Babylon. God revealed a plan for the end of captivity, which came true.

God's plan for the Israelites after He allowed them to be captured and taken into slavery shows His forgiveness and control over what happens on earth. As God told Jeremiah that the Israelites were like "clay in a potter's hand, so you are in My hands," [22] and we, like the Israelites, are in His hands.

The prophet Zechariah predicts events involving Jesus, and beyond, even to the end times. [23]

God has control over our lives. But unlike the Israelites, Jesus intercedes for us so that we can follow God's plan. Jesus knew God's plan and carried it out—even to a horrible death on a cross—to pay the debt for our sins sand make us acceptable for an eternal life. God gave us a plan for our salvation through the life, death and resurrection of His Son.

Knowing that, we should repent, thank Jesus, and follow Him into God's kingdom.

CHAPTER FIVE

"This is the history of [the origin of] the heavens and of the earth when they were created, in the day [that is, days of creation] that the Lord God made the earth and the heavens—it was very good."
Genesis 2:4 AMPSB

God's Creation

Outside of God's spiritual realm there was nothing but dark space, absent of anything that humans would know or could understand. Nothing! From that God created, possibly with a Big Bang (according to scientists) a formless and void earth covered by a deep primeval ocean from matter He made.

Then God spoke and said, "Let there be light." (Genesis 1:1-3) Awesome! From nothing to a world, a whole universe, a new kingdom as we humans know it.

Why create a kingdom anywhere outside of God's spiritual world? The Bible tells us He wanted to produce a universe for His glory.

"O Lord, our Lord, how excellent (majestic and glorious) is Your name in all the earth! You have set Your glory on (or above) the heavens. (Psalm 8:1 AMP)

"The heavens declare the glory of God, and the firmament shows and proclaims His Handiwork." (Psalm 19:1 AMP)

"This is what the Lord says, 'Heaven is My throne and earth is My footstool. Where, then is a house that you could build for Me? And where will My resting place be?' " (Isaiah 66:1 AMP)

" 'For all these My hand has made. So all these things came into being [by and for Me],' declares the Lord. "
(Isaiah 66:2 AMPSB)

Paul's Letter to the Romans states:

"For ever since the creation of the world His invisible nature and attributes, that is, His eternal power and divinity, have been made intelligible and clearly discernible in and through the things that have been made (His handiworks). So [men] are without excuse [altogether without any defense or justification]." (Romans

1:20 AMP)

Proverbs proclaims:

> "The eyes of the Lord are in every place, keeping watch on the evil and good." (15:3 AMP)

And Paul's Letter to the Hebrews states:

> "By faith we understand that the entire universe was formed at God's command, that what we now see did not come from anything that can be seen." (11:3 NIV)

These verses and others tell of God's awesome creation, producing from nothing a vast universe.

Quantum Physics and God's Creation

Quantum physicists support the Hebrew 11:3 passage as they have found evidence of small invisible particles that make up all things created on the earth.

When did the beginning occur and how was the creating done? Why this planet?

In Genesis Chapter 1 God created (by forming from nothing) the heavens and the earth. He said, "Let there be light," separated the light from the darkness (invisible), placed water on the earth, and made the conditions (visible) of the creation so that human life in His image could build His kingdom here.

We don't know why God chose this planet, and we don't know of any other He selected, but He told us in Genesis 1 that it was good and He was happy with His creation.

It was God's choice to create the earth to build an earthly kingdom and set the desire for eternity in the human heart (yours and mine).

> "He has made everything beautiful and appropriate in its time. He has also planted eternity [a sense of divine purpose] in the human heart [a mysterious longing which nothing under the sun can satisfy, except God]—yet man cannot find out (comprehend, grasp) what God has done (His overall plan) from the beginning to the end." (Ecclesiastes 3:11 AMPSB) {Hopefully we know more now than when Ecclesiastes was written.}

One of our biggest challenges is trying to understand and describe the infinite (God's world) and the finite (mankind's) in human terms. The science of quantum physics is being developed to try to explain how God created the visible world from the invisible pieces of atoms, protons and smaller particles. One of the major findings is that everything created follows a mathematical process.

In "Quantum Glory," Pastor Mason explains how "one specific mathematical pattern"—called the Divine proportion, the Golden Section, the Golden Mean or the Golden Ratio—detected from quantum theory, has been used by God to create everything in the universe. The Golden Ratio (Mean or Divine Proportion) is expressed as the Greek letter "fye," with a numerical value of 1.6180339. 1

Mason states it probably is not surprising that such a discovery has been made through quantum physics in the atomic age. Creation by an omniscient, omnipresent and omnipotent Divine Being with the mathematical precision used to make the universe provides a means to comprehend His intelligent design. We can only marvel at the awesomeness of His creation and let it move us to worship His power and omnipotence.

The Bible tells us of God's creation, but discovery of the Divine Ratio reveals the magnitude and exactness He used to accomplish it, possibly in His mind before the actual event. 2

Mason explains that God formed the quantum particles from which He created the material world as written in the book of Colossians 1:16:

> "For by Him all things were created that are in heaven and that are on earth, *visible and invisible*, whether thrones or dominions or principalities or powers." 3

Mason further states that not only did God create the heavens and earth but He also monitors it:

> " 'The Lord *watches over* the foreigner and *sustains* the fatherless and the widow.' (Psalm 1:46:9 NIV) In the same way God looks upon all that He has made and He sustains His entire creation with His watchful gaze and His powerful word." (as written in Hebrews 1:3 NLT) 4

Clearly we do not understand all that God has done to create the universe. But we do know that He made it as well as all the particles we use to sustain and enhance our lives. In Revelation the apostle John wrote:

> "Worthy are You, our Lord and God, to receive the glory and honor and dominion, for You created all things; by Your will they were (brought into being) and were created." (4:11 AMP)

God's Explanation

In the Book of Job, God questions Job's understanding of his knowledge of the earth, and then describes all the things He did to make the universe that is beyond Job's (and our) understanding and why He made it.

God asks Job whom he thought he was questioning: His wisdom; where he was when He made the universe, and did he know the dimensions He used to make it, could he direct the movement of the stars, and did he know the laws of the universe? And could he regulate the earth? (Job 38:1-7, 31, 33, 42 AMP)

While Job could not answer these questions, he did believe because he answered God telling Him he knows God could do all those things beyond his knowledge and understanding. Job repented and regained favor with God.

Psalm 8 reveals God's idea for creating the kingdom on earth. The psalmist lists all the things God made, drove the enemies away, established a judgment seat to evaluate the world in righteousness to show all we are but men and He alone is God, yet has made man "a little lower than God" and placed him on earth to have dominion over the kingdom.

Pastor Davis' book includes a quotation from Dr. Dave Martin, who writes that God is the architect of the visible and invisible realms and that the same principles apply in both. [5] I think God intended earth to be a kingdom like the invisible spirit kingdom and, although Satan destroyed that plan, Revelation confirms there will be a "New Kingdom" in the end times.

Mason substantiates God's continuing presence with His creation from the beginning::

> "Virtually every book in the Old Testament describes some level of supernatural intervention by God." [6]

God was active with His creation from the making of Adam, His questions of Adam and Eve's nakedness, and His forcing them to leave the Garden of Eden. He wrestled with Jacob, spoke with Moses, give him the Ten Commandments, guided the exodus to the promised land and visited earth on many occasions in the Old Testament.

The New Testament tells of His life on earth as Jesus from His human birth to His ascension to Heaven after His death and resurrection..

Man's Understanding to Date

The evidence clearly indicates that a superior being created the universe. But just how it was made, and the source of the matter and energy required, are unknown.

Davis offers this explanation in "Quantum Christianity":

"Big Bang or not, even science has difficulty explaining within their present understanding of their laws surrounding energy and physics or how physical matter existed before the Big Bang.

"As I understand it, within the Big Bang theory lies the assumption that all matter and energy in the physical universe existed in a compacted, ultra-dense form, which exploded and released our universe into what is *physicality*. Science concedes that they don't understand where this matter came from or how matter originated, only that there are consistent physical laws surrounding it after its inception. So, in a nutshell, science does not know beyond theory and Christians cannot speculate beyond their biblical theoretical justification of when and how they believe it all originally manifested." [7]

Author Miller writes that someone beyond this physical universe had to create and sustain it:

"Even if creation began with a Big Bang, Paul (the apostle) might argue today, someone had to load the universe and pull the trigger. In a physical universe, it's impossible for something to come from nothing. So there's more than a physical dimension at work in creating and sustaining the universe." [8]

Scientists and clergy have debated how and when the earth was formed. The basic difference in theories relates to the time and matter that it took to form the earth. Scientists and some biblical scholars believe in a Gap theory, which Davis explains:

"In essence, the Gap theory says there's an indeterminable amount of time represented between Genesis 1:1, 'In the beginning God created the heavens and the earth,' and Genesis 1:2, 'The earth was without form, and void, and darkness was on the face of the deep. And the spirit of God was hovering over the face of the waters.' " [9]

According to Genesis 1:26-27, God created mankind on the sixth day; on the seventh day God rested. In Genesis 2:7, God created a man from the dust of the earth and blew the Holy Spirit into his nostrils after the seventh day. The question has been whether the creation of a man (Adam) in Genesis 2 was an explanation of how it happened in Chapter 1—or did it occur (as a special creation) at a different time from the event in Chapter

1?

Another consideration is how much Moses would have known about a creation that took place thousands or millions of years before he wrote Genesis. God might not have revealed to Moses (revelatory day theory) what He had created before Adam, since the text was *about the Jewish people, not the history of creation.*

Holman's Old Testament Commentary of Genesis addresses the creation story timing issue this way:

> "The events recorded in Genesis stretch historically from creation to Joseph's death. If the genealogies in Genesis are taken as 'closed' (that is with no gaps), then the minimal period from the end of creation to Israel's entry into Egypt would be some 2,328 years, dating the creation of the world at some 6,176 years ago.
>
> "This figure is arrived at by adding the 2,002 years {date of publication of Holman's book} of the Christian era, plus the 1,446 years (taking an early date for the exodus) back to the exodus, plus 400 years of slavery in Egypt, plus 2,328 years from the entry into Egypt back to Adam. If there are gaps, then the time period could be extended considerably and made to fit more closely with the more commonly accepted belief among conservatives that mankind had been on the earth some 10,000 years (Egyptian history appears to go back to 3500 B.C.). The period covered by the creation account itself is of course subject to much controversy."[10]

The question of timing might also revolve around the interpretation of the Hebrew word "*yom.*" There are several meanings of the word, clouding whether the author (Moses) meant one day (24 hours) or a longer period. Christian apologists believe that the author meant one 24-hour day (Creation *in situ* theory). The secular belief based on geology (the indefinite age theory) defines it as a long time (possibly millions of years) based on the geological record found to date.

Davis relates:

> "How the universe began, when exactly it took place, whether or not conscious observation is a necessity in order for it all to be collapsed from wave to particle form, how it all interconnects, and what holds it all together are biblical and scientific issues we don't have absolute answers for yet. Still we {theologians and scientists} argue as though we know the infinite truth from both sides of the fence." [11]
>
> "Amongst the scientific community, because of the compounding evidence, the theories of divine design or

intelligent design are becoming less and less a doubt." [12]

The word "day" in the Bible means different lengths of time in various books. Simply put, the word has multiple meanings. In Genesis 1 God called the light "day" without specifying a duration. In Chapter 1 "day" is used to describe light as a 12-hour period and a 24-hour period. In Chapter 2 it appears to mean all of creation. In 2 Timothy it seems to refer to an era and in 2 Peter and Psalms 90 a thousand years. While Genesis is not a record of science it is similar to "biological and zoological sciences." [13]

The author of the Zondervan Handbook to the Bible writes that Genesis Chapter 1 is not a "chronological account" of God's creation. The story doesn't tell when, how and what God created to form the heavens and the earth. The term "day" is not defined as a specific period of time, and the story should be viewed as the creative and powerful ability of God, not a scientific truth of creation. [14]

Scientific Evidence

We can, however, start with our limited understanding of what God has revealed to us in geology, astronomy, physics, science and the word passed through the Bible to estimate the earth's age. Scientists believe, based on geologic history, that the earth is very old. Geologists have carbon dating results showing the earth millions of years old. Some calculate its age as at least 4.5 billion years. Other sources speculate the earth is much older, perhaps 13 or 14 billion years, according to the TV show "Big Bang Theory." [15]

In "Quantum Christianity," Davis writes:

> "Science dates the earth at 4.54 billion years, plus or minus 1 percent, while on the other hand, some Christian apologists (one who offers an argument in defense of something controversial) date the earth at 6,000 years." [Six thousand is only .00013215859 percent of 4.54 billion years] {calculated by adding the dates from Adam to Abraham as 2,000 years, and agreeing that Abraham lived 4,000 years ago}.
>
> "Couple this with the Christian apologetic theory of dinosaurs existing in tandem {with humans} in the last 6,000 years (pre-2348 B.C.) with what we understand to be Modern Man and that they were destroyed in the great flood of Noah, versus the most widely accepted scientific theory of the dinosaurs being destroyed by a significant ice age occurring on earth after a possible collision of an asteroid with the earth 65 million years ago, and we see additionally why this gap between perspectives continues to increase exponentially." [16]

Obviously, the length of a day and the time of creation are subject to varied opinions and controversy. The Bible does not specify exactly when, how or from what God created the universe. Our understanding is determined by gleanings over the eons.

Holman's Commentary on Genesis states:

"The period covered by the creation account is subject to much controversy. If present scientific 'facts' are accepted, then the earth is about 4,500,000 years old. Interpreters who believe such 'facts' are compelled to interpret the words of Scripture in light of such accepted 'facts.' In addition, the days of creation are seen as short, long, or unrelated to time...

"The Hebrew word *yom* (day) is used three ways in Genesis 1 and 2: (1) Twelve–hour period of daylight. (Gen. 1:5,14,16,18) (2) Twenty-four-hour day (Gen. 1:14) (3) the entire "six-day" period of creation (Gen. 2:4)...

"Major views about the length of the 'days of creation': (1). Literal twenty-four-hour-day. (2). Day-age (or geologic-day) view. (3). Literal days with intervening ages view. (4). Revelatory-day view."[17]

Davis explains further:

"The truth is, as it pertains to the beginning and life on earth, we don't really know what happened, when it happened, or how it happened. This is why we develop theories based upon our understanding of the evidence that we have been presented. As knowledge and understanding increase, so do the depth of the theories and possibilities of how everything seems to connect." [18]

Who Was at Creation?

Some versions of the Bible start with God saying "Let Us create the heavens and earth." To whom was God speaking? Genesis tells us that:

"God said, ' Let us (Father, Son and Holy Spirit) make mankind in Our image, after Our likeness, and let them have complete authority over the fish of the sea, the birds of the air, the (tame) beasts, and over all of the earth, and over every thing that crepes upon the earth.' "
(1:26 AMP)

Although Christ (God's Son) was invisible to man until He was born into human form (Jesus), John's gospel states that Christ was the Word in the beginning and "became flesh (human, incarnate)" and lived among us "full of grace (favor, loving-kindness) and truth." (1:1,14 AMP)

Some biblical scholars think that angels might have been with God when the heavens were created and the earth formed, as hinted in Genesis 2:1 NIV.

Job records that:

> "All the Sons of God (angels) shouted for Joy" when the heavens and earth were created. (38:7 AMP)

Holman's Commentary states:

> "The creation of angels is not mentioned in Genesis 1, just the items that are part of mankind's natural world. Some interpreters believe that Job 38:7 suggests that angels were created at the same time as the stars, while others would see angels already created and present at the creation of the earth (and in fact that Satan had already fallen before the creation of mankind)." [19]

While there are differing opinions and theories as to when the earth was formed, there is one consistent belief—God created the earth and placed mankind in it.

Father Rohr believes that:

> "Creation is the *First Bible*, and it existed for 13.7 billion years before the *Second Bible* {Christ on earth} was written." [20] {emphasis added}

CHAPTER SIX

"By faith [that is, with an inherent trust and enduring confidence in the power, wisdom and goodness of God] we understand that the worlds (universe, ages) were framed and created [formed, put in order, and equipped for their intended purpose] by the word of God, so that what is seen was not made out of things which are visible."
Hebrews 11:3 AMPSB

Creation or Happenstance? [1]

Were the earth and heavens created or did it just happen, possibly with a big bang? It might have happened with a big bang, but if so, it was not necessarily by random act.

Pastor Mason expounds:

> "Big-bang cosmologists point out that our big bang was the just right big bang because if the mathematical and physical constants of the Universe were not precisely predetermined, the big bang would have immediately imploded in upon itself! It is as though the condition of the laboratory were perfectly prepared before the scientific test was conducted.
>
> "If the constant of the gravitational force were even minutely weaker or stronger by just 0.1 part per million, the universe would not exist! Because the ratio of one constant to another is even more fine-tuned, a slight variation in the gravitational constant would send a cascading effect throughout the fabric of the cosmos such that our universe could not possibly come into being." [2]

The power and the precise care to create the universe exceeds our ability to comprehend. Man has long attempted to learn how the earth was formed, and many discoveries have been made to determine how the laws govern life on earth through the science of physics (in recent times the science of quantum physics). Mason explains:

> "Physics concerns itself with matter, energy, force, motion, space, time, gravity, mass and electric charge. Quantum physics concerns itself with the study of the constituent elements of

nature which are divided into discrete units or packets of energy called 'quanta.'

"Those who believe in the inspiration and authority of the Bible believe and accept that there is a personal God who created the heavens and the earth. As such we believe that this God is the Creator of everything that is now being discovered in the frontier science of quantum physics. We also believe that the only correct interpretation of the science of quantum physics will come in the light of the revelation of the Bible." [3]

Pastor Davis cites a pertinent belief of astronomer Allan Sandage, winner of the Craford Prize in astronomy (equivalent to the Nobel Prize), in "Quantum Christianity":

"I find it quite improbable that such order came out of chaos. There has to be some organizing principle. God to me is a mystery but is the explanation for the miracle of existence, why there is something instead of nothing." [4]

The Evidence of Creation

Several things exist that support a creation instead of a happening. There was light on the first day, according to the Bible.[5]

The Holman Commentary observes:

"The light created on Day 1 of creation does not appear to be the light from the sun since this celestial body was introduced on the fourth day (Genesis 1:14-18)." [6]

That must have been God's light until He created the sun. on the forth day. There are periods of night and day as the earth rotates about the sun. There is sky and breathable atmosphere. There is water. There is land and a suitable climate for life to exist. There are seasons, and there are rain and snow to replenish the water on earth. There are vegetation, fruit-bearing trees, and seeds of all kinds that support life.

Pastor Hamilton points out that:

"Oxford mathematician John Lenox notes that the odds for the self-organization of life on earth are in the neighborhood of 1 to 10 to the 40,000 power." [7]

All these things can occur because of the distance the earth is from the sun (God's third day). [8] The sun, the stars and the moon were set to provide seasons, periods of night and day (God's fourth day). [9]

The moon keeps the earth from tumbling on its axis. The moon is 1/400th the size of the sun, and 1/400th the distance from the earth to the sun, and can just cover the sun during an eclipse as viewed from earth. [10]

Again, the probability of these exact events "just happening" is infinitesimally small. No other planet in our solar system that has been discovered to date can support life.

Davis finds the interaction of trees and other plants intriguing, but not surprising and it only reiterates:

> "what seems to me to be the *rule* as it pertains to the unity and interconnectedness of God's creation. The soil nourishes the plants that provide the oxygen that is breathed in by the animals who exhale the carbon dioxide that feeds the plants, all receiving their energy from the sun and water, and completing the circle of life and exampling absolute interdependence of all living things within the earth."[11]

As noted in Chapter 5 of Stephen Miller's "The Complete Guide to the Bible" and revisited here for emphasis:

> "In a physical universe, it's impossible for something to come from nothing. So there's more than a physical dimension at work in creating and sustaining the universe."[12]

God has been and is at work! The earth didn't just happen. Only God had the ability to create and sustain it and, as Revelation reveals, completely destroy it.

CHAPTER SEVEN

"Then God said, 'Let the earth bring forth living creatures according to (limited to, consistent with) their kind.' ... Then God said, 'Let us (Father, Son, Holy Spirit) make man in Our image, according to Our likeness [not physical, but spiritual personality and moral likeness]' ..."
Genesis 1:24,26 AMPSB

Life is Created

According to Genesis 1, on the fifth day of creation, God made animal life, and on the sixth day men and women. (20-27 AMPSB)
Davis writes:

> "The truth is, as it pertains to the beginning and life on earth, we don't really know what happened, when it happened, or how it happened. This is why we develop theories based upon our understanding of the evidence that [has] been presented. As knowledge and understanding increase, so do the depth of the theories and possibilities of how everything seems to connect." 1
> {reinserted for emphasis}

Christian Professor Hugh Ross documents in his book, "The Creator and the Cosmos," that bonding of more than 40 different elements is required to create life. In addition, bonding depends on the strength of an exact ratio [not over 4% stronger or 10% weaker] of electrons and protons. Without the exact balance of elements, electrons and protons, life would not be possible (when life was first created and now). .2

A Correlation

Comparing the biblical and geologic records reveals a great correlation between them. In the first four days (periods) of creation, according to Genesis, 3 God created the heavens and earth from an empty, formless, dark space. He created light and the land, water and plants.

Holman's Old Testament Commentary advises that:

> "The first couple of days (periods) of creation will bring order to this matter, while the next several days will bring fertility and

fullness."₄

Considering the energy that God must have used to create the universe, there likely was an extremely long period of cooling off for the earth to support life.

The Bible relates that the first living creatures grew in the sea and birds flew in the sky. Geology supports a period of time when only living creatures populated the sea and the sky. (God's fifth day) ₅ That period in the geologic history is called The Paleozoic Era, estimated to have begun about 600 million earth years ago and lasting about 370 million years of earth days. ₆

Land animals began to appear in the following period for the next 160 million years during the Mesozoic Era as described in Genesis 1:24. This epoch included the dinosaurs and other living creatures preceding man. The question arises: Why dinosaurs? Was it in His plan that eventually mankind would need the decayed bodies (as oil) to improve human life?

Theories abound about the dinosaurs' demise. Is it possible that natural events [climate change, viruses, fires] occurred, not necessarily caused by God, that destroyed the dinosaurs before the first humanlike beings appeared? As revealed later, if Satan was the guardian of the prehistoric world, was it destroyed when he began to sin and could not manage the kingdom according to God's plan?

The following period, The Cenozoic Era, records the appearance of beings similar to mankind, such as the Homo erectus and other hominid species (Cro-Magnon, Neanderthals, and Homo Sapiens Neanderthalensis). These life-forms appear to be much like modern man, though lacking his thinking power and intelligence.. (See Chart 1)

Evolution?

In the 1800s, the theory of evolution became popular for explaining how different species and man developed. While there are similarities within each species, their variations can be explained as adaptive changes through the mating process. (God told the animals He created to multiply. Genesis 1:28 AMPSB)

One of the theories touted was that man evolved from the apes. While there are some similar features, it would be impossible, according to the Bible, as God created man and woman the same time he created the animals (the sixth day).

According to scientific study, it would be impossible for the "biological changes needed to transition from a primarily arboreal monkey adjusted to life in the trees to a walking, running, hunting, gathering, intelligent, talking human being." ₇

According to Genesis 1, the animals God made were wild animals, cattle, and everything that creeps on the earth., then man, but both on the sixth day. (1:25-26) While He gave man authority over the animals He created, (1:28) they were not given as help mates (domestic) as those made for Adam in Chapter 2:19. There appears to be a difference in God's intentions by creating some animals in certain time periods and others later on, perhaps suggesting varying reasons and time periods in creation.

Mankind Is Created
"So God created man in His own image, in the image and likeness of God He created him; male and female He created them."
Genesis 1: 27 AMPSB

Genesis records God's creation of mankind in His image and likeness:

"God said, 'Let Us [Father, Son, and Holy Spirit] make mankind in Our image, after Our likeness, and let them have complete authority over the fish of the sea, the birds of the air, the [tame] beasts, and over all of the earth, and over everything that creeps upon the earth.'

"So God created man in His own image, in the image and likeness of God. He created him, male and female He created them.

"And God blessed them and said to them, 'Be fruitful, multiply, and fill the earth, and subdue it [using all its vast resources in the service of God and man]; and have dominion over the fish of the sea, the birds of the air, and over every living creature that moves upon the earth."
(Genesis 1:26-28 AMP)

Mankind was charged to ensure God's kingdom would thrive on earth. Thus, mankind was given complete authority and charged essentially to build and control God's earthly kingdom. Note that to this point in Genesis, God had not created mankind from the earth or breathed His spirit into mankind's nose, as recorded in Genesis 2:7.

Geological discovery shows that what science (as opposed to religion) calls "first man" was found to exist 1.3 billion years ago, called Homo erectus. The species Homo erectus shared a great many anatomical and cultural features with modern man, including efficient upright walking, the use of fire, specialized tools and probably complex social interactions. [8]

Modern man (Homo sapiens) is estimated to have appeared around 20,000 years ago. For many Christians and Jews, the true modern "first man" (human-spirit) did not arrive until the birth of Adam, 6,000 years ago.

The Bible calls both human creations in Genesis 1:27 and 2:7 man, sparking questions as to differences in the two, or if they are in fact two varying creations. I believe there were two different creations in two separate time periods, and God made Adam (second creation) for a special purpose. Genesis 1:27 states that God created man and woman in His image and likeness, but excludes breathing His Spirit into them. Only in Chapter 2 when God created Adam did He breath His spirit into him.

Genesis 2 records that God was finished with creation after the "seventh day" (note Adam was not yet created):

> "Thus the heavens and the earth were finished, and all the host of them.
>
> "And on the seventh day God ended His work, which He had done; and He rested on the seventh day from all His work, which He had done.
>
> "And God blessed (spoke good of) the seventh day, set it apart as His own, and hallowed it, because on it God rested from all His work which He had created and done.
>
> "This is the history of the heavens and of the earth when they were created. In the day that the Lord God made the earth and heavens." (Genesis 2:1-4 AMP)

Genesis 2:4 is stated in several ways in various translations, but with the same meaning:

> "This is the account of the heavens and the earth when they were created." (NIV);
>
> "These are the generations of the heavens and of the earth when they were created, in the day that the Lord God made the earth and the heavens." (KJV);
>
> "Here is a summary of the events in the creation of the heavens and earth which the Lord God made." (TLB)

All these translations, and many others, indicate that God had finished His creations of the earth and placed the animals, men and women, on it before the seventh day. Some biblical scholars believe it is possible that God established an earthly kingdom before the birth of Adam, and that the angel Lucifer was sent as the guardian angel to control the kingdom.

> "No information is given to us about what happened before the creation of the physical universe, though John 1:1 speaks of this time. (In the beginning [before all time] was the Word (Christ) and the Word was with God, and the Word was God Himself. He was [continually existing] in the beginning [co-eternally] with

God). It is possible that the rise, rebellion and judgment of Satan transpired before the events of this chapter." 9 {Chapter 2}

When God created the heavens and earth, He called His creation very good. If Satan was the guardian of the earth in the beginning as alluded to in Ezekiel 28:14-17, it would have been possible for Satan to cause death and sin from the very start. There is no clear biblical account of when Lucifer fell from grace, but he is not banished from God's kingdom until Revelation. (12:9 AMPSB)

It would have been possible then for Lucifer to be guardian of God's earthly kingdom before Adam, and that would explain his presence as Satan at the Garden of Eden. If Lucifer turned to sin while guardian of God's creation, it would also explain death of the early animals and early mankind. The Bible does not reveal what happened to the early creation, so we are left with just geological evidence.

Perhaps God destroyed the first creation because it was evil just as He did with the flood in Noah's day, only 10 generations after Adam's, because:

> "The Lord saw that the wickedness (depravity) of man was great on the earth, and that every imagination or intent of the thoughts of his heart were only evil continually.
>
> "The Lord regretted that He had made mankind on the earth, and He was [deeply] grieved in His heart.
>
> "So the Lord said, 'I will destroy (annihilate) mankind whom I have created from the surface of the earth—not only man, but the animals and the crawling things and the birds of the air— because it [deeply] grieves Me that I have made them.' "
> (Genesis 6:5-7 AMPSB)

This theory would explain the geological record and Lucifer's (Satan's) earthly existence when God created Adam.

To Know God

In order to understand man as created by God, we first must know God. We cannot meet God face to face, but in John's Gospel God's Son Jesus told His disciples:

> "If you had known Me, you would have known My Father. From now on you know Him and have seen Him.
>
> "Whoever has seen Me has seen the Father.
>
> "Do you now believe that I am in the Father and the Father is in Me? " (John 14:7, 9-10 AMP)

We have not met Jesus personally, but we know Him from His word. Jesus the Christ and God are one.

We know from the Bible that God cannot stand evil, sin and disobedience to His will. Dr. William Barclay, a renowned pastor in Scotland in the 1950s, wrote in his book, "Letter to the Romans":

> "God gave man free will (to choose between good and evil), and God respects that free will.
> "We {now} would say there is a moral order in this world, and the man who transgresses the moral order law, soon or late, is bound to suffer. The conclusion is clear—*that moral order is the wrath of God at work.*" [10]

Paul's Letter to the Romans reveals God's reaction to sin:

> "(I will send wrath) from heaven against all the godlessness and wickedness of men who suppress the truth by their wickedness, since what may be known about God is plain to them, because God has made it plain to them. For since the creation of the world God's qualities—his eternal power and divine nature—have been clearly seen, being understood from what has been made, so that men are without excuse." (1:18-23 NIV)

Yet, Paul goes on to say every man is a sinner, that no man could ever put himself back into a right relationship with God through his own efforts, that every man is God's debtor, and that all grounds for self-satisfaction and boasting in one's own achievements are forever gone. In other words, man has no excuse for his sins, but can be absolved of the consequences if he accepts Jesus Christ as his savior because He died on the cross to atone for our sins.

Scientists Attempt to Create Life

In his novel, "Origin," Dan Brown identifies several actual attempts by scientists to create life to disprove God's necessity for that purpose.

In the 1950s chemists Stanley Miller and Harold Urey conducted experiments to determine how humans were created. Apparently, they thought that by recreating a mixture of elements that make up human anatomy, similar to the conditions at the dawn of earth's creation, human life could be developed.

Their mixture of boiling chemicals known as *"primordial soup to simulate "Creation"… using only science"* failed to produce life. That experiment has been considered as proof that life cannot be created without God's evolvement. [11]

Physicist Jeremy England at MIT does not rule out it may be possible for life to be created if the laws of physics are followed, but notes that "life began because of those laws." [12]

"If the laws of physics are so powerful that they can create life...(consider) who created the laws?" [13]

Dr. Constance Gerhard, a biochemist at Stanford University, believes mankind can't create life because there is no known way for inanimate chemicals to form a living being. Even cells themselves cannot form to create a living being, as such a formation is against the laws of entropy. (Entropy is the law of physics denoting the tendency of an energy system to run down). [14]

All efforts by scientists to create life without God have come after He created the universe—primordial soup, laws of physics, entropy, dissipation or spread of energy, etc. Miller and Urey did not create the chemicals placed in their primordial soup, God did. Jeremy England did not create the laws of physics, God did. Without God's matter and His laws of physics man cannot create anything; even love comes from Him.

As the joke goes, when an atheist challenged God to a test in creating life (the atheist able to clone animals): God reaches down, takes a handful of dirt, and creates another Adam. The atheist reaches down and takes a handful of dirt to clone a life, but God says, "No, get your own dirt." It's God's world; man is just part of the creation. Man did not and cannot create human life without God's hand.

Equally absurd is not to accept the geologic evidence that God created the earth long before the first human-spirit [Adam in 6000 B.C.].

Professor Marcia Bjornerud, a geologist professor at Lawrence University, in her book "Timelessness," writes, considering all the geological evidence that has been discovered around the world to date and if one believes in God, then there is a choice that must be made. Either God created a prehistoric world, or He created a "young earth a few thousand years ago" and planted all the geologic evidence around the world as a "devious and deceitful creator," including planting fossil beds and minerals, knowing they would be tested in laboratories. "Which is more heretical?" [15]

The geologic evidence supports the creation story in Chapter 1 of Genesis, showing the awesome power and miraculous imagination of God's plan to create a world and begin life. The record of the creation and history of God's chosen human-spirits starts in Genesis, Chapter 2.

CHAPTER EIGHT

"And by the seventh day God completed His work which He had done, and He rested (ceased) on the seventh day from all His work which He Had done."
Genesis 2:2 AMP

God's Day

Some believers and nonbelievers agree God could not have created the earth in seven days as geologic evidence shows. The length of a "day" is subject to question again due to the geologic record. Further, the length of the seven days stated in Genesis is debated as a week in earth days.

Genesis does not mention the length of a day or refer to a week. It only states seven days, not defined as 24-hour days or seven consecutive earth days.

First, as geologic history shows, the earth was not created in "earth days" as it did not exist on the first day, but was made on God's schedule.

Revisiting Genesis 1:

> "In the beginning God created the heavens and the earth. Now the earth was formless and empty, darkness was over the surface of the deep, and the Spirit of God was hovering over the waters.
>
> "And God said, 'Let there be light,' and there was light. God saw that the light was good, and he separated the light from the darkness. God called the light 'day' and the darkness he called 'night.' And there was evening, and there was morning—the first day." (1:1-5 NIV) {Note that God called the light day and the darkness night without stating any length of time. The duration for each came after the earth was fully formed.}

The earth was still formless when God provided the light and darkness. The sun and moon, which did not yet exist, were created on the fourth day.[1] It was God's "day and night," not man's, as the earth and man did not yet exist. [2]

And as geologic history reflects, God's day must be significantly longer than earth's 24-hour day. The psalmist says God is above time:

> "For a thousand years in Your sight are like yesterday when it is past, Or as a watch in the night." (90:4)

CHAPTER SIXTEEN

"The Egyptians made the Israelites serve rigorously, [forcing them into severe slavery]."
Exodus 1:13 AMPSB

Land of Slavery

God appeared to Jacob, reiterated his name as Israel, and blessed him.

" 'I am God Almighty. Be fruitful and multiply; A nation and a company of nations shall come from you. And kings shall be born of your loins. The land which I gave Abraham and Isaac I will give to you, and to your descendants after you I will give the land.' " (Gen 35:11-12 AMPSB)

Jacob had 12 sons, six with Leah, two with Rachel, two with Bilhah, and two with Zilpah. This dozen formed the 12 tribes of Israel. ₁

Abraham's great-grandson (Jacob's son) Joseph was sold into slavery by his jealous brothers. Joseph was taken from his homeland to Egypt. ₂ While in captivity, Joseph continued to worship God. ₃ Joseph interprets the Pharaoh's dream and is given a high post in his house. ₄

God uses Joseph as part of His plan to save His people. Joseph rises in power and is placed in charge of Egypt's agricultural production. When famine strikes his homeland, his father Jacob, brothers and all his descendants move to Egypt. ₅

Joseph received and placed them in land suited to graze sheep. There they worked and lived and multiplied until their offspring became so numerous that the rulers of Egypt feared a Jewish takeover. The Jews were enslaved, ₆ and remained captive for 400 years until God and Moses convinced the Pharaoh to set them free.

God chose Moses as leader of the Jewish slaves from his birth. Faced with the Egyptian edict that all children 2 and younger were to be executed to slow the growth of the slave population, ₇ his mother placed baby Moses in a reed basket and floated it to where an Egyptian princess bathed. ₈

God used a baby, not even in the bloodline of Jesus, to implement His plan. Moses may be the only other infant recorded as part of God's plan.

Moses was taken into the Pharaoh's household and raised as a son. There he was educated; perhaps the most educated Hebrew of his time. He fled Egypt after killing an Egyptian who was beating a Hebrew slave. ₉

Although 2 Peter refers to the end times, the reference to God's time is a fact that Peter urges us to remember:

> "But by His word the present heavens and earth are being reserved for fire, being kept for the day of judgment and destruction of the ungodly people. Nevertheless, do not let this one *fact* escape your notice, beloved, that with the Lord one day is like a thousand years, and a thousand years is like one day." (3:8 AMPSB)

The correlation between the uncertainty of how time is determined, geologic history (as described in Chapter 7) and Genesis Chapter 1, leads logically to the conclusion that God's word does contain the possibility that the earth existed before Adam.

Time and Bible History

Skeptics might say the Bible was written after the fact to explain the earth's geological history. But it was written billions of years after the earth was formed— and necessarily after man was created.

The Bible reveals that God gave Adam a language in which to speak with Him. It is unknown when verbal language first developed into writing. Early attempts to record earthly events were in picture form.

The Greek alphabet was developed and used by the Hebrews and Phoenicians about 2000 B.C. The Roman alphabet was developed in Jesus' time, about 2000 years later.

Moses, writing in Hebrew about 1500 B.C., is credited as writing the Torah. (See Chart 2) Moses is credited with having written the first five books of the Bible plus many of the psalms.

The apostle Peter's second letter warns the early churches that false prophets were discouraging believers because God's second coming had not come true. Peter reminds them of Psalm 90:4 and tells them not to lose hope because God will come in *His time*.

> "Nevertheless, do not let this one fact escape you, beloved, that with the Lord one day is as a thousand years and a thousand years as one day." (2 Peter 3:8 AMPSB)

While the secular interpretation and some religious interpretations differ, both agree that God created the earth. We have to understand that while God guided Moses in writing the first five books of the Bible, man has interpreted that writing through the ages. Further, the extent of the written word (Hebrew vocabulary) at that time was limited..

One missed interpretation of a word or its use based on the vocabulary of that time could change the meaning to today's understanding. For example, if the word "day" (Hebrew "yum") in the beginning would have been interpreted "period," there might not be any difference in the secular and Christian understanding of the beginning of the book of Genesis.

In Chapter 5, the biblical scholar's "Gap Theory" explains why there is thought to be an indeterminable amount of time represented between Genesis 1:1 and Genesis 1:2, and between other "days" of the creation story. In light of geological evidence, the "Gap Theory" appears relevant and supports the claim "God's Day" is determined by God, not our 24-hour day.

CHAPTER NINE

"Who shall ever separate us from the love of Christ? For I am convinced [and continue to be convinced—beyond a doubt] that neither death, nor life, nor angels, nor principalities, nor things present and threatening, nor things to come, nor powers, nor height, nor depth, nor other created things, will be able to separate us from the [unlimited] love of God, which is in Christ Jesus our Lord."
Romans 8:35, 38-39 AMPSB

God's Love

Why did God create this solar system and especially earth? I believe God made the earth to establish His kingdom in a consultant relationship with man. Pastor Davis writes:

> "We {mankind} are meant to exercise our 'rule' only in union with God, as he acts with us. He intended to be a constant companion or co-worker in the creative enterprise of life on earth. That is what His love for us means in practical terms." [1]

Why did He create mankind in His image? We know that God created Adam with His divine breath from His love. Placing His divine breath in man makes him part spiritual and part human. God directed the human part to establish His kingdom on earth and made it possible for the spiritual part to join Him in the afterlife.

There is no guarantee that the spirit part will join God, but He provided a way conditioned on belief in Jesus.

> "For God so loved the world that he gave his one and only Son, that whoever believes in him shall not perish but have eternal life. For God did not send his Son into the world to condemn the world, but to save the world through him." (John 3:16 NIV) or:
> "For God so loved the world, that he gave his only begotten Son, that whoever believeth in him should not perish, but have everlasting life." (John 3:16 KJV)

God Chose Us

Through His love, God must feel the pain and disappointment that each

59

of His creations suffers. He made mankind to rule the earth in constant companionship as co-workers with Him; He created each of us for more than we know we can do.

> "And Jesus said, [You say to Me] If You can do anything? [Why,] all things can be (are possible) to him who believes!" (Mark 9:23 AMP)

Paul's Letter to the Ephesians gives us an idea why God created mankind:

> "May blessing (praise, laudation and eulogy) be to the God our Father of our Lord Jesus Christ (the Messiah *and the Word*) Who has blessed us *in Christ* with every spiritual (given by the Holy Spirit) blessing in the heavenly realm.
> "Even as [in His love] He chose us [actually picked us (believers) out for Himself as His own] in Christ before the foundation of the world, that we should be holy (consecrated and set apart for Him) and blameless in His sight, *even* above reproach, before Him in love." (1:3-4 (AMP)

Pastor Nabeel Qureshi expresses it clearly:

> "In the beginning of the Christian worldview is the one God, Yahweh. He exists as three persons who love each other perfectly. Thus, the one God is love in his very essence. Out of this love, God created mankind in his image, that God might love man and man might love God.
> "That is who God is, almighty yet most humble, the center of the universe yet selfless. He created mankind so he could delight in us, and we in Him, with selfless love.
> "But in order for this love to be valuable, it must be voluntary, so God gave man the choice to love or reject him. When man disobeys God, it is tantamount to rejecting God. In rejecting the Source of Life, we bring death upon ourselves. This bears repeating: The result of sin is death because it is a rejection of the Source of Life." 2

God is Love

God is love, unconditional love, so strong that He gave His Son to die on the cross to atone for our sins. His love is a love of forgiveness. Through the death of His Son, all of our sin is forgiven when He is accepted as our Lord and Savior.

In their book, "Kelly Tough," Erin with Jill Kelly express God's love as unknown unless we know Jesus:

> "We cannot know love unless we know God. And we cannot know God unless we have been drawn to Him through His Son, Jesus, by the power and work of the Holy Spirit."

> "I find that what man considers love and what God considers love, are radically different. Human love is limited and inadequate to meet the deeper needs of the human heart. We ache for love, but worldly love can't fill a soul. Only God's love can. Everything about God and His love reaches in from the eternal as He makes loving decisions that result in our highest good without compromising truth, reality, or what is right. His love is selfless and sacrificial—period." [3]

God's love for each of us has been expressed in the Christian song "Reckless Love." The lyrics tell us that God chose us. He knew us before we were born and expresses His never-ending love to get us to join His kingdom. He continues to seek us, to invite us to join His kingdom and to love Him as He loves us. Once we join the kingdom, He continues to watch over us with His Spirit, and when we falter He returns us to the fold. We do not earn His love, He gives that freely without strings. There is nothing that can prevent God from saving us except ourselves. [4]

Christian author John Eldredge in His book, "Waking the Dead," concludes that our heart is the source of our emotions, creativity, courage and faith, and that God looks at our heart not our physical appearance, to test our faithfulness to Him. [5]

Without God's love, life has no meaning. In God's plan, His love is essential to make His kingdom possible for mankind.

CHAPTER TEN

"Then the Lord God formed [that is, created the body of] man from the dust of the ground, and breathed into his nostrils the breath of life; and the man became a living being [an individual complete in body and spirit]."
Genesis 2:7 AMPSB

Adam Is Created

Genesis 1 (all translations) ends with God's completion of the creation of the earth and heavens in six days (periods), and on the seventh (day or period) He rested. Chapter 2 of Genesis starts with God causing rain "so plants of the field would spring up." God *then* made Adam from the dust of the ground and breathed His spirit into the man's nostrils to give him life. God created a human in His image and likeness and added His Spirit making him more than human; he became a human-spirit, different than all beings formed before. Awesome! 1

Some biblical scholars and Bible versions [the New American Bible] consider there was only one man created when the earth was formed, and Adam was that man. If that is so, there would be no prehistoric world.

I don't think God would have left out a major component of adding His spirit (the gift of a spiritual life) to the man He created in His "image and likeness" in Chapter 1. Without God's Spirit man would be just another mammal. If Adam was the man created in Chapter 1, then all of pre-historical life before 6000 B.C. could not have occurred.

However, since there is evidence that humans (Homo erectus–minus God's spirit) did exist before 6000 B.C., it is logical to believe that God made Adam after the initial creation of the earth for a *special purpose.*

The First Human-Spirit

Genesis 2 records the birth of Adam and the planting of the Garden of Eden:

> "Then [The time came when (TLB)] the Lord God formed man from the dust of the ground and breathed into his nostrils the breath or spirit of life, and man became a living being.
> "And the Lord God planted a garden toward the east in Eden [delight]: and there He put the man whom He had formed (framed, constituted).

"And out of the ground the Lord God made to grow every tree that is pleasant to the sight or to be desired---good (suitable, pleasant) for food; the tree of life also in the center of the garden, and the tree of knowledge of [the difference between] good and evil and blessing and calamity.

"And the Lord God took the man and put him in the Garden of Eden to tend and guard and keep it." (Genesis 2:7-9, 15 AMP)

Pastor Davis elaborates:

"Considering the interaction that God displayed with Adam in the Garden (Genesis 2), it seems apparent that He was directly accessible to Adam for instruction much like a consultant., mentor, or advisor would be working alongside the new CEO of a corporation. Adam and subsequently his offspring, it seems, were given the authority to rule the earth and it appears the original intent was that he would do it with the direct help and instruction of God, and as a result, the kingdom of God would be established in the earth.

"In this, God's rule and lordship would be established in and through His creation who was created in His image and they would willfully have an intimate relationship and knowledge of Him.

"However, in order for man to have a willful relationship that established God's kingdom (His way of doing things) on the earth, there would have to be an option for them to willfully choose something outside of His kingdom, or *free will* would only be an illusion." ₂

Pastor Mason adds:

"Human beings are 'creative' in a secondary sense. We are endowed with creative and imaginative abilities to manipulate and shape the world around us because we are made in the image and likeness of God. But God has not endowed human beings with ultimate creative power to speak things into existence in a way that only God can.

"This is what the Lord says about Himself: 'I am God, and there is no other; I am God, and there is none like Me.' (Isaiah 46:9) "We are dependent beings who need the gift of spiritual grace and power that only comes through acknowledgment of our absolute dependency upon God to be the strength of our life.

" 'My grace is sufficient for you, for my power is made perfect in weakness.' (2 Corinthians 12:9 NIV)

"When God chose to create the world He decided to make a very specific kind of world in which those who were made in His own image and likeness were uniquely endowed with the ability to speak and hear. This is a fundamental aspect of what it means to be created in the image of God." [3]

In Genesis 1 on the sixth day (period) God created mankind, male and female in His image and likeness. (*Note the text does not say he breathed His spirit into their nostrils.*) (1:27 AMP) The meaning of "in Our image, and likeness" has been interpreted variously in biblical texts. Most would agree that image does not mean physical beings, and some a spiritual personality (belief in a higher power) and moral likeness. Some texts interpret the terms to distinguish (indicate) man a higher being than animals. A footnote in the Amplified Study Bible, Page 3, indicates the phrase could also mean "Let us make man *as* Our image," stating "God placed mankind as living symbols of Himself on earth to represent His reign," based on interpretation of Hebrew grammar None of the texts in Chapter 1 states God blew His Spirit into the humans He created.

Yet, in Genesis 2 the text states God finished the creation, rested on the seventh day. Afterward, (some passage of time) God did not find a man to "till the ground" so He created a new man (Adam) in His image and likeness from the dust of the earth. At this time, He added breathing the breath of life (God's spirit) into the new man, thus creating a 'human-spirit' individual. (2:2-8 AMP)

Not only did He create a special human-spirit man, Adam, He also planted a special garden for him to live in, one providing everything needed to sustain life, making Adam unique, the first member in the line of human-spirit beings.

"THIS IS the book (the written record, the history) of generations of [the descendants of] Adam. When God created man, He made him in the likeness of God [not physical, but a spiritual personality and moral likeness]." (Genesis 5:1 AMPSB)

Why didn't God take a "man" [Genesis 1:27] He had created earlier to work the ground instead of making a new one? Looking forward to when God would destroy the earth by flood, He needed an heir of the man who had received His Spirit to establish a bloodline for sending His Son, Jesus Christ, into the world.

The flood wiped out all mankind, except the bloodline from Adam (Noah and his sons and their wives). Following the flood, all mankind would be human-spirit individuals, thereby making it possible for their spirits to be saved for eternity with God. In creating Adam as a special human-spirit being, He established the birthright of His Son Jesus from Adam, to Noah, to Abraham, to King David to Jesus and eventually to us. (See Appendix C)

Scientific Evidence

Scientists recognize but cannot explain a period in the development of man marked by a dramatic change in his intelligence, called the "Great Leap Forward."

The brains of human creatures became smaller but higher functioning. The most plausible explanation to date links this spurt to God's having added His breath into Adam's nostrils, thereby giving him life, a soul, ability, and the freedom to choose good or evil.

Thus while science estimates God's creation of mankind in His image and likeness at 100,000 to 200,000 years ago, it was not until (possibly) only (religious belief) 6,000 years ago that He created Adam as the "Great Leap Forward."

With God's breath in Adam's creation, his descendants became spiritual beings as well as simply human beings. It is the spiritual part of man that God wants to save for the spiritual world.

In his book, "The Phenomenon of Man," Pierre Teilhard de Chardin states that we are spiritual beings experiencing (life as) human beings who must now experience human life [because of Adam's sin]. 4

There are also differences in the strict literal religious interpretation and the secular view of God's creation of man as recorded in Genesis 1 and 2. The religious belief is that God created one man (Adam) from which all human development emerged, and Adam was the man created in Genesis 1.

The secular belief is that the mankind created in Genesis 1:27 was representative of an earlier type preceding Adam., and Adam was a completely different type of man who was created in Chapter 2 as a human-spirit thousands of years after his predecessors.

Why bring the question up at all.? The only apparent explanation in the different interpretations of God's creation of man in Genesis Chapter 1— with the supporting geological evidence, and God's creation of Adam in Chapter 2— is that God needed a human-spirit to carry out His plan.

Adam's Job

Adam was tasked to live in the garden and care for God's creation. He was also directed to name the animals (domestic, tame) God created for him (suitable helpers) in the garden. Adam was allowed to eat from all the trees in the garden *except* the Tree Of Knowledge.

It is interesting to note that the verse, Genesis 2:16, granting Adam permission to eat fruit from all but the Tree Of Knowledge (of good and evil), did not mention the Tree Of Life, as there were two trees in the garden's center.

Later God drove Adam from the garden so he would not eat of the tree of life and be like "Us" (Father, Son and Holy Spirit), and live eternally but in a fallen sinful condition. Think what would have happened if Adam and Eve had partaken from the Tree Of Life instead of the Tree Of Knowledge. Obviously Satan was at work! (Genesis 3:22 AMPSB)

On the other hand, if Adam and Eve had chosen fruit from the Tree Of Life, the Tree Of Knowledge would have remained in the garden, and as occurred in the spirit realm [Satan falling out of grace] it would be possible for man at some point to be tempted and eat the forbidden fruit, at Satan's prompting, and the outcome would be the same—man again in a sinful state. Adam and Eve would then be fallen angels, like Satan. As a result God's plan would have to be restarted.

Although created in God's image and likeness with His Spirit, man was not given the ability to "create with the spoken word" as God can. [5] It wasn't until man received the Holy Spirit from Jesus that he was able to create by the spoken word and perform spoken healings and other physical acts as Jesus did. [6] Fortunately, the Holy Spirit in mankind places him higher in the spiritual world than Satan. [7]

However, as Pastor Mason notes:

> "Unless the Holy Spirit establishes in our hearts a deep and intimate oneness with Christ and the Father, we will never enter into the level of supernatural ministry that Jesus has prepared for His followers to walk in." [8]

Adam was created to establish God's kingdom on earth. God gave him all the power and knowledge to rule the kingdom (Garden of Eden) when He placed His Spirit in Adam.

Based on Ralph Allan Smith's "The Covenantal Structure of the Bible," Pastor Davis writes:

> "Adam was commissioned by God to rule the earth and establish the kingdom of God to the manifested glory of God in the world. Although Adam's position was compromised (by Satan in the garden), he was still responsible to God for his leadership in priestly, kingly, and fatherly duty, but he was also open to satanic temptation in a new way. He now had an internal sympathy with Satan's sinful rebellion against God. Therefore, for Adam to stand with God meant a lifelong war with Satan and a war against the sin in his own heart. From this time, Adam's work included the fight to reclaim for God what Satan had stolen. For Adam to have authority in a fallen world meant that he must fight, either for God or against

Him.   Authority also included the pain of perseverance in a sin-cursed world." [9]

Created in God's Image and Likeness

"Let Us (Father, Son, Holy Spirit) make Man in Our image, according to Our likeness
[not physical, but a spiritual personality and moral likeness]."
Genesis 1:26 AMPSB

God said He created mankind in His image and likeness. Additionally, Genesis reveals that God created Adam from the dust of the earth and breathed into his nostrils the breath of life, making him and all his descendants part divinity—spiritual and human beings.

But just what is God's image? Here's Pastor Davis' take:

"I've heard it speculated that God created Adam the perfect genetic specimen. And that would seemingly make sense when considering the perspective that God was first creating man in His image and likeness and that He intended to populate an entire race of people through the offspring of a single set of parents. (Even science agrees that all of mankind likely came from a single mother genetically, although they would argue that she existed between 140,000 and 280,000 years ago.)" [10]

The speculation might be based on the fact that before the great flood, many of the offspring were reported in the Bible to have lived as long as 900 years. Further, it is probable that Adam and Eve had the same gene structure as God's earlier creation, with the only differences being they had His Spirit and a more intelligent brain than predecessors.

From Genesis we know that Adam was made almost God like, but to prevent Adam and Eve from returning to the Garden of Eden and eating from the Tree Of Life, He had to drive them away.

"And the Lord God said, 'Behold, the man has become like one of Us [Father, Son and Holy Spirit], to know [how to distinguish between] good and evil *and* blessing and calamity, and now, lest he put forth his hand and take also from the tree of life and eat, and live forever.'

"Therefore the Lord God sent him {Adam and Eve because they had His Spirit in them} forth from the Garden of Eden to till the ground from which he was taken.

"So [God] drove out the man; and He placed at the east of the Garden of Eden the cherubim and a flaming sword which turned every way, to keep *and guard* the way to the tree of life." (Genesis 3:22-24 AMP)

There is no other reference in the Bible to reveal when the Garden of Eden vanished.

So what is God's image and likeness? Admittedly we do not know, but we do know His aversion to sin. Image and likeness must include free will, as Lucifer and other angelic beings were thrown out of heaven because they sinned or chose to go with Lucifer when he was ejected. So mankind automatically receives a free will when they are created in God's image and likeness.

The Bible records Moses' two (the second with Aaron) meetings with God when he received the Ten Commandments, but there is no record of Moses (or Aaron) seeing God. They only heard His voice from a cloud. Later Jesus said "whoever saw me has seen the Father" [meaning spiritually, not physically].

We know that He loves us and wants us to worship Him, enjoy His creation, and join Him in eternal life. Knowing God spiritually is all we need to be part of His kingdom.

Skeptics would argue that if God is sinless and loves us, why does He allow evil things to befall us? Pastor Hamilton writes in his book "Half Truths":

> "The reason most things happen is not because God willed them, but because of the decisions we make or the laws that govern nature and our interaction with them.
>
> "God has a will and plan for humanity.
>
> "But even in all these terrible occurrences, God has a way of forcing good to come from tragedy when we trust Him with it.
>
> "But Christians believe that in Jesus, God came to walk among us, showed us and taught us who God is and who we are meant to be." [11]

We know God from His word (the Bible) and from the teachings of His Son Jesus the Christ. The Bible gives us a clear picture of God's nature from the written word about Jesus. We resemble Adam and need a spiritual relationship with God to live as He wishes.

CHAPTER ELEVEN

"And the rib which the Lord God had taken from the man He made (fashioned, formed) into a woman, and He brought her and presented her to the man."
Genesis 2:22 AMPSB

Woman Is Created

After God placed Adam in a garden He had created, God charged him with its care.

> "Now the Lord said, 'It is not good (sufficient, satisfactory) that the man should be alone; I will make him a helper mate suitable, adapted, complementary) for him.'" (Genesis 2:18 AMP)

God took a rib from Adam's body and created a woman. Adam named her Eve. She also had God's spirit since He created her from Adam's body. The woman was to be a helper and companion for Adam and for procreation of mankind.

The Original Sin

Adam and Eve disobey God by eating forbidden fruit from the Tree Of Knowledge (of Good and Evil), thus beginning sin on earth. However, it was Satan who convinced Adam and Eve to disobey God, and thus taking control of the earthly kingdom.

Pastor Davis elegantly states:

> "With the establishment of the kingdom of sin on the earth also came a separation from the original intent of God for man to live in the full benefit of His kingdom through an intimate relationship with Him and institution of His principles. Sin created a separation between God and man that separated man from the benefit of living within the fullness of God's kingdom on the earth. This doesn't necessarily mean that all of the physical or spiritual laws that were instituted for man to function within his rule over the earth were now gone, but the benefit of God's direct and intimate interaction with man was. He would now only communicate to them through priests, prophets, an occasional angelic visitation, or when securing a covenant with

man (as the case of Abraham). ₁

In Romans the apostle Paul reminds us that with Adam's sin, all mankind following him are sinners.

> "Therefore, just as sin entered the world through one man, and death through sin, and in this way death came to all men, because all sinned." (Romans 5:12 NIV)

Adam at first refused to eat fruit from the Tree Of Knowledge (of good and evil) because God told him that he would die if he did so. ₂ Satan prompted the serpent (note the power of Satan to have a snake speak) to convince Adam and Eve to eat from that tree, telling them they would not die as God had warned. ₃ Perhaps Satan was hoping that Adam and Eve would die, thereby destroying the human-spirit bloodline.

God does not have Adam and Eve die immediately, but punishes their (and all mankind's) disobedience by causing Eve and all women to suffer great pains in child-bearing, and man to obtain food through painful toil all the days of his life.₄ Adam lives for 930 years. (Genesis 5:5 AMP) There is no mention of Eve's life-span.

Adam and Eve have three male children, Cain, Abel and Seth. Cain kills Abel and is punished by God. Cain's genealogy extends for only five generations. The genealogy (history of future generations) of mankind begins with Seth (the family tree of the human race). ₅

Genesis records the life-span of Adam and Seth's off spring as hundreds of years, until God decides:

> "My spirit shall not strive and remain with man forever, because he is indeed flesh [sinful, corrupt—given over to sensual appetites]; nevertheless his days shall yet be a hundred and twenty years." (Genesis 6:3 ANP)

However, Noah found favor with God and lived for 950 years. ₆ Others who pleased God lived longer than 120 years with His grace. (For example, Terah, Abram's father, died at 205). ₇

Eve was the first woman human-spirit because she was created from Adam. The genealogy presented in the Bible follows the male line, even though most had wives and daughters. Although not listed in the bloodline, the women who bore the bloodline to Jesus were of great importance in God's plan. Noah's wife bore the three sons who's wives began the generations through which *"the whole earth was populated and scattered with inhabitants."* ₈

God's faithful servant Abram (later Abraham) took his wife Sarai to Egypt when a famine struck their homeland. Sarai was very beautiful and caught the eye of the Pharaoh. Abram told the Egyptians that Sarai was his sister because he was afraid that [otherwise] the Egyptians would kill him [for her]. Pharaoh took Sarai into his harem with the intent of marrying her. When Pharaoh learned that Sarai was Abram's wife he sent them from Egypt. Abram and his wife traveled throughout the Middle East, eventually reaching the land of Canaan. ₉

Sarai asked Abram to have children with her maid, Hagar, because she was infertile. ₁₀ Hagar bore a son, Ishmael, through whose lineage many nations were born [other than Jews].

God made an everlasting covenant with Abram and his descendants, promising him to be "the Father of many nations"; promising him a son, changing his name to Abraham, and giving him and his descendants the land of Canaan "as an everlasting possession." God only required Abraham and his descendants to "keep and faithfully obey" Him. ₁₁

God then told Abraham to change Sarai's name to Sarah (Princess) and made it possible for Sarah to bear a son.

> "I (God) will bless her, and indeed I will also give you a son by her. Yes, I will bless her, and she shall be a *Mother* of nations; kings of peoples will come from her." (Genesis 17:15-16 AMPSB)

Sarah bore a son Isaac at age 90. Isaac's birth continued the bloodline to King David and Jesus.

The Book of Ruth gives a clear picture how God continues the bloodline of the chosen Israelites through non-Jews. Ruth was a Moabite woman who married an Israelite living in the land of Moab. Her husband died along with his brother and father, leaving Ruth and her sister-in-law, Orpah, with the father's wife, Naomi. Naomi chose to return to Canaan. Orpha opted to remain in Moab, but Ruth wanted to go with Naomi. Naomi urged her to stay in Moab, but Ruth replied:

> "Do not urge me to leave you or to turn back from following you; for where you go, I will go, and where you lodge, I will lodge. Your people will be my people, and your God, my God."
> (Ruth 1:16 AMPSB)

When they reach Canaan, Ruth meets Boaz, marries him and bears a son, Orbed (father of Jesse), extending the bloodline to David (the king of Israel and ancestor of Jesus the Christ). (Ruth 4:13-22 AMPSB)

David fathered many sons with concubines before becoming king and, after being crowned, "took more concubines," siring many more sons, one of whom was Nathan, 12 through whom God established the bloodline to Mary, Jesus' mother.

Later, King David has a son with Bathsheba, Uriah's wife, and has Uriah killed in order to marry her. They conceive a son, named Solomon through whom God establishes the bloodline to Joseph, earthly father of Jesus. 13

Mary, a virgin girl, betrothed to Joseph (both descendants of King David), became "with child by [the power of] the Holy Spirit." 14

An angel of the Lord appeared to Joseph and told him to marry Mary, as the Holy Spirit had conceived the child. The angel said:

> "She will give birth to a Son, and you shall name Him Jesus (The Lord is salvation), for He will save His people from their sins.
> "All this happened in order to fulfill what the Lord had spoken through the prophet [Isaiah]:
> " 'BEHOLD, THE VIRGIN SHALL BE WITH CHILD AND GIVE BIRTH TO A SON, AND THEY SHALL CALL HIS NAME IMMANUEL'— which, when translated, means, "GOD WITH US." (Matthew 1:21-23 AMPSB)

Although the birth of Jesus took place thousands of years after the first woman spirit, Eve, it is recorded here to show the bloodline connection of Eve with Jesus. More will be revealed in the chronological record of the Jews.

God chose the women mentioned here to implement His plan. Many other women through daily life contributed to making God's plan a reality, and (I believe) He will call on many more until the end times to implement that plan.

CHAPTER TWELVE

"Now the serpent was more crafty (subtle, skilled in deceit) than any living creature of the field which the Lord God had made. And the serpent (Satan) said to the woman, "Can it really be that God has said, 'You shall not eat from any tree of the garden?' "
Genesis 3:1 AMPSB

Conflicting Spiritual Kingdoms

While mankind was beginning to establish God's planned kingdom on earth, Satan was busy setting up shop as well.

The book of Ezekiel describes Lucifer, the fallen angel:

" 'You were the model of perfection, full of wisdom and perfect in beauty.

" 'You were in Eden, the garden of God; every precious stone adorned you; ruby, topaz, and emerald, chrysolite, onyx and jasper, sapphire, turquoise and beryl.

" 'Your settings and mountings were made of gold; on the day you were created they were prepared.

" 'You were anointed as a guardian cherub, for I ordained you.

" 'You were on the holy mount of God; you walked among the fiery stones.

" 'You were blameless in your ways from the day you were created till wickedness was found in you.

" 'Through your widespread trade you were filled with violence, and you sinned.

" 'So I drove you in disgrace from the mount of God, and I expelled you, O guardian cherub, from among the fiery stones.

" 'Your heart became proud on account of your beauty, and you corrupted your wisdom because of your splendor.

" 'So I threw you to the earth.' " (28:12-17 NIV)

Pastor Mason theorizes:

"There was a brief season after the initial creation where beauty and perfection characterized everything that God had made. Even Lucifer, the glorious light-bearer appointed as the "covering cherub" over the Garden of Eden was *perfect in beauty* until he fell

73

into the sin of pride. ...

"This once perfect angelic being was so beautiful that he fell into sinful pride, and so began the descent of God's creation into the abyss of death and destruction with all of its attendant ugliness. Lucifer, the resplendent angel who once reflected the glory and beauty of the Lord, had become Satan who is now identified as the Destroyer.

"This once perfect fallen being is now hell-bent on destroying everything that is beautiful in God's creation. His first mission in the Garden of God was to win the allegiance of Adam and Eve and to convert them to the dark side. The moment Adam and Eve rebelled against God the human race descended into an abyss of sin and destruction." [1]

Pastor Davis amplifies:

> "It's not until Isaiah 14, Ezekiel 28, and Jesus' own account of Satan in Luke 10 that we have clarity surrounding the character of Lucifer, the former angel being cast from heaven for his rebellion against God. If Satan was present in the Garden of Eden, then his being cast from heaven must have taken place *before* the existence of man on earth, as there is no record of it in the six accounted days of creation." [2]

In the Ezekiel passage above, Lucifer is referred to as the guardian of earth, possibly indicating he was placed here long before Adam. It appears his fall from grace must have occurred while guardian of pre-historic earth. Perhaps after his fall God decided to create a new man, a human-spirit.

In 1 John the apostle wrote:

> "The one who practices sin [separating himself from God, and offending Him by acts of disobedience, indifference, or rebellion] is of the devil [and takes his inner character and moral values from him, not God]; for the devil has sinned *and* violated God's law from the beginning. The Son of God appeared for this purpose, to destroy the works of the devil." (3:8 AMPSB)

God and Satan have been overseeing the creation since the outset. God created a spiritual-human world. Satan cannot create either world, so must rely on taking God's creations to form his spiritual-human counter and opposing world. From his debut in the Garden of Eden, Satan has worked to deny humans of the wonderful benefits of living in God's kingdom.

Davis explains:

"If the devil can't make you bad, he'll just try to make you busy. I wonder if this may be the case in many aspects of our kingdom involvement with God."{So true!} ₃

Paul's letter to the Ephesians states that Satan roams the earth like a lion looking for opportunities to cause man to sin.
Mason expands:

> "Satan seeks to destroy that which is beautiful in order to wipe out the very memory of God from the human heart and to lock humanity into chains of darkness and deception.
> "There is considerable biblical evidence that sickness and disease is regarded as the work of the devil. (1 John 3:8)
> "The satanic kingdom is an invisible spiritual kingdom inhabited by millions, perhaps even billions, of dark spirit beings.
> "Satan and his demonic hordes **do not** have the capacity to **create** in the quantum world, but they do have the capacity to manipulate, to interfere with and to corrupt matter at a biological level."₄ {Amen, brother!}

Davis observes:

> "In the Bible, we also see spiritual references to kingdoms that parallel these previously cited physical examples (various man-made kingdoms), with the Kingdom of God and the kingdom of darkness established and operating in this physical realm. In the Old Testament book of Daniel, the prophet prays to God and then goes weeks without an answer. When an angel appears to him, he says:
> " 'Do not fear, Daniel, for from the first day that you set your heart to understand, and to humble yourself before your God, your words were heard: and I have come because of your words. But the prince of the kingdom of Persia withstood me twenty-one days; and behold, Michael, one of the chief princes, came to help me, for I had been left alone there with the kings of Persia.' Daniel 10:12-13 (NKJV)
> "It was obviously God's will that Daniel receive an answer from Him about what he prayed, yet there was something other than what God *willed* standing in the way of Daniel receiving what was released to him. This opposition was directly connected to the establishment of another kingdom in the earth with some form of spiritual leadership and authority that could contend with the

progress of an angel of God reaching Daniel with his answer. In this case, it was the prince of the kingdom of Persia." [5]

Everything Happens for a Reason

Clearly, as recorded in Daniel, a conflict between the two kingdoms had been ongoing since man's creation. But in Daniel, the conflict must have been so tremendous that God's angel delivering an answer to Daniel was detained. Is it possible that such battles continue today and delay answers to our prayers?

Pastor Kinley reminds us:

> "In our culture that calls evil good and good evil, we may sometimes forget that there are bad people who do horrible things and deserve to be arrested and removed from society. We forget that man is not basically good but inherently evil." [6]

So it is clear, many bad things happen because we are innately evil. Certainly those things are not of God. While we are sinners, I believe most want to be good and do God's will, but as Jesus said, "the spirit is willing, but the body (flesh) is weak." (Matthew 29:41 AMPSB)

Mason writes re: those who say that everything is of God:

> "But according to biblical revelation everything is not God. God chooses to clearly differentiate Himself from *all* that He has made.
>
> "According to biblical worldview there is a realm that is identified as 'spirit' that is definitely not a part of God. For example, there are created spiritual beings such as angels and archangels that constitute an invisible order of created beings, and some of these spirit beings are revealed to be the enemies of God. Satan and the entire demonic realm appear to be the dark counterparts of God's holy angels and archangels. Both God's angels and the entire host of invisible demonic beings are identified as 'spirit beings.' Angels and demons are living spiritual beings that deserve the designation of 'spirit.' But in stark contrast to pantheistic (the doctrine that all forces, manifestations, etc. of the universe are God, the worship of all gods) teachings, neither the angels nor the demons are revealed to be part of God. They are created beings.
>
> "Then there is what we call the 'spiritual realm.' This is another plane of reality that exists in a hidden and invisible dimension. Within the sum total of what we call the spiritual realm there are two realms: one of darkness and the other of

light." [7]

Paul's letter to the Ephesians recognizes the conflict:

> "For our struggle is not against flesh and blood, but against the rulers, against the authorities, against the power of this dark world and against the spiritual forces of evil in the heavenly realms." (6:12 NIV)

Many Christians explain tragic human events as part of God's will. Yet as stated above there are two kingdoms, one of love and the other of sin. Why would a loving God cause harm to His creation?

Davis queries:

> "If everything that happens is 'just God's will' then why would He tell us to pray? ...If God already knows the desires of our heart and wants to give us good gifts like a good father, or if God's will is going to be done anyway, then why the need to ask {or give mankind free will}?" [8]

Davis quotes fellow Pastor Jurgen Matthesius:

> "Some believe that God does whatever He wants, whenever He wants because He's God. They speak these things ignorantly, not knowing that God has bound himself to both His word and His laws, which He will not violate." [9]

God must share the pain with man when tragic events occur, since He made us in His image and likeness. However, He works all things out according to His plan.

> "And we know [with great confidence] that God [who is deeply concerned about us] causes all things to work together [as a plan] for good for those who love God, to those who are called according to His plan and purpose." (Romans 8:28 AMPSB)

In "Half Truths," Pastor Hamilton agrees that everything happens for a reason:

> "if in saying it, we mean that we live in a world of cause and effect. Actions create consequences.
> "If we examine the notion that everything happens for a reason, the first problem is that it eliminates the concept of

personal responsibility for our actions. If everything happens according to God's immutable plan, then whatever I do must have been God's will."10

Inherent in God's creation of man in His image and likeness is the ability to choose good or evil, a free will. He is not responsible for our every action or the actions that we create. While we hope He would interfere or change our bad decisions, He does not magically do so, but He has given us the Holy Spirit to guide our choices. If God were responsible for all actions then His plan to destroy evil could not succeed.

However, since Satan remains active, he acts to lead us astray and relies on us to fall for his deceit. Although Satan will try to direct man, he must rely on him (us) to accept his interference.

When tragedy occurs Davis questions:

"Yet, I wonder if this (God watches and weeps at every tragedy) is exactly what has happened between God and man. What if the greatest, most dividing satanic deception in the history of man has been to convince man that God is watching on in agreement and compliance with our tragedy?

"I wonder if the heart of God is torn apart with every injustice and untimely death and brutality that is committed. I wonder if He is constantly speaking, begging His creation to hear His voice and just hoping that some of His children—even one of His children—will hear Him and make a difference by raising up and joining their authority with His omnipotence, and as a result, changing their world for His glory." 11

God watches, and as stated in Paul's epistle to the Romans:

"We are assured *and* know that [God being a partner in their labor] all things work together *and* are [fitting into a plan] for good to *and* for those who love God and are called according to [His] design and purpose." (8:28 AMP)

Because God works things out after a tragedy, we want to say He caused (or let it happen) for His purpose. God is not the cause, but He picks up the pieces after we fail. He is not complicit in our tragedies.

Davis explains it this way:

"Perhaps a great many of experiences that we attribute to God *allowing or putting on us* are simply cause and effect. The cause being the establishment of kingdoms other than the kingdom of God in this earth, and the result being the direct or indirect wages of the establishment of those ungodly kingdoms." [12]

The Conflict in the Future

When we look at the atrocities happening in the world and compare them with what the Bible says about God, it just does not equate that He is complicit in such events. As with Adam, the evil one still exists and is active in human events today.

Mason examines the conflict through the apostle Paul's writings in 2 Corinthians 4:4, noting, there is a veil between the spiritual worlds, and Satan blinds the unbelieving so we cannot see God's glory.[13]

So why didn't God destroy Satan for interfering with His plan to establish an earthly kingdom? We don't know for sure, but Francis A. Schaeffer in his book, "A Christian Manifesto," includes an excerpt from Heney De Bracton's *De Legibus et Consuetudinibus* (circa 1250):

"God in His sheer power could have crushed Satan in his revolt by use of that sufficient force, though many ways were open to Him, for His ineffable redemption of the human race, the true mercy of God chose this most powerful way to destroy the devil's work, He would not use the power of force but the 'reason of justice.' But because of God's character, justice came before the use of power alone. Therefore, Christ died that justice, rooted in what God is, would be the solution. Therefore, power is not first, but justice is first in [God's] society and law."[14]

In Revelation, Satan, who was given access to heaven during his time on earth, will revolt against God and be driven from heaven forever, taking many angelic beings with him. The war will continue on earth until God destroys him and his host of followers. [15] Ultimately God will destroy Satan, and all who follow him or do not believe in God will be thrown into a lake of fire. [16]

Adam and Eve's acceptance of Satan's temptation introduced sin into God's kingdom.[17] Satan tempted God's chosen people throughout the Jewish people's history. Satan tried to tempt Jesus in the wilderness "after He had gone without food for forty days and forty nights. He became hungry."[18] While Jesus did not yield to Satan's temptation, he continues to temp mankind today. Only faith in God through Jesus and the Holy Spirit helps us to resist that temptation. We cannot escape Satan's power alone.

Until Satan is destroyed we have to live with his presence in our lives. The analogy of the devil sitting on one shoulder and the Holy Spirit on the other describes our dilemma, each one encouraging us to follow their path.

God gave us one advantage: He wrote what is right and wrong on our hearts. [18] We have the free will to choose our path.. We just have to listen to our heart, as God's servant Job did.

The Book of Job

"There was a man in the land of Uz whose name was Job; and that man was blameless and upright, and one who feared God [with reverence] and abstained from and turned away from evil [because he honored God]. ...Then Satan asked the Lord, 'Does Job fear God for nothing?' "
Job 1:1, 9 AMPSB

Although he was not one of them, Job's book appears in the same section of the Bible as God's prophets.

> "It is a story that is not part of the flow of the history of Israel. ... Its primary subject matter is the most basic question man has of God: Why do we suffer?"[19]

Job records a "man blameless and upright; he feared God and shunned evil."[20] The book contains the dialog between God and Satan concerning the loyalty of Job to God, no matter what disasters befell him.

Job remains faithful to God and is rewarded many times over what he lost. [21] Job is perhaps the only Old Testament character (besides Enoch and Elijah whom God took directly to heaven) who expressed belief in an afterlife.

> "(But as for me), I know that my Redeemer lives, and that in the end he will stand upon the earth. And after my skin has been destroyed, yet in my flesh I will see God: I myself will see him with my own eyes—I, and not another. How my heart yearns within me." (Job 19:25 NIV)

The book is important because it records God and Satan conversing about the earth and mankind. Job illustrates how Satan is always trying to cause evil. It also reinforces God's action in creating the earth when He speaks directly to Job asking where he was "when He laid the earth's foundation."[22]

Job is thought to have been a contemporary of Abraham. [23]

Job and Us

The book of Job has great bearing on our understanding of the relationship among God, Satan and mankind. Job was:

> "blameless and upright, he feared God and shunned evil.
> "One day the angels came to present themselves before the Lord;

Satan also came with them." (Job 1:1, 6 NIV)

Thereafter God and Satan, two spiritual beings, competed in testing Job's faith. This heavenly contest is significant as it validates the existence of Satan and the battle between God and Satan for man's soul. The conflict also reveals the power Satan imposes on mankind. Satan causes other nations to steal Job's livestock and kill his family. He also creates a storm to destroy his house and gives Job sores from head to toe.

But God did not allow Satan to kill Job, showing that He was ultimately in control. In spite of Job's friends and wife, who blamed God for causing Job's fate and urged him to cease loving Him, Job remained faithful to God. The lesson for us is to listen to God with your heart, not your friends.

I think Job's story was included in the Bible to tell us that God allowed Satan to demonstrate the power he is capable of using to achieve his will. We need to know his power as Satan continues to use it against us. Satan uses others to do his will; apparently he even has the power to alter the weather, and to inflict illnesses. These powers are beyond our ability to fight unless God is with us and prevents Satan from destroying us. Think about it. Many people die each year from these causes, yet others are saved. Why?

Like Job, there is a battle for our souls, with the outcome ours to choose. Davis writes:

> "From the beginning, the devil has attempted to dissuade man from believing in the benefits of the kingdom of God or the consequences of living outside of it." [24]

Job's faith never wavered even after his wife and friends counseled turning away from God. As a result, God restored Job's wealth several times over. [25] We can be like Job if we truly believe and worship God.

CHAPTER THIRTEEN

"Now having been asked by the Pharisees when the kingdom of God would come, He replied, 'The kingdom of God is not coming with signs to be observed or with a visible display; nor will people say, "Look! Here it is!" or, "There it is!" For the kingdom of God is among you [because of My presence].' "
Luke 17:20-21 AMPSB

God's Kingdom

When God created the heavens and the earth He proclaimed His creation very good.

Although we do not know for sure why God created our universe, the Bible unmistakably states that His intent was to establish a kingdom on earth for His glory:

"The heavens are the heavens of the Lord, but the earth He has given to the children of men." (Ps 115:16 AMPSB)

Psalm 8 goes further:

"When I see and consider Your heavens, the work of Your fingers, the moon and the stars, which You have established, What is man that You are mindful of him? And the son of [earthborn] man that You care for him? Yet, You have made him a little lower than God, and You have crowned him with glory and honor. You made him to have dominion over the works of Your hands; You have put all things under his feet." (8:3-6 AMPSB)

Pastor Davis in "Quantum Christianity" writes:

"As I read the Scripture (Luke 17:20-21) again, I realized the kingdom of God is not a place at all, but an *experience* where we aren't seeking an end goal, in the kingdom, but rather we are seeking a way of life and an experience that alters our reality." [1]

Who among us has made something of value, or wished we could, and when it was good, tried to protect it from being destroyed? It was God's creation and He began to watch over it. God appeared on earth throughout the history of the Old Testament to maintain His kingdom and guide His followers' ways.

Pastor Qureshi recounts:

> "Starting with the third chapter of Genesis, the very beginning of the Bible, we find God walking in the garden where Adam and Eve were (Gen 3:8). In Genesis 18, God appears to Abraham as a man and talks with him. In Exodus 34:5-6, God stood with Moses and walked in front of him. In Exodus 24:9-11, Aaron, Moses, and seventy-two-elders all saw God at the same time and even dined with him. In an even more tangible experience, Jacob wrestled with God in Genesis 32:24-28. In Exodus 13:21, when the Hebrews needed guidance in the desert, God personally led them as a pillar of smoke by day and pillar of fire by night. In another, rather important account, God commanded the Hebrews to make him a tabernacle, a place where he would descend and "dwell among them." (Ex 25:8-9 NIV) After they built it, God filled the tabernacle with his glory (Ex 40:34). These many appearances of God on earth are often called theophanies." [2]

God Is Here

God never stopped appearing on earth. Jesus lived on the earth for 33 years. After Jesus' crucifixion and resurrection, and just before He ascended into heaven, He left (sent, or gave) the Holy Spirit to all believers. The Holy Spirit is still here and active in our lives. [3]

Mankind's sinful nature changed God's planned kingdom as noted by Pastor Davis:

> "With the establishment of the kingdom of sin on the earth also came a separation from the original intent of God for man to live in the full benefit of His kingdom through an intimate relationship with Him and institution of His principles. Sin created a separation between God and man that separated man from the benefit of living within the fullness of God's kingdom on the earth." [4]

In spite of man's sinful nature, God continues to control His Kingdom today, and will forever. Why does God want to save a sinful mankind and specifically our spirits, yours and mine, and those of all mankind throughout earth's history? Is it to win the battle of Good vs. Evil? What does He want with our spirit? What we know is that He loves us so much that He sent His Son to provide the means for us to be saved for His spiritual world, and He is willing to fight for us to save us from permanent death. ₅

The Earthly Kingdom

What should God's kingdom on earth look like?
As Davis pictures it:

> "Within God's kingdom rule (His way of doing things) on earth, we have a specific understanding of how to function and what it looks like, but we also have present at the same time, in direct proximity and opposition to God's kingdom, a well established kingdom of darkness, where people are directly influenced by evil and destructive principles that are in opposition to the kingdom of God." ₆

From Scripture we learn that God expects us to maintain orderly lives, love one another and fight evil. Through the centuries man has established governments to maintain order and carry out His plan. God expects the citizens to obey those governments that are established on His principles.

> "Be submissive to every human institution (government) *and* authority for the sake of the Lord. whether it be to the emperor as supreme,
> "Or to governors as sent by Him to bring vengeance (punishment, justice) to those who do wrong and encourage those who do good service.
> "For it is God's will *and* intention that by doing right [your good and honest lives] should silence (muzzle, gag) the ignorant charges and ill-informed criticisms of foolish persons.
> "[Live] as free people, [yet] without employing your freedom as a pretext for wickedness; but [live at all times] as servants of God.
> "Show respect for all men [treat them honorably], Love the brotherhood (the Christian fraternity of which Christ is the head). Reverence God. Honor the emperor {head of state}."
> (1 Peter 2:13-17 AMP)

In his book, "A Christian Manifesto," Francis A. Schaeffer writes:

> "God has ordained the state as a *delegated* authority; it is not autonomous. The state is to be an agent of justice, to restrain evil by punishing the wrongdoer, and to protect the good in society. When it does the reverse, *it has no proper authority*. It is then a usurped authority and as such it becomes lawless and is tyranny.

"When a government is not established on God's commandments, its citizens will fail to live to the fullness of what God expects for His kingdom. When governing bodies do not operate under God's delegated authority, they should be challenged and changed though not necessarily destroyed by their citizens." 7

"When in the Course of human events it becomes necessary for one people to dissolve the political bands which have connected them with another...they should declare the causes which impel them to (the) separation....that whenever any Form of Government becomes destructive of these ends (Life, Liberty and pursuit of Happiness) it is the Right of the People to alter or abolish it and to institute new government ..." (The Declaration of Independence, thirteen united States of America, July 4, 1776)

Many of our ancestors have fought and died to maintain God's kingdom throughout history. God directed Adam to establish His kingdom on earth, and as members of His kingdom we are expected to continue to maintain it.

CHAPTER FOURTEEN

"For God knows that on the day you eat from it (the Tree of Good and Evil) your eyes will be opened [that is, you will have greater awareness], and you will be like God, knowing [the difference between] good and evil."
Genesis 3:5 AMPSB

The War with Evil Begins

Satan's appearance as a talking snake enticing Adam and Eve to eat the forbidden fruit of the Tree of Knowledge, when eaten, began the battle of good and evil on earth.

Being created in His image (with the gift of free will), has been problematic for mankind. Satan has continued to challenge man to sin, knowing that free will has proved, and will continue to prove, difficult for mankind.

Pastor Davis states in "Quantum Christianity":

"(But) in Genesis 1, we discover it's not a perfect universe. Satan had rebelled and had been cast out of heaven, and with him a portion of the fallen angels took dominion over the earth. God could have destroyed the devil and his host with a word, but instead He chose to defeat darkness through his delegated authority—those (man) made in His image who were (and are) lovers of God by choice. And since man was given the keys of dominion over the planet, the devil would have to get his authority from them. And as it was in the beginning, it seems consistent and important to realize that even today, Satan is empowered through man's agreement." [1]

"I believe that it's possible there is a war ensuing (whether we are aware of it or not) for the heart of mankind and there are casualties often resulting in human experiences that are directly connected to that war, even when (and maybe *especially* when) man is not aware of it." [2] {emphasis added}

Paul's epistle to the Ephesians identifies the enemy:

"For our struggle is not against flesh and blood, but against the rulers, against the authorities, against the powers of this dark world

and against the spiritual forces of evil in the heavenly realms."
(6:12 NIV)

The existence of evil has caused man an unending battle to appreciate all God has done for him. From the very start, man has failed to recognize God as his creator, choosing evil over good. The story of Adam and Eve tells us that God disciplined them for ignoring His direction. ₃

Mankind's choice of the Tree Of Good And Evil over the Tree Of Life, ignited a war between good and evil, that continues today. Mankind, as recorded in the Bible, has not done what God intended, but through all the tragedies, He has continued to forgive our sins through His grace and love for His creation. ₄

God's Covenant

The entire Bible describes the covenant relationship of God and His creation of man and the universe. Adam fails to listen to God, is punished and forced to leave the garden and till the soil for survival. Romans tells of God's plan and His love from the very beginning:

> "{He} was already planning a means to redeem man and re-establish His relationship with him." (5:12-21 AMP)

Davis states it this way:

> "The redeemer and promised Savior who was foreshadowed in Genesis 3:15 would be the One who would again fulfill the purpose of God in creating the world by establishing the kingdom rule of God in the earth." ₅

Adam's son Cain kills his brother Abel because he believes their father and God favored Abel over himself. Abel's murder is the first recorded in the Bible. Cain's sin is the second sin [after Adam and Eve's] so recorded. Some people might say it was God's will that Cain kill Abel, but the Bible does not support it. Cain chose to kill Abel, not God.

God Reacts Directly with Man

The significance of this record is that God talked directly with Cain, but did not direct his actions.

God asks:

> "Where is your brother Abel?" Cain replies: "I don't know....
> Am I my brother's keeper?" God punishes Cain with a curse that
> takes away his work of the soil and drives him from the land to

be a "restless wanderer on the earth." (Gen 4:9-12 NIV)

Throughout Genesis and the rest of the Old Testament, God speaks directly to humans. God spoke to Adam. He spoke to Cain. He spoke directly to the prophets, and in all cases He was correcting them or charging them to follow His commandments.

There is sufficient evidence that what happens on earth by man's hand is not God's will. If the opposite were the case, that would be saying that God tells man to sin, or God's will includes sin.

Most of the time mankind has not done what God expects. Things happen as a result of cause and effect, not because of God's will. Man is personally responsible for his actions; God does not control us like puppets.

Thinking everything that happens is God's will would make Him responsible for the sin in the world and every horrible act His fault. The truth is God does not orchestrate every action of man; the existence of evil causes man to sin, not God. [6]

God spoke directly with Adam and his son Cain, but not until Adam's son Seth, some 130 years later, is it recorded that anyone began to worship God. As noted in Genesis:

> "Man began to call on the name of the Lord [in worship through prayer, praise, and thanksgiving]." (Gen 4:26 AMPSB)

It is important to note man's first recorded worshipping of God. There appears to be no record of God again talking directly with Seth's offspring until He spoke to Noah, 10 generations [1,000 years] after Adam.

From Adam and Eve to Noah, mankind—with some exceptions, such as Enoch and Elijah—continued to choose evil over good. (God actually took Enoch and Elijah directly to Heaven without them experiencing death on earth. These are the only deaths discussed in the Old Testament where anyone else went straight to Heaven). [7]

God:

> "saw how great man's wickedness on earth had become, and that every inclination of the thoughts of his heart was only evil all the time. The Lord was grieved that he had made man on the earth, and His heart was filled with pain. So the Lord said, "I will wipe mankind, whom I have created, from the face of the earth—men and animals, and creatures that move along the ground, and birds of the air—for I am grieved that I have made them.' But Noah found Grace (favor) in the eyes of the Lord." (Gen 6:5-8 NIV)

A Contingency Plan

Although God was disappointed by what became of His creation, He had a contingency plan. God (by a covenant) directed Noah, a true follower of God, to build an ark to save the farm animals and some wild beasts of the earth before God flooded it. 8 The flood was the punishment God gave to destroy the prevailing sin. Noah's ark was a means of salvation for him and his family.

Thousands of years later God provided another way for man's salvation, His Son the Christ.

> "Salvation is found in no one else, for there is no other name under Heaven given to men by which we must be saved." (Acts 4:12 NIV)

God flooded the earth and destroyed all life except Noah and his family and all the creatures Noah had placed on the ark as God commanded. God could have, but did not completely destroy the earth and mankind with the flood because of His covenant with Adam. In Genesis 3:15 God explains that He had a plan for man's redemption, a contingency plan for when he fell to sin. From a woman's seed a savior would overcome sin and redeem man from sin. This was *God's plan from the very beginning* to save mankind!

The Bloodline Continues

Although grieved, because He loved Noah for his faithfulness, God made a covenant with Noah and his descendants to carry out His plan. God's promise:

> "I now establish my covenant with you and with your descendants after you and with every living creature that was with you—the birds, the livestock and all the wild animals, all those that came out of the ark with you—every living creature on earth. I establish my covenant with you: Never again will all life be cut off by waters of a flood; never again will there be a flood to destroy the earth." (Gen 9:10-11 NIV)

The rainbow is the token or sign of a covenant or solemn pledge between Noah and God and for all generations. As a result, the flood ended, and mankind essentially started over with Noah's family.9 Thus, if the flood covered the whole world {some biblical scholars believe it may have only covered the world then known to man}, the entire world population is descended from Noah's sons. 10

Those descendants created many nations as they spread throughout the earth after the flood. 11

At that time all the nations spoke one language enabling them to gather to build a tower (city of Babel) to the sky to become like God.

God saw what was happening and said:

> " 'Come, let Us (Father, Son, Holy Spirit) go down and confuse and mix their language, so that they will not understand one another's speech.'
>
> "So the Lord scattered them abroad from there over the surface of the entire earth; and they stopped building the city.
>
> "Therefore, the name of the city was Babel—because there the Lord confounded the language of the entire earth; and from that place the Lord scattered *and* dispersed them over the surface of all the earth." (Gen 11:7-9 AMPSB)

Although the descendants from Adam to Noah were not Jews exclusively, the Bible's authors included their history with that of the Jews. The Jewish race starts with Abraham, who does not appear in the Bible until hundreds of years later. [12]

The genealogy from Adam through Seth to Noah is important because it:

> "helps us understand God's plan for the world. The corruption of the human race threatens the godly line.
>
> "The human race can be divided into two classes, the godly who listen to God and the ungodly who reject God.
>
> "Each descendant of Adam and Eve must choose whether he or she will listen to God or rebel against Him." [13]

We are descendants of Noah and therefore must choose which path we want to follow, God's or the evil one's.

CHAPTER FIFTEEN

*" 'I will establish My covenant between Me and you and your
descendants after you throughout their generations for an everlasting
covenant, to be God to you and to your descendants. I will give to you
and to your descendants after you the land in which you are a stranger
[moving from place to place], all the land of Canaan, as an everlasting
possession [of property]; and I will be their God.' "*
Genesis 17:7-8 AMPSB

God's Chosen People and His Covenants

God selected Abram [later Abraham] to establish a connection with
mankind. Since the birth of Adam, God had spoken with his descendants,
sharing His will for them, but there was not an intimate father-child
relationship with them until Abram expressed his reverence for God.
Pastor Mason illuminates:

> "God revealed Himself to Abraham and so began a journey of
> unfolding revelation as God began to reveal Himself and His
> purposes for the creation which He himself has made for His own
> glory."[1]

Rabbi Donin explains perhaps why God chose Abraham to establish a
Covenant:

> "(But) Abraham is credited with being the founder of the world's
> first monotheistic faith because unlike others whose monotheism
> was like an oasis in a spiritual wilderness which dried up and
> disappeared with their deaths, Abraham devoted himself to the
> propagation of the faith. He succeeded in passing this faith on to
> his son, Isaac, and Isaac in turn passed it on to his son Jacob
> (Israel), the latter to his twelve sons, the heads of the Tribes of
> Israel, and thence into the stream of Israel's history and the history
> of mankind. 'For I have known him, that he may instruct his
> children and his posterity to keep the way of the Lord by doing
> what is just and right...' (Gen 18:19)
>
> "This ability of Abraham to transmit his faith may be what most
> qualified him in the sight of God as the person with whom to

establish a 'Covenant' that involved eternal responsibilities in bringing the name of the Lord to all the peoples of the world." [2]

Abraham had two sons, Ishmael to Hagar his maid, and Isaac to Sarah, his wife. Ishmael was forced to leave Abraham and settle in lands east of Egypt with his offspring. They were excluded in the covenant. [3] The offspring of Ishmael are listed in 1 Chronicles 1:29-31. There is no further biblical record of Ishmael.

God made a covenant with Abraham and his offspring [Isaac's], selecting them as His chosen people, promising them His care as long as "he and his descendants kept the covenant by worshipping God." [4]

God gave Abraham and his descendants the land of Canaan [modern Israel] as their homeland via the covenant. In return He demanded that his descendants worship Him. God selected Abraham, (because he obeyed God) and his descendants as His people, promising He would be their God.[5]

God's plan for the Jewish people is written in the book of Deuteronomy:

> "For you are a holy people [set apart] to the Lord your God; and the Lord has chosen you out of all the peoples who are on the earth to be a people for His own possession." (14:2 AMPSB)

The New Covenant

God's covenant with Abraham is one of His most important agreements. His word made in the covenant with Abraham would control the future of mankind until a new covenant was made, almost 2,000 years later. God promised to care for Abraham and his descendants. God could not send a savior [Jesus Christ] later as a descendant of Abraham if he broke the original covenant.

However, when He did send His Son Jesus, God made a new covenant, executing the old, but providing a new relationship with God. The new covenant gives *everyone* the opportunity to continue a relationship with God after death through God's grace, if they accept His love.

Pastor Davis (in "Quantum Christianity") describes God's unbreakable covenant, from His perspective, as Him calling His people in love, and them responding to that love as expressed by loyalty to the covenant.

> "The kingdom of God... is a *covenantal kingdom*. Everything that is available to man within the kingdom of God is a direct result of God's covenant promises toward man. In essence, man's covenant with God is the *Constitution* of the kingdom of God." [6]
>
> "This model of love continues through every covenant

established between God and man throughout the Old Testament and is finally completely fulfilled in the *new and final* covenant through Christ." 7

In Hebrews, the apostle Paul explains the certainty of God's promise (covenant). God made a promise to Abraham that He kept in spite of the unfaithfulness of his heirs because He cannot lie. In like manner God has made a promise (covenant) with us by sending His Son to atone for our sins in order for us to be acceptable in His kingdom. 8

Jewish Early History with God
The Old Testament contains the history of the Jews' relationship with God and their life in light of the covenant. The story of Lot and his wife showed how serious God was when His people failed to keep the covenant: He destroyed the cities of Sodom and Gomorrah and turned Lot's wife into a pillar of stone for not obeying His directions. 9

God instructed Abraham to sacrifice his first-born son, Isaac, perhaps to test Abraham's faith. Abraham took Isaac to be sacrificed, but because he obeyed God, Isaac was spared from death. 10

Isaac's son, Jacob, steals his brother Esau's birthright, flees to live with Laban, Isaac's brother, marries Laban's daughter Rachel and dreams of a stairway to Heaven to seek and receive God's blessing. 11

While returning to his homeland (Canaan), when Jacob was alone:

> "a Man (manifestation of God) [came and] wrestled with him until daybreak." (Gen 32:24 AMPSB)

Jacob's name is changed by God to Israel:

> "Your name shall no longer be Jacob, but Israel; for you struggled with God and with men and have prevailed." (Gen 32:28 AMPSB)

Jacob meets Esau, who forgives him, and they part to different lands. Esau and his offspring establish the kingdom of Edom. 12 Jacob returns to Beth-el Canaan with his family. 13

Jacob's return to the land of Canaan is significant at this point in Jewish history as it continues the establishment of Israel as the land given by God to Abraham for him and his descendants.

Years later Moses returned to Egypt as God asked him to seek release of the Hebrew slaves. Having lived in the Pharaoh's household, through God's power, Moses was able to convince the Pharaoh to allow the Jewish slaves to leave Egypt with God's help (the 10 plagues). [10]

God chose Moses to lead the Jews out of slavery, later gave him the Ten Commandments [11] and guided his writing of the Torah (first five books of the Old Testament). God had a plan for Moses' life, from birth, as He has and will continue to have for all people.

Escape to the Promised Land

" I promise to rescue them from the drudgery and humiliation they are undergoing, and to take them to the land ....flowing with milk and honey.' "

Exodus 3:17 NLB

After escaping, Moses led God's people [Exodus 12:37 puts their number at about 600,000 men plus women and children; some biblical scholars estimate possibly 3 million in all] from Egypt back to the land of Canaan where Jacob had lived, wandering the desert for 40 years because of the Jewish disobedience to God's covenant. [12] The logistics to support this many people at that time must have been horrendous—but not for God.

Miller records in his "Complete Guide to the Bible":

> "During that time, God organizes the people into a nation. He gives them hundreds of laws—religious, civil, and criminal. These laws set up a system for worship and for running the country, with God as king." [13]

Miller continues with the Jewish creed that Moses shared with the exiting slaves:

> "Listen, O Israel! The Lord is our God, the Lord alone. And you must love the Lord God with all your heart, all your soul, and all your strength. And you must commit yourselves wholeheartedly to these commands that I am giving you today [Ten Commandments]. Repeat them again and again to your children." (Deuteronomy 6:4-7 NLT) [14]

Earlier in Deuteronomy, Moses assembles the Israelites to tell them of a new covenant made with God:

> "Hear, O Israel, the statutes and ordinances which I speak (the Ten Commandments) in your hearing this day, that you may learn them and take heed and do them. The Lord our God made a covenant with us in Horeb. The Lord made this covenant not with

our fathers, but with us, who are all of us here alive this day."
(5:1-3 AMP)

God dictated the Ten Commandments to Moses to show how all people must live to maintain His favor, a relationship to be continued generation after generation. (The commandments define the difference between good and evil and form the basis for our laws today.)

Moses was denied the privilege to lead the Israelites into the Promised Land because he had disobeyed God by misusing the powers given him. [15] Moses dies [16] and Joshua leads God's people into Canaan.

The Land of Canaan [17]

"…a land now occupied by the Canaanites, Hittites, Amorites, Perizzites, Hivites and Jebusites."
Exodus 3:17 NLT

Why did God select the land of Canaan for His chosen people? The Bible starts with Adam and Eve in the Garden of Eden, thought to be in the Tigris and Euphrates River valley in modern Iraq. [18] The Bible tells us that God removed Adam and Eve from the garden after their sin. [19]

Adam and his descendants must have remained in the area near the Garden of Eden, until God made a covenant with Abraham, giving the land of Canaan for him and his descendants. While the river valley terrain appears more suitable for human life, God chose land along the Mediterranean Sea.

The land of Canaan is not very big, but its position between the sea and the desert at the eastern end of the Mediterranean Sea renders it a strategic site in the Middle East. The land supports agriculture and livestock production, allowing farming for grain, vineyards for grapes and orchards for fruit crops. The plains, hills and pasture lands provide grazing for sheep and cattle. The Lake of Galilee is rich in fish, and the Dead Sea contains salt and minerals. [20]

While suitable, why here? The Zondervan Handbook to the Bible explains God's plan to give Abraham the land of Israel because it would sustain the nation promised to him. Although not all generations lived in the promised land, Abraham's descendants were numerous and continued to return to the land God gave them over 4,000 years ago. Israel is and has been the home of the Jews ever since. [21]

Genesis and the rest of the Old Testament describes how God had to overcome obstacle after obstacle to fulfill His plan for the Israelites:

*Abram [Abraham] was forced to move to Egypt when famine struck Canaan, [22] but returned many years later. [23]

*Abraham's grandson Jacob also moved his family to Egypt because of famine. [24]

*The Israelites remained in Egypt as slaves for more than 400 years until being led by Moses back to Canaan, God's promised land. [25]

*Joshua led the Israelites in taking the land from the Canaanites, [26] after which it was divided among the 12 tribes of Israel but never called the nation of Israel until King David's rule in 1010-970 B.C. [27]

*The history of Israel is filled with foreign forces taking the land from the Jews after they disobey God. During the period of the Judges (roughly 1220 to 1050 B.C.) wars were fought with Cushan-Rishataim, Moab, Philistines, Jabin and Sisera, Midianites, Amalekites and Ammonites. [28]

*The Israelites held the land until the invasion of the Assyrians in 729 B.C. when many Jews were taken as captives to Assyria. The Babylonians defeated the Assyrians in 604 B.C. and again in 597 B.C. attacked Judah, destroying Jerusalem and taking survivors captive to Babylon. In 539 B.C. the Persians conquered the Babylonian Empire and freed the Jewish captives to return to Israel.

*Alexander the Great conquered the entire Middle East in 334 B.C., followed by the Romans about one century B.C. [29]

During the Middle Ages the Holy Lands were invaded by European Templars, the Arabs and the Turks. The land remained in the Ottoman Empire (Turks) from 1516 to 1919. [30]

Following World War I, the Jewish homeland was occupied by the British and remained in their control through World War II.

In 1946, Jews from around the world returned to Israel to fulfill God's promise to Abraham made thousands of years before. After several years of fighting with the modern inhabitants, the United Nations in 1947 "approved a plan to partition Palestine into a Jewish and Arab state over the Arabs' objections. In May 1948, Israel was officially declared an independent state." [31]

God kept His word and provided the "Promised Land" to the Israelites time and time again for more than 4,000 years.

CHAPTER SEVENTEEN

" I will give to you [Abraham] and to your descendants after you the land in which you are a stranger [moving from place to place], all the land of Canaan, as an everlasting possession [of property]; and I will be their God.' "
Genesis 17:8 AMPSB

Israelites and God in the Promised Land

During the exodus, God asks the Israelites to build Him a "Holy Sanctuary" so He could live among them (a tent tabernacle). ₁ Later, the Israelites built a temple in Jerusalem. Knowing the Israelite tendency to sin, God asks them to:

> " 'Consecrate yourselves and be holy, because I an holy.' "
> (Leviticus 11:44 AMPSB)

In The Third Book of Moses, called Leviticus, God shows the Israelites how He wants them to express devotion and gives them a method to atone for their sins.

God set the rules for giving animal sacrifices to make them acceptable to Him. The ritual of animal sacrifices is the Old Testament's method of substituting atonement for sinful human behavior.

> " 'The life of the body is in its blood,' God explains: 'I have given you the blood on the altar to purify you, making you right with the Lord. It is the blood, given in exchange for a life, that makes purification possible.' " (Leviticus 17:11 AMPSB)

Later we see and can understand why God sacrifices the blood of His Son, Jesus the Christ, to make us "right with the Lord." This is a *very important concept* in understanding what God expects from His creation.

God also told them as His chosen people to love your neighbor as yourself 2 and to maintain allegiance to God and He would bless them and would dwell among them, but if they break their contract and disobey Him, He will scatter them among all nations from one end of the earth to the other. 3

The Disobedient Generations

The generation after Joshua's did not know or worship God. They worshipped idols [Baals] like their non-Jewish neighbors. ₄

For the next 3,000 years God sent upright men and women chosen from the people, called judges, ₅ to lead the Israelites to freedom.

But the Israelites continued to disobey God and worship idols. God scattered them as He had warned as punishment.

The judges, Ezra and Nehemiah, led the Israelites back to Israel and out of Babylonian captivity, and in thanks to God, established a new temple in Jerusalem.

The era of judges was when:

> "people turned from God to worship idols, they were punished, after which they returned to God in repentance, only to slip back again into the old sins." ₆

Miller elaborates:

> "Each time the Israelites repented of their sins and asked God for deliverance from their attackers, God sent a leader called a 'judge.'
>
> "That word's a bit outdated now since we associate judges with court cases. The Hebrew term had a much broader meaning, which included 'ruler' or 'leader.' 'Tribal ruler' is probably a better way of describing them." ₇

Miller further describes this as a period when:

> "The Israelites get locked into a cycle they can't seem to break. It goes like this: They sin, usually by worshipping idols of Canaan; God punishes them, usually by sending an oppressor such as raiders or a bully nation that forces the Israelites to do as they're told (or be taken into slavery). The Israelites repent and ask God to help them; He forgives them and sends a hero (judge or prophet) who stops the oppression. This happens over and over—at least a dozen times." ₈

While God punishes His people's disobedience, He forgives when they repent.

Although not a judge per se, Esther was able to save the Jews in exile because she was wife of the king of Persia. If God had not led Esther into the King's harem, the Jews in exile might have been eliminated as a people. The Jewish holiday, The Feast of Purim, was instituted to "remind the Jews of God's deliverance from their day of destruction." [9]

Judges such as Gideon, Samson and Samuel led God's people against their enemies to preserve their freedom. During this period, God led Ruth [non-Jewish] to return with her mother-in-law to Canaan where she married Boaz, thereby continuing the bloodline leading to Jesus. Their son, Obed, became the father of Jesse, who was the father of David (the ancestor of Jesus Christ).[10]

The Time of Kings

"Then all the elders of Israel gathered together and came to Samuel at Ramah and said to him, 'Look, you have grown old, and your sons do not walk in your ways. Now appoint us a king to judge us [and rule over us] like all the other nations.' "
1 Samuel 8:4-5 AMPSB

War between nations became a way of life for the Israelites, since they did not do as God asked. Time after time, the Israelites would turn from God to worship false gods. As a result they lost wars, were captured, taken from their homeland, and enslaved elsewhere. (After numerous enslavements they would return to their homeland.)

In 1050 B.C. the Israelites asked God to give them kings to rule the land in hope that they would gain God's favor to protect them from enemies. The Israelites pressured God's last judge, Samuel, to ask Him for a king to lead the people as in other nations. [11] Samuel, feeling he has failed to lead the Israelites as God expected, asks God, who grants their request, with reservations:

> "The Lord said to Samuel, 'Listen to the voice of the people in regard to all that they say to you, for they have not rejected you, but they have rejected Me from being King over them. Like all the deeds which they have done since the day that I brought them from Egypt even to this day—in that they have abandoned (rejected) Me and served other gods—so they are doing to you also.' " (1 Samuel 8:7-8 AMPSB)

Sounds kind of like us; we want God's favor but not His guidance.

God has always been King of the universe and He returns as Jesus, King of the Jews—and the entire world—to prove it!

Saul, as the first king of Israel, reigned for 42 years [12] and died in battle with the Philistines. [13] Kings David and Solomon were two of the subsequent leaders considered the greatest of all, both of whom God blessed. They wrote most of the Books of Psalms and Proverbs and introduced music in the worship of God.

Psalms is "a collection of songs that literally covers hundreds of years of

Jewish history from the patriarchs through the post-exilic period. The Book of Psalms is practical and personal as well as dramatic and magnificently beautiful. The Psalms teach how to pray, how to grieve, how to rejoice, and how to worship…It is the prayer book for all who believe in the God of the universe."[14]

Proverbs, in contrast, is a book of wisdom passed from generation to succeeding generations on how to deal with life's daily problems. [15] Though written for Jews in biblical times, it remains practical advice for addressing today's problems.

Even though God blessed them, both kings eventually sinned. King David has the general of his army placed in battle so he is killed in order to marry the general's widow, Bathsheba. [16] David's son, Solomon, rules more than 40 years in peace. God blessed Solomon with the gift of wisdom. Next to Jesus, fully God and fully man, He made Solomon the second wisest man ever to live. [17]

Miller points out that even Solomon, in his wisdom, questions the value of life and why we are on the earth:

"What's the point of life—why are we humans here?…

"He (Solomon) looks in all the logical places, where people measure their worth: by the work they do, the wealth they accumulate, the education they gain, the pleasures they seek, and the relationships they cherish"… (concluding:) 'Everything is meaningless.'…

"That said, he reaches a surprising conclusion. Instead of urging us to eat, drink, and party like there's no tomorrow, he suggests that we live in a way that would express gratitude to the one who gave us life. 'Honor God,' he says, and 'do what he tells you.' " (Ecclesiastes 12:13 THE MESSAGE) [18]

To honor God, Solomon has Israel's first permanent temple built in Jerusalem. After its completion, the Lord appears to Solomon and tells him:

" 'I have heard your prayer and supplication which you have made before Me; I have consecrated this house which you have built by putting My Name and My Presence there forever. My eyes and My heart shall be there perpetually.' "
(1 Kings 9:3 AMPSB)

Solomon's "700 wives; princesses, and 300 concubines, turned his heart away from God," [19] and in old age he is lured to worship their idols. For his sin, Israel is split into two nations, Israel and Judah. [20]

Four hundred years later, Babylonian invaders in 586 B.C. destroy the temple Solomon built, take prisoners to Babylon, essentially erasing the Jewish nation from the world map. Israel would not resurface as a nation for more than 500 years when the Persians would destroy the Babylonians and free the Jews from exile. [21]

The Temple Is Rebuilt

Fifty years later (in 536 B.C.) the Persians defeat the Babylonians and hold the captives in Persia. As part of God's plan, Esther convinces the king not to wipe out the Jewish captives as planed by the king's officials. God's plans save the Jews in exile from extinction in Persia.[22] The King of Persia releases the Israelites from captivity. [23]

Over the next century the Jews return to Israel and begin to rebuild the temple destroyed by the Babylonians. The temple is not as grand as the one built by Solomon, but it lasts 500 years, longer than any other. .... (Solomon's temple, 400 years; or Herod's in Jesus' time 100 years). [24]

Besides rebuilding the temple the Jewish leaders required the returning Jews to end marriages to pagans made while in captivity, because those unions were determined to have led Jews to worship idols. [25]

Yet, the sins of the Israelites became so pervasive that God left the temple, making it just a house of worship. The Romans subsequently destroyed the structure in A.D.70.

God's Love Never Wavers

Even though God gave them kings, such as David and Solomon and their successors, the Israelites did not understand that God is sovereign and demands that mankind obey His will and worship *only* Him. Even though King David did not obey God's will, He still followed the covenant made with Abraham in sending His Son, Jesus, through David's bloodline. (See Appendix C)

Only a loving God could send His Son to atone for our sins enough to want us to spend eternity with Him.

The books of Chronicles emphasizes that worship and repentance by God's people is the way to maintain a connection with Him.

"O give thanks to the Lord, for He is good; for His mercy and loving kindness endure forever!" (1 Chronicles 16:34 AMP)

CHAPTER EIGHTEEN

"Then I heard the voice of the Lord, saying, 'Whom shall I send, and who will go for Us?' Then I said, 'Here am I. Send me!' "
Isaiah 6:8 AMPSB

Time of Prophets

Prophets were men called by God to carry out His plan at a specific point in time. God's prophets (roughly 800 to 400 B.C.), including Isaiah, Jeremiah, Ezekiel and Daniel, served to bring the Israelites back to God after they fell away. Sixteen prophets are named in the Bible. The prophets foretold the consequences to the Jewish nation for disobeying God, and taught them that through repentance, they could restore a connection with Him.

The books of the prophets are not in chronological order as in the rest of the Bible. The books of Jonah (770-750 B.C.), Amos (763-750 B.C.), Hosea (750-722 B.C.), Joel (700s? B.C.) and Micah (742-687 B.C.) would appear before the book of Isaiah (740-700 B.C.) followed by Nahum (663-612 B.C.), Zephaniah (640-621 B.C.), Habakkuk (612-586 B.C.), Jeremiah (627-586 B.C.), Obadiah (586-553? B.C.), Zechariah (520-518 B.C.), Haggai (520 B.C.) and Malachi (400s), if arranged in sequence of service.[1] All of these prophets lived before or during the Jewish exile in Assyria, Babylon, or Persia. All were part of God's plan to return His chosen people to Israel and rebuild a temple.

The Reason for a Temple
What is the significance and why was God so insistent on building a temple in the Old Testament? In Exodus, God asks Moses to erect a mobile temple for Him and the Ark of the Covenant.

> " 'Have them build a sanctuary for Me, so that I may dwell among them. You shall construct it in accordance with everything that I am going to show you, as the pattern of the tabernacle and the pattern of all its furniture. They shall make an ark of acacia wood two and a half cubits long, one and half cubits wide, and one and a half cubits high.' " (Exodus 25:8-10 AMPSB)

In Leviticus, God instructs the Israelites to sacrifice animals to atone for their sins:

> " 'For the life of the flesh is in the blood, and I have given it to you on the altar to make atonement for your souls; for it is the blood that makes atonement, by reason of the life [which it represents].' " (Leviticus 17:11 AMPSB)

The procedure established by God for reconciling sinners to Himself (atonement) involves these elements: A sin of humanity (Isa 6:7); Blood must be shed (Lev 16:14,18); Substitutionary sacrifice is offered (Lev 4: 13, 20); Guilt is transferred to the substitute (Lev:1:3-4); Forgiveness is granted (Lev 4:26, 31, 35).

But it is not just any blood: "so that you may by accepted—it must be a male without blemish from the cattle, the sheep, or the goats." 2 The animals must not be: "stolen or crippled or sick." 3

It is the sacrifice of blood that makes mankind acceptable to God in the Old Testament.

> " 'He shall lay his hand on the head of the burnt offering [transferring symbolically his guilt to the sacrifice], that it may be accepted for him to make atonement on his behalf.' "
> (Leviticus 1:4 AMPSB)

Sacrifices had to be made in the temple. A permanent temple was not available until King Solomon built one in Jerusalem about 480 years after the Israelites entered the land of Canaan:

> " 'Behold, I [Solomon] intend to build a house (temple) to the Name of the Lord my God, just as the Lord said to my father David:' " " 'Your son whom I will put on your throne in your place shall build the house for My Name *and* Presence.' "
> (1 Kings 5:5 AMPSB)

The Babylonians destroyed Solomon's temple in 586 B.C. God instructed the Jews returning from Babylon to:

> " 'Go up to the hill country, bring lumber and rebuild My house (temple) that I may be pleased with it and be glorified.' "
> (Haggai 1:8 AMPSB)

The replacement temple built in 515 B.C. remained until the Romans destroyed it in A.D. 70. Construction and furnishing of all the temples took more than a 1,000 years. 4

The temple was important not only for making sacrifices to atone for their sins but also served as a place for spiritual renewal, religious education, and a compassionate hand when facing personal crises. 5

God required the Jews to give a tenth of their income (crops and animals) to the temple to sustain the ministries. 6 (Today's concept of giving God one-tenth of our earnings probably originated in this period.)

After the Romans destroyed the replacement temple (A.D. 70) there was no place to make animal sacrifices. 7

The Jews replaced (animal) sacrifices with prayer, as many believe was predicted:

> "Accept our good sacrifices of praise instead of bulls" (Hosea 14:2 CEV); "Accept my prayer as incense offered to You, and my upraised hands as an evening offering." (Psalm 141:2)

The New Testament Sacrifice

In the New Testament, God provided the ultimate sacrifice to atone for mankind's sins through the death and resurrection of His Son Jesus Christ:

> "Whom God displayed publicly [before the eyes of the world] as a [life-giving] sacrifice of atonement *and* reconciliation (propitiation) by His blood [to be received] through faith. *This* was to demonstrate His righteousness [which demands punishment for sin], because in His forbearance [His deliberate restraint] He passed over the sins previously committed [before Jesus' crucifixion].
>
> "It was to demonstrate His righteousness at the present time, so that He would be just and the One who justifies those who have faith in Jesus [and rely confidently on Him as Savior]."
> (Romans 3:25-26 AMPSB)

No longer must we make burnt blood sacrifices to be acceptable to God. We simply must believe that Jesus died and rose from the dead to pay for our sins, to make us acceptable to Him.

The Wisdom Books

In the five books called "the Writings" (Psalms, Proverbs, Job, Ecclesiastes, and the Song of Solomon) are recorded thoughts and prayers of the people of that era, many of which still apply today.

"The Psalms teach us how to pray, how to grieve, how to rejoice, and how to worship. ... It is the prayer book for all who believe in the God of the universe. Jesus used it as such, and so should we.

"The Proverbs are part of what are commonly called the wisdom literature of the Bible. Each society needs a way to pass on what it understands to be the best way to live to succeeding generations. Biblical wisdom literature provided that means for the Jewish community. The Proverbs contain nuggets of truth that endure not only in the Jewish culture, but also make sense [on a wider scale] today. It contains basic wisdom on how to deal with the most common everyday issues that we face. Transcending personality and culture, the simple truth is that if people followed the advice of Proverbs, many of their problems would be reduced dramatically." [8]

The rest of "the Writings" express man's relationship with God at that time in history. God offers a similar relationship with us today. Accordingly, much of our worship today comes from these writings.

Continuing the Plan

The prophet Isaiah foretold of God's plan (740 B.C.) to send a savior, named Jesus, for mankind, telling of His birth, death and Resurrection. It is not hard to understand God's people's frustration in looking for the messiah long before He came—or that Jesus was widely accepted as the savior when He *did* arrive. Thankfully we have had 2,000-plus years of believers passing the truth to reassure us.

From 750-500 B.C. the Jewish people were in exile in Babylon and Persia because of failing to worship God. So He had the prophet Jeremiah send a letter to those in exile stating that after 70 years He would keep His promise and return them to Israel, stating:

" 'For I know the plans and thoughts that I have for you,' says the Lord, 'plans for peace *and* well-being and not for disaster (evil) to give you a future and a hope.' " (Jeremiah 29:11 AMPSB)

Throughout the Bible God has made agreements with and plans for the Israelites. God made His plans known through the prophets. Jonah did not want to do what God asked, yet he eventually obeyed. A key point of the Book of Jonah is to show that God is willing to change His mind when people repent. [9]

Jonah's mission was to urge the Assyrians living in Nineveh to repent from their wickedness or God would destroy their city. [10] Jonah chose to flee from God to avoid facing the fierce Assyrians. Under God's direction,

Jonah eventually went to Nineveh, the Assyrians *did* repent, and He did not destroy the city.

An important point with this example of God's love is that it applies to people other than His chosen nation, and that if *anyone* repents and believes in God, He will omit His punishment.

As written in the Book of Joel:

> "Rip your heart to pieces [in sorrow and contrition] and not your garments. Now return [in repentance] to the Lord your God. For He is gracious and compassionate, Slow to anger, abounding in loving kindness [faithful] to His covenant with [His people]; And He relents [His sentence of] evil [when His people genuinely repent].
>
> " 'It shall come about after this (you know I am your God) That I shall pour out My Spirit on all mankind.' " (Joel 2:13, 28 AMPSB)

Biblical experts debate the significance of Jonah's story, citing these points:

> "God's love isn't limited to Jews; God is eager to forgive (all) and slow to punish. His justice is balanced by His merciful grace; Everyone and everything yields to God; wind and waves, pagans and prophets." [11]

A Kingdom Divided
"And Israel has rebelled against the house of David to this day."
2 Chronicles 10:19 AMPSB

After King Solomon died, some of the northern tribes of Israelites could not live under the rule of the son who succeeded him, Rehoboam. [12] (This is the same period, [900-400 B.C.], when the prophets were actively trying to get the Israelites to continue worshipping God as described above). So the land was divided with Israel in the north and Judah to the south in the land of Canaan.

The Kingdom of Israel existed for 200 years as a separate nation with 19 kings, many seizing power via violence. Rehoboam's son, Jeroboam, was among the kings who found favor with God. But continuing disobedience to God was punished by a foreign nation invading the country and enslaving many.

The Kingdom of Judah continued for another 200 years because the people continued to worship God, but many of the later kings were wicked and foolish. Prophets continued to warn the misbehaving rulers to repent, but their warnings went unheeded and the country again was overrun by foreign powers and the people enslaved. Jerusalem was taken by the Babylonians and the country was essentially wiped from the map. 13

Israel and Judah suffered battlefield defeats because their land was divided into two kingdoms, and they failed to worship God. The temple in Jerusalem built by King Solomon was destroyed. The people could not understand that God was sovereign and demanded their obedience to His will.

So the Israelites lived under foreign rule (Assyria, Babylon, Persia, Greek) until about 163 B.C., when foreign oppression was broken by Jewish patriots, called the Maccabees. They lived in peace for a period of 100 years until the Romans conquered them in 63 B.C. No matter how many prophets God sent to warn the Israelites they failed to abide by His commandments. 14

Pastor Davis explains it this way:

"From the beginning, God's intent was for man to rule this earth through the establishment of His kingdom. Even when man veered from God's intent for him, in His love, God orchestrated a plan for redemption and restoration to their original purpose and intent by Him. A New Covenant of Grace through Christ would establish eternal undivided connectivity and relationship with God. Through this New Covenant, man can, in spite of himself and in spite of sin, experience the intimate relationship with God that he was created to have. As a result, man also has the covenantal authority to establish the kingdom of God as true heirs and undefiled representative of that kingdom."15

The Old and New Testaments and Us

All the books of the Old Testament remain important today, as they show that God is in control of life on earth and heaven in spite of the evil one. Further, as God told the Israelites long ago, live your lives as though I am watching, because *I Am*. The New Testament reveals God's plan of salvation through His Son and the ultimate destruction and defeat of evil.

The New Testament begins with the Gospel According to Matthew, even though chronologically Mark's is thought to have preceded it. Miller believes Matthew appears first because:

"…. Matthew—better than any other Gospel about Jesus—picks up where the Jewish Bible leaves off. Malachi closes the Old Testament with a promise: God will send a Messiah to fix Israel's problems and bring peace and joy to the people. Matthew opens the New Testament by declaring that this promise from centuries past is now fulfilled: The Messiah has come at last.

"And Matthew does it convincingly, quoting one ancient Jewish prophecy after another an explaining how Jesus fulfills each promise—57 in all." [16]

The Revelation to apostle John (by divine messenger), ending the New Testament, was written for all future generations and offers a last chance for man to seek a good relationship with God to receive eternal life.

During the Old Testament era, God established a relationship with man if he accepted Him as his God and obeyed His commandments. God gave many second chances when repentance followed failures. Lack of repentance brought disaster.

Since the New Testament was written, Jesus has offered a relationship with Him as a savior, available to all who believe in Him. He is now the final judge of our relationship with Him, and when we leave this world, He determines our fate. He only asks we believe and repent of our sins to be acceptable to Him. Lack of belief and repentance is the path to disaster.

CHAPTER NINETEEN

*"For this day in the city of David there has been born for you a
Savior, who is Christ the Lord (the Messiah)."*
Luke 2:11 AMPSB

A Savior Is Given

After the Romans conquered Israel, God sent His only Son, Christ, to
live among His people to show them what life in the Creator's kingdom
can be, to save their souls, and to bring them to a new life with Him. His
primary message was the re-establishment of God's kingdom on earth. The
angel Gabriel had told Mary, a descendant of King David:

> " 'You will conceive and give birth to a son, and you will name
> him Jesus. He will be very great and will be called the Son of the
> Most High. The Lord God will give Him the throne of His
> ancestor David. And He will reign over Israel forever; His
> Kingdom will never end!' " (Luke 1:31-33) 1

Jesus lived on earth for 33 years, instructing people how to maintain
God's kingdom by loving one another and Him. When asked what God
was like, Jesus answered: "Whoever sees Me sees Him who sent Me."
(John 12:45 AMP)
Earlier in John:

> "In the beginning was the Word, and the Word was with God,
> and the Word was God.
> "The Word became flesh, and made His dwelling among us. We
> have seen His glory, the glory of the One and Only who came from
> the Father, full of grace and truth." (John1:1, 14 NIV)

Jesus is referred to as (and is) the Word (*with* God), and thus was a
critical part of earth's development from the start. The Son of God, Christ,
was at the creation. He came to earth millions of years later as the baby
Jesus.
Christ came to earth as Jesus to help restore God's kingdom on earth.
He came to tell mankind what God's earthly kingdom was intended to be,
and what life can be in the heavenly spiritual kingdom. 2
During His brief earthly life, three years of it in recorded active

ministry, Jesus won many followers, but not the Jewish religious order of the time.

Asked by a Jewish Pharisee lawyer to state "the greatest commandment in the law," Jesus re-emphasized and reiterated God's command as recorded in the Book of Leviticus 3 (written 1,400 years earlier when God gave the commandment to His chosen people):

> "Love the Lord your God with all your heart and with all your soul and with all your mind. This is the first and greatest commandment. And the second is like it: Love your neighbor as yourself. All the Law and the [writings of the] Prophets hang {depend} on these two commandments."
> (Matthew 22:36-37 NIV)

Jesus told His disciples that command applies to all people, not only Jews just because it is part of Jewish law.

In "Quantum Christianity" Pastor Davis writes:

> "God's plan was always redemption. Because of God's love for mankind and His desire to have a relationship with we who were created in His image and likeness, God integrated a sin-contingency plan into our existence that would restore our relationship and authority back to a place where we could directly communicate with Him and live in the authority that He created for us to live in, free from the dominion of sin in our lives. In essence, giving us the opportunity to choose for ourselves what kingdom we would want to participate in establishing and ultimately be ruled by and freeing us from the default bondage that would otherwise by our reality. According to the Bible, this sin-contingency plan for redeeming man was established in the very beginning of creation. Revelation 3:18 refers to Jesus as 'the Lamb (the intended sacrifice for sin) slain from the foundation of the world.' " 4 {repeated for emphasis}

When God created the earth, according to Genesis, He planned an earthly kingdom for man. Satan foiled that plan {possibly from the beginning of creation (1John 3:8)} and especially when He tempted Adam to disobey God. Although God created man to establish His kingdom on earth, man failed.

After sending judges, kings, prophets and great leaders, God's kingdom was still not established to His liking. Therefore, God sent His Son (Christ) to establish a way for us to build the kingdom through belief in Him.

Miller relates:

> "God's agreement with Abraham, which set the Jews apart as his chosen people, has expired (with the birth of Jesus)—just as the Jewish Bible said it would. God had promised to make a new covenant."{ See Jeremiah 31:31-36} 5

Pastor Kinley emphasizes the need for belief in Him from the apostle John's description in Revelation:

> "John's description of this Jesus is pretty intimidating as it tells us He is the eternal God. The implications of such a claim are beyond profound, and if true, effectively exclude and disqualify every other religious founder, philosopher, and belief system in history. He alone possesses ultimate credibility. Scripture, and Jesus Himself, repeatedly assert this claim that He alone is God." 6

Summarizing the plan from Dr. Mark Chironna's book, "Stepping Into Greatness: Finding the Flow of Your Intended Destiny," as cited in Davis' book:

Adam was placed in authority in God's earthly kingdom as a gift.

God hoped Adam would learn from Him to rule according to His plan.

Adam sinned, resulting in loss of his authority and dominion over the kingdom, and becoming a slave to sin.

God could not restore the kingdom with Adam's descendants as they carried his original sin.

God could not just take control without violating His own principles.

So to restore the kingdom to man's control, God sent His Son.

Jesus was born from a heavenly seed free of sin.

Satan no longer had sole control of earth, as God's kingdom was begun again. 7

Jesus the Son

Jesus asked His disciples, "Who Am I?"

Simon Peter replied, "You are the Christ the (Messiah, the Anointed) the Son of the living God."

Matthew 16:16 AMPSB

God placed His son on earth in human-spirit form. He placed Him in a virgin's womb so that He would be born as a human being, one with the spirit of God, not some mythical being. God is the Father of Jesus because any human father would be subject to sin as in all mankind. Birth from a woman impregnated by God, not a human, would produce a sinless child.

Davis neatly explains:

> "Jesus had to be a man in order to restore what was lost (control of the earth kingdom) because it was man (Adam) who was given authority by God and man who submitted his authority to the kingdom of sin." [8]

God chose this time in history to send His Son to earth because most of the known world was united under a common language and connected by a road system, which made travel easier and safer under Roman rule.

Pastor Mason quotes Psalm 2 to help grasp (God's perspective):

> "'I have installed my King (Jesus) on Zion, my holy hill.' I will proclaim the decree of the Lord: He said to me 'You are my Son; today I have become your Father. Ask of me, and I will make the nations your inheritance, the ends of the earth your possession. You will rule them with an iron scepter; you will dash them to pieces like pottery.'
>
> "Therefore, you kings, be wise; be warned, you rulers of the earth. Serve the Lord with fear and rejoice with trembling. Kiss the Son, lest he be angry and you be destroyed in your way, for his wrath can flare up in a moment."
> (Psalm 2:5-12 NIV) [9]

Jesus is the most important human-spirit individual in world history. He was crucified to atone for mankind's sin to make us right with God. Author Steven M. Miller points to God's change in covenants from biblical verses to explain His rationale to save mankind.

> **Old Covenant:** "For the life of the flesh is in the blood, and I have given it to you on the altar to make atonement for your souls; for it is the blood that makes atonement, by reason of the life [which it represents]." (Leviticus 17:11 AMPSB).
>
> **New Covenant:** "(All) are being justified [declared free of the guilt of sin, made acceptable to God, and granted eternal life] {when they believe and have faith} as a gift by His [precious, undeserved] grace, through the redemption [the payment for our sin] which is [provided] in Christ Jesus." (Romans 3: 24 AMPSB)
>
> "But God clearly shows and proves His love for us by the fact that while we were still sinners, Christ died for us. Therefore, since we have now been justified [declared free of the guilt of sin] by His blood, [how much more certain is it that] we will be saved from the wrath of God through Him." (Romans 5:8–9 AMPSB) [10]

He rose from the dead, [11] thereby making mankind acceptable (sin free) to God. Not only is He the most important human-spirit; He is God's Son.[12] Jesus is Christ; Christ is Jesus. Not only a Son, according to the Book of John Chapter 1, He is God, as the Triune God. [13]

The Triune God

For many people it is quite difficult to imagine that one being, albeit a spiritual being, can be three persons in one. An analogy with water gives some hint of the concept:

The chemical formula for water is $H2O$. Water can be a liquid, a solid (ice) or a vapor (steam). Yet it is still $H2O$; the matter does not change, just the physical state. God's gift of water is the only liquid needed to sustain an earthly life. Belief in Jesus is all that's necessary to attain eternal life.

In his book, "No God But One," Pastor Nabeel Qureshi captures the concept this way:

> "...*Person* is not the same as *being*. Your being is the quality that makes you *what* you are, but your person is the quality that makes you *who* you are. For example, we are humans. That is *what* we are. That is why we are called human *beings*. But what we are is not the same as *who* we are....
>
> "Unlike a human being, which has only one person, God has three persons. He is one being, Yahweh, in three persons: Father, Son, and Spirit. He's more than able to exist like that because He is God. If we say God must have only one person, like humans, then we are making God in our image."[14]

From the beginning God the Father, God the Son and God the Holy Spirit created heaven and earth from the spirit realm. (Genesis 1:1) On earth, God the Son told His disciples that He and the Father were one, and God the Holy Spirit would come to earth to be with His followers forever. (John 14: 11,16) Upon His Ascension, God the Son joined God the Father in the afterlife, sitting on the judgment seat to create a New Heaven. (Revelation 21:7).

The Son of God is Crucified

"When they came to the place called The Skull, there they crucified Him."
Luke 23:33 AMPSB

Many refuse to believe Jesus was crucified and rose from the dead. Besides the actual events witnessed by Jesus' family and the apostles, and the accounts of the Crucifixion in Scripture, there is ample historical evidence that Jesus appeared before the Roman prefect Pilate, was sentenced to death, beaten and hung on a cross where He died.

Qureshi records many of the important historic figures that confirm the sentence:

"Gerd Ludemann is a German scholar who so doubted the Bible that he infamously said, 'The person of Jesus himself becomes insufficient as a foundation of faith.'... (But he goes on to say) 'The fact of the death of Jesus as a consequence of crucifixion is indisputable, despite hypotheses of a pseudo-death or a deception which are sometimes put forward. It need not be discussed further here.' " (Ludemann's book is " What Really Happened to Jesus.")

"Paula Fredriksen, another well-known scholar who frequently challenges Christian beliefs, also concludes similarly to Ludemann, positing, 'The single most solid fact about Jesus' life is his death: he was executed by the Roman prefect Pilate, on or around Passover, in the manner Rome reserved particularly for political insurrectionists, namely crucifixion.'

"In fact, the evidence is so strong that at least one Muslim scholar agrees. ...(In) his book, '*Zealot*,' Reza Aslan makes it abundantly clear that Jesus 'was most definitely crucified.' " [15]

Qureshi sums up the historical evidence as:

"The basis of any historical case must be the primary sources, and in this case (Jesus' death), the sources are unanimous, diverse, early, and plentiful: Jesus died by crucifixion. Starting almost immediately after Jesus' death, *over a dozen authors and traditions* recorded the death of Jesus by crucifixion, including Christians, Jewish, and Roman sources, and their testimony was unanimous. For more than one hundred years, no record even suggests that Jesus survived death on the cross or otherwise circumvented his execution. This coheres well with what we know of crucifixion practices, in that there is no person in recorded history who ever survived a full Roman crucifixion. Positing that Jesus did not die on the cross would have served the agenda of the early Christians and those opposed to their message, but such a suggestion appears inconceivable." [16]

Mel Gibson's movie, "The Passion of the Christ," portrays the excruciating process of crucifixion (20th Century Fox DVD 2004).

The Resurrection

"The Lord has really risen and had appeared to Simon [Peter]."
Luke 24:34 AMPSB

Qureshi similarly examined the historical record of Jesus' resurrection focusing on two facets:

> 1) "Jesus' followers truly believed the risen Jesus (Christ) had appeared to them.
> 2) "People who were not followers of Jesus truly believed the risen Jesus had appeared to them.
>
> "Historians are also convinced that Jesus' followers came to believe that they had seen the risen Jesus. Their reasons are manifold.
>
> "First, the proclamation appears extremely early in church history. First Corinthians 15:3-7, the "news flash" Christian creed that reported Jesus' death within a few years of his crucifixion, also contains a formulation of the people to whom he appeared. It reports 'that Christ died for our sins according to {in accordance with} the Scriptures, he was buried, he was raised on the third day according to the Scriptures, and that *he appeared to Peter, then to the Twelve, then he appeared to more that five hundred brothers at the same time, of whom most remain until now, though some have fallen asleep. Then he appeared to James, then to all the apostles....*
>
> "Second, the proclamation of Jesus' resurrection invites verification from eyewitnesses. For example, while reporting the above creed about twenty years after Jesus' death, Paul says that most of the five hundred eyewitnesses are still alive, as if to say, 'If you want to talk to the eyewitnesses of the risen Jesus, there are over 250 to choose from.' " [17]

Jesus is God

"Believe Me, that I am in the Father and the Father is in Me; otherwise believe [Me]
because of the [very] works themselves [which you have witnessed]."
John 14:11 AMPSB

Again, to believe that Jesus is God, the historical records must be re-examined. Qureshi writes:

> "When people who were skeptical of Jesus' claims asked for a sign, he said that the one sign he would show them is his resurrection." [18]

During a Feast of Dedication, in discussion with the Jewish leaders after restoring sight to a blind man, Jesus was asked if He was the Messiah. Jesus replies that He has told them many times through His works (miracles), which only the Father (God) could do, yet they did not believe. He then adds bluntly:

> " 'I have told you so, yet you do not believe. The works that I do in My Father's name testify concerning Me [they are My credentials and the evidence declaring who I am]. ...
> " 'I and the Father are One....
> " 'But if I am doing them (that is, the miracles that only God could perform), even if you do not believe Me or have faith in Me, [at least] believe the works [that I do—admit they are the works of God], so that you may know and keep on knowing [clearly— without any doubt] that the Father is in Me, and I am in the Father [that is, I am One with Him].' " (John 10:25, 30, 38 AMPSB)

Jesus tells His disciples that He will die and rise from the dead in three days— exactly what He did. Who but God knew and could tell them? 19
Qureshi cites more evidence in the Gospel of John:

> "There can be no doubt that Jesus is presented as divine in the this Gospel. From the outset, John emphatically declares that Jesus is God, that he has always existed, and that he is the very means of all creation. (1:1-3). Thus the first three verses of John's gospel introduce Jesus as 'God, the Eternal One through whom the universe was created.' "John's prologue concludes by calling Jesus 'The only begotten God.' " (1:18).
> "As John's gospel progresses, the Christology is unpacked and elaborated. Jesus is worthy of the honor due to God (5:23); he asks people to have faith in him as they have faith in God (14:1); he claims to be the enabler of salvation (5:21) and the earthly manifestation of God (14:8); he is the king of another world (18:36-37); he assumes dominion over all things (3:35); and he claims to be able to do whatever people ask in his name after he is gone, more or less implying that he has omniscience, omnipotence, and omnipresence (14:13). In addition, he admonishes his opponents that his identity is central to salvation (8:24) and that he perpetually pre-exists Abraham (8:58), in both of these cases using the divine name Yahweh from the Old Testament, the "I Am." In what some consider the climax of the gospel, a disciple realizes who he is and exclaims affirmation, 'My Lord and my God!' to which Jesus responds, 'Because you have seen me, you have believed; blessed are those who have not seen and yet have

believed.' " (20:28-29 NIV) [20]

All the other gospels include references to the works of Jesus that only God could accomplish including fulfilling Old Testament prophecies.

Jesus the Holy Spirit

"...Regarding His Son, who, as to the flesh [His human nature], was born a descendant of David [to fulfill the covenant promises],and [as to His divine nature] according to the Spirit of holiness was openly designated to be the Son of God with power [in a triumphant and miraculous way] by His resurrection, from the dead: Jesus Christ our Lord."
Romans 1:3-4 AMPSB

The third part (spiritual-being) of the Triune God is the Holy Spirit. Again historical Scripture validates the Holy Spirit as being in Jesus and God. The Holy Spirit was present at the creation of the earth and universe:

> "God said, 'Let Us create man in Our image, according to Our likeness (not physical, but a spiritual personality and moral likeness).' " (Genesis 1:26 AMPSB)

The Holy Spirit guided Moses during the exodus from Egypt toward the promise land. [21]

God sent the Holy Spirit to Mary to impregnate her with Jesus. [22]

Saul was filled with the Holy Spirit after Jesus stopped him on the way to Damascus, converting Saul to the apostle Paul. [23] (See footnote on Paul) [24]

Before Jesus was taken to die on the cross, He told His disciples that He would send the Holy Spirit to explain so that they would understand all that He had told them (probably to assist in writing the gospels) and most importantly, for us and all believers and followers of Jesus. [25]

In sum, historical evidence shows Jesus died on the cross, rose from the dead, appeared to His disciples and 500 others, and sent the Holy Spirit to guide those who believe in Him, as Christ. The Holy Spirit, Christ and God are one.

Our Savior

"Therefore, since we have now been justified [declared free of the guilt of sin] by His blood, [how much more certain is it that] we will be saved from the wrath of God through Him."
Romans 5:9 AMPSB

Because He paid for our sins, our spirit can now reside with God eternally. Without the Resurrection Jesus would have been just another prophet. He rose from the dead because He was God's contingency plan to save mankind. Christ was so important that time has been determined from His birth. He is the savior of God's earthly kingdom and all of mankind. He was with God when the earth was formed and He came to earth in human form to wrest God's kingdom from Satan's control.

During His life on earth of 33 years—the last three in ministry—Jesus performed many miracles: healing the sick, casting out demons, restoring sight to the blind, and raising followers from the dead. 26

Jesus' friend Lazarus died four days before He visited the grave. Jesus called Lazarus from the grave and Lazarus rose four days after dying. 27

This miracle is proof that Jesus can reverse death. For believers, this signals everlasting life with the Father. If Jesus can raise a man from death to life on earth, imagine what He can do for us later on. The Son had the same creative power as His Father, but Jesus told followers that He could not employ it without God.

Jesus said:

> " 'I tell you the truth, the Son can do nothing by Himself; He can do only what He sees His Father doing, because whatever the Father does the Son also does. For the Father loves the Son and shows Him all He does. Yes, to your amazement He will show Him even greater things than these.' " (John 5:19-20 NIV)

Although the religious leaders had Jesus crucified, He rose from the dead according to God's plan so that he who believes in Him has his spirit saved for eternal life. Once and for all eternity, the Israelites have a chance to live forever: Jesus left the door open, if only they would believe.

As a sign of God's covenant with Abraham and his descendants, He said they were to be circumcised. But God did not provide salvation only for the Israelites (those that are circumcised). Jesus died for *all* people.

The apostle Paul explains in his letter to the Romans that Abraham received God's blessing because he trusted God, and through God's grace Abraham had a right relationship with God. (4:9-12 AMP)

In Barclay's, "Letter to the Romans," he writes that Abraham actually was uncircumcised when God established His covenant:

> "Abraham was not, in fact, circumcised until fourteen years after he had answered God's call, and had entered into a unique relationship with God. Circumcision was not the gateway to a right relationship with God; it was only the sign and seal that a man had already entered into that relationship.

(Therefore,) "Abraham is not the father of those who have been circumcised; he is the father of those who made the same act of faith in God as he made. He is the father of every man who in every age takes God at His word as he did. ...

"And all the great promises of God are made not to the Jewish nation, but to the man who is Abraham's descendant because he trusts God as Abraham did....

"The descendants of Abraham are not members of any particular nation, but those who in every nation belong to the family of God." [28]

After Jesus' resurrection, He reappeared on earth and breathed the Holy Spirit into the disciples and those gathered with them, charging them to spread the gospel throughout the world. [29]

Pastor Mason bluntly explains that:

"The power source that sustains the universe is the power of the Holy Spirit." [30]

Paul writes in his letter to the Ephesians:

"In reading this (divine revelation given to Paul) then, you will be able to understand my insight into the mystery of Christ, which was not made known to men in other generations as has now been revealed by the Spirit to God's holy apostles and prophets. This mystery is that through the gospel the Gentiles are heir together with Israel, members together of one body, and share together in the promise in Christ Jesus."
(Ephesians 3:4-6 NIV)

Not only did Jesus charge His followers to spread the good news of His kingdom, but He also empowered them with the Holy Spirit so they could do miracles as He had.

" 'That they all may be one, [just] as You, Father, are in Me and I in You, that they also may be one in Us, so that the world may believe *and* be convinced that You sent Me.

'I have given to them the glory and Honor which You have given Me, that they may be one; [even] as We are one:

'I in them and You in Me, in order that they may become one *and* perfectly united, that the world may know *and* [definitely] recognize that You sent Me and that You have loved them [even] as You have loved Me.' " (John 17:21-23 AMP)

During the Last Supper, Jesus gave His disciples, a special blessing with the bread and wine, which became a sacrament and ordinance for His church throughout the ages for believers (the Lord's Supper or communion). Jesus asked that believers continue to take communion as a remembrance of Him. ₃₁

After Jesus' resurrection, His apostles began the task to establish churches to spread that good news, thereby starting Christianity. The apostles also wrote the books of the New Testament.

Pastor Mason expands:

> "The ultimate purpose of the coming of Christ was to reveal the glory of God to all flesh. But the coming of Jesus was just the beginning. He commissioned His disciples to perpetuate the ministry of the Father's glory to the ends of the earth. The same glory that the Father imparted to Jesus was imparted to His disciples. In John 17 Jesus prayed to the Father, 'The glory which You gave Me **I have given them**, that they may be one just as We are one.' (John 17:22)   Paul said, 'He called you by our gospel for the obtaining of the glory of our Lord Jesus Christ.'   (2 Thessalonians 2:14)…
>
> "In the same way, Jesus continues to lavish His glory upon His disciples so that they can continue to release and reflect His glory in the earth. The ministry of the church is a ministry of heaven's glory." ₃₂

Jesus' followers (disciples) spread the good news of His death and resurrection not only with the Jews, but also with the gentiles (non-Jews). Although the gospel was ordained to be given to the Jews, it was not received by the Jewish nation. Dr. Barclay laments:

> "The tragedy of the Jew was that the great task of world evangelization that he might have had, and was designed to have, was refused by him. It was therefore given to the Gentiles, and, in the end, God's plan was, as it were, reversed, and it was not, as it should have been, the Jew evangelized the Gentile, but the Gentile who evangelized the Jew—a process which is still going on." ₃₃

Miller, in his "Complete Guide to the Bible," writes that the apostle Paul, a Jew:

> "Believes that the good news he's delivering about Jesus is the next step for the Jewish faith. It's where God wants to take

them—away from the laws of His old covenant agreement with them and into the era of a new covenant. In this new arrangement, the Holy Spirit guides people toward holiness." 34

"Jews have to be fully convinced of this (Jesus *is* the Messiah whom the prophets said would come to save Israel and the world) because Christianity radically changes the Jewish religion. It changes their worship practices, the way they seek forgiveness, and even the way they approach God. Everything changes with Jesus.

"But in a religion in which traditions and rituals are treated as holy—and have been for well over a thousand years—these sacred practices die hard.

" 'But die they must. 'Christianity,' says the Hebrews writer, is the next step in God's plan of salvation. And it's a step the prophets predicted. They said the covenant, or agreement, God made with the Jews would be replaced.' That old agreement required Jews to observe the laws and worship rituals God gave Moses.

" 'But this is the new covenant I will make with the people of Israel… I will put my instructions deep within them, and will write them on their hearts.' (Jeremiah 31:33; quoted in Hebrews 8:10)

"When God speaks of a 'new' covenant, the Hebrews writer explains, 'it means He has made the first one obsolete. It is now out of date and will soon disappear.' " (Hebrews 8:13) 35

But many Jews did not (and still do not) believe that Jesus was the Son of God, the Messiah, thinking that God would not come to earth as a human [and He was not a triune God].

In the Revelation to John there is reference to God's angels returning to Israel to save Jews:

"Then I heard the number of those who were sealed (having the seal of God): 144,000." (12,000 from each of the 12 tribes of Israel)

"Some believe that refers specifically to Jews—that there will be a great revival among the Jews, and that many will be saved. Some say (others argue) that there will be exactly 144,000 Jews saved—perhaps to be evangelists for the rest of the great multitude." 36

Jesus the Christ
"And the Word (Christ) became flesh and lived among us; and we [actually] saw His glory, glory as belongs to the [One and] only begotten Son of the Father, [the Son who is truly unique, the only One of His kind, who is] full of grace and truth (absolutely free of deception)." [Is 40:5]
John 1:14 AMPSB

At creation, in the beginning, Christ was with His Father, God. ₃₇ God sent His Son, Christ, to be born of Mary to become a human spirit. God, through the angel Gabriel, told Joseph, Mary's betrothed, that the child she was carrying was from the Holy Spirit, and the child should be named Jesus (meaning Immanuel—God with us). ₃₈ Thus, to accurately identify who Jesus was, we must call Him *Jesus the Christ.*

Father Richard Rohr further explains:

> "Christ is God, and Jesus is the Christ's historical manifestation in time. Jesus is a Third Someone, not just God and not just man, but God and human together." ₃₉

Therefore, Christians worship Jesus because He is "the Christ," not because He was a great man, rather that He was God with us. When Jesus died on the cross, His human spirit became Christ again with His Father as one.

Many Christians are waiting for Christ's second coming, as prophesied in Revelation. Rohr feels that they may be missing God's point at this time in earth's history:

> "The Christ Mystery [humans became anointed] anoints all physical matter with eternal purpose from the very beginning. Many are still praying and waiting for something that has already been given to us three times: first in creation; second in Jesus, "so that we could hear Him, see Him with our eyes, watch Him and touch Him with our hands, the Word who is life," (1 John 1-2); and third, in the ongoing beloved community (what Christians call the Body of Christ), which is slowly evolving throughout all of human history. (Romans 8:18ff.) We are still in the Flow. …
>
> "For me, a true comprehension of the full Christ Mystery is the key to the foundational reform of the Christian religion, which alone will move us beyond any attempts to corral or capture God into our exclusive group. As the New Testament dramatically and clearly puts it: 'Before the world was made, we have been chosen in Christ…claimed as God's own, and chosen from the very beginning' (Ephesians 1:3, 11) 'so that He could bring everything together under the headship of Christ.' " (1:10).
> *If all of this is true, we have a theological basis for a very natural religion that includes everybody. The problem was solved from the beginning.* ₄₀

Or, as the Father of Orthodoxy, St. Athanasius (269-373), wrote when the church had a more social, historical and revolutionary sense of itself:

"God was consistent in working through one man to reveal himself everywhere, as well as through the other parts of His creation so that nothing was left devoid of His Divinity and his self-knowledge...so that the whole universe was filled with the knowledge of the Lord as the waters fill the sea." 41

CHAPTER TWENTY

" 'You will receive power and ability when the Holy Spirit comes upon you; and you will be My witnesses [to tell the people about Me] both in Jerusalem and in all Judea, and Samaria, and even to the ends of the earth.' "
Acts 1:8 AMPSB

The Battle for God's Kingdom: The Spread of Christianity

After Jesus' death and resurrection, He commissioned the apostles ₁ to spread the gospel (good news of the Savior of mankind). This command from Jesus (an order that Christians believe today) became what followers know as the "Great Commission:"

> " 'Go therefore and make disciples of all the nations [help the people to learn of Me, and obey My words], baptizing them in the name of the Father, and of the Son and of the Holy Spirit.' " (Matthew 28:19 AMPSB)

The work to spread the gospel of salvation was not without peril. Jesus foretold His disciples that they would be persecuted and killed for choosing to follow Him. (John 15:18-21 NIV) The apostles established congregations called "The Way," later called Christians. ₂ Early Christians met in people's homes, until Rome legalized Christianity ₃ throughout the Middle East, Italy, Gaul (France), Spain and as far east as India.

The leader of a new church usually was one of Jesus' apostles. They wrote letters (epistles) to the established congregations to monitor their faith and endurance to continue to worship God in spite of persecution and difficult circumstances, thereby giving us 22 of the 27 books of the New Testament. The exact dates when the books of the New Testament were written is unknown, but biblical scholars estimate the dates to be a period around the destruction of Jerusalem in A.D. 70. ₄

The apostle Paul wrote 14 of the 22 books to the congregations in Asia Minor and the Middle East. The fact that he wrote so many of the books led some non-Christians to believe that Paul had taken control of Christianity to establish a Pauline religion.

Pastor Qureshi explains:

"Not only do Muslims (and nonbelievers) disagree that Jesus actually died on the cross, they consider the entire foundation of Christianity to be questionable because a man (Paul) who was not a disciple and who never even saw Jesus successfully infiltrated the ranks and hijacked the early church. The religion taught by Jesus became the religion about Jesus, and what was a religion about following God's law and worshipping God alone became a religion that ignored the law and worshipped a man alongside God. Though Christianity originally looked much more like Islam (and other monotheistic religions), it (because of a questionable foundation) has been lost forever because of Paul.

"The common Muslim assertion that Paul hijacked Christianity, imposed his own teachings and corrupted the true religion not only goes against the biblical record but also is unwarranted from a historical point of view and (thus) enjoys very little scholarly support." [5]

During the new church's first 300 years, followers were persecuted by foes of what then was called The Way,' (later Christianity). Qureshi states:

"The church held no political or military power in the first three hundred years, subsisting on faith and perseverance in the face of persecution. Christian martyrdom did not mean dying with sword in hand, but laying down one's life instead of one's faith." [6]

The Catholic Church is Formed
In A.D. 312, the Roman soldier Constantine became the first Roman emperor to embrace Christianity. A year later he published the Edict of Milan, granting all living in Roman lands religious freedom, with Sunday a day of worship. Christians began to build churches for the established congregations after Rome legalized Christianity. [7]

In 325 A.D. Constantine held a meeting of church leaders at Nicaea to establish Christ's divinity.[9] Constantine moved the center of the Roman Empire to the old Greek city of Byzantium (Constantinople; today Istanbul) in A.D. 330, thereby establishing the Byzantium Empire as a religious state. The emperor was not only ruler of his people, but also God's representative on earth. (The empire fell to the Turks in 1453.) [8]

The church in Rome continued as the center of Christianity in the west, and after long arguments with the church in Byzantine—and others throughout the east—it eventually became the base of the Catholic religion. Christianity was essentially split east to west, a divide that continues to this day. [9]

126

The Catholic Church now had both power and military might. Christians were continually being killed in the east for their beliefs and religious freedom. 10

Christianity was known as a religion of peace despite Jesus' words:

> "Do not think that I have come to bring peace on the earth; I have not come to bring peace, but a sword [of division between belief and unbelief]." (Matthew 10:34 AMPSB)

The apostle Paul described what's expected of a Christian soldier:

> "Put on the full armor of God [for His precepts are like the splendid armor of a heavily armed soldier], so that you may be able to [successfully] stand up against all the schemes *and* the strategies *and* the deceits of the devil. For our struggle is not against flesh and blood [contending only with physical opponents], but against the rulers, against the powers, against the world forces of this [present] darkness, against the spiritual *forces* of wickedness in the heavenly (supernatural) *places*." (Ephesians 6:11-12 AMPSB)

Faced with knowing Jesus, and in light of the Scriptures, for the first time Christians had to deal with religious killing. Previously, wars and killing were conducted mostly for wealth, power and freedom.

The Crusades

In the 10th century "holy wars" broke out between Christians and Muslim sects in Jerusalem and surrounding areas (The Holy Lands). To protect Christians in that region and others on their pilgrimages—and responding to cries for help from the Byzantine church—Pope Urban II instituted the First Crusade in A.D. 1095. 11

Pastor Qureshi elaborates on the fate of Christians in the Holy Lands:

> "Attacks [were made] on Christian lands from the mid-600s through the year 1095 and well beyond. By the time the Byzantine emperor asked for the pope's help, *two-thirds of the Christian world had been captured by Muslims.*" (Note, much of the land was in fact the land God had given to Abraham. and later again to Moses [the land of Canaan].) 12

Thus while Christians were fighting for control of the Holy Lands, they were actually fighting to reclaim the land for the Israelites. After 850 years, including two world wars and the Holocaust, through the resilience of God's chosen people, the Israelis retook the land in 1946. No piece of real estate, the heart of God's kingdom on earth, has been fought over more often in human history.

Crusaders

Crusaders were mostly Christian knights, fellow soldiers, and common people. 13 The society of the Templars (God's Holy Warriors) was subsequently formed to provide a qualified armed force. The Templars established a religious order with a strict ethical code, believing in what Jesus taught them through Scripture, especially that: His followers should not fight, but turn the other cheek if struck; those that lived by (habitually drew) the sword would die by the sword; 14 and all humans are to obey the Fifth Commandment not to kill. 15

Qureshi explains the Crusaders' dilemma:

> "Jesus' teachings were so peaceful that they posed a problem for early Christians who felt obligated to defend the oppressed with violence. Because Jesus made no clear allowance for war, such Christians developed an elaborate notion of 'just war' starting with Augustine at the turn of the fifth century. Delineating stringent conditions of war, Augustine argued that fighting could be within the will of God, but it remained a necessary evil and something that required penance." 16

The Templars were in a quandary. Fellow believers were being slaughtered, but Christian ethics, as they understood them, dictated a peaceful solution. The Templars formed a strict religious code to *kill* only those who were persecuting Christians, never others (noncombatants).

As the Templars researcher Dan Jones put it:

> " 'This armed company of knights may kill the enemies of the cross without sinning,' stated the rule [code], nearly (and neatly) summing up centuries of experimental Christian philosophy, which had concluded that slaying humans who happened to be 'unbelieving pagans' and 'the enemies of the Son of the Virgin Mary' was an act worthy of divine praise and not damnation. Otherwise, the Templars were expected to live in pious self-denial." 17

Qureshi explains further:

> "When launching the Crusades, Christians relied on the arguments of Augustine and other similar perspectives to vindicate their defense of the Byzantines, and they initially did

treat their wars as a necessary evil to combat a greater one. It was during the Crusades, though, that holy war started to be seen positively, itself a means of gaining forgiveness. In this, they were going far further than Augustine.

"This idea gained popularity, as a contemporary historian wrote, 'God has instituted *in our time* holy wars, so that the order of knights and the crowd running in their wake…might find *a new way* of gaining salvation.'

"So it was not until the Crusades, over a thousand years after Jesus, that Christians saw holy war as a positive endeavor that, instead of being a sin requiring penance, would actually forgive crusaders of their sins." [18]

For the next 200 years Christians and Muslims fought for control of the Holy Lands as documented in the "New Book of Knowledge." [19] Unlike battles between good and evil, holy wars are fought with each side thinking it is good and the other evil, each fighting for their God. That fight continues today (2020).

The church in Rome eventually became the Roman Catholic Church. St. Jerome (340?-420) translated the Bible from the original texts in Hebrew (Old Testament) and Greek (New Testament) to Latin. The church formed a separate political body governing Christian affairs throughout Europe. Catholicism continued to grow, erecting monasteries manned by monks and nuns, and by the Middle Ages were predominant over most of Europe and the British Isles. [20]

The Reformation

In 1517 Martin Luther, a German Augustinian monk, questioned many practices of the Catholic Church. Rather than remedy the issues Luther raised, the pope chose to deem Luther a heretic. [21] Luther broke from the Catholic Church and formed a new one (Lutheran), thereby igniting the Protestant Reformation.

Luther translated the Bible from Latin to German and mass-produced it for distribution to the German population. This was the first publication utilizing the Guttenberg press.

"The New Book of Knowledge" notes that:

"Luther's translation of the Bible into German was of great importance in the early days of the Reformation. For the first time people could read the Bible for themselves in their *own* language, rather than hearing it read in church in *Latin*." [22]

Within the next 200 years other reformers began to form Protestant churches across Europe. During the reign of Henry VIII, many English clergy who tried to translate the Latin Bible into English were captured and burned at the stake, as heretics. John Wycliffe and William Tyndale began the translation, and John Rodgers finished and published it in 1611 during the reign of King James of England; the King James version remained the only Bible in English until much later. [23]

In 1620 a Protestant group traveled to North America seeking religious freedom. The Americas became the land of religious freedom. Christianity and other religions spread from the Atlantic to the Pacific.

In 1732 John Wesley formed a group of friends in England to share a strict form of Christian living. The disciplined nature of the new method of serving God became known as "Methodism." He served as a missionary in North America in the early mid-1700s, returning to England to lead the Methodist movement. The United Methodist Church became the largest Protestant congregation with over 9 million members worldwide. [24]

Despite numerous setbacks—the holy wars; the great plague (the Black Death of 1346), world wars and natural disasters—Christianity has grown to claim more than two billion members today. As of 2020, the Bible has been translated into 2,400 of the world's 6,000 languages, and distributed to at least 78 countries. [25] Considering there are least one billion nonbelievers, implementing Jesus' commandment is far from accomplished. [26]

Pastor Kinley writes that Christianity's success has resulted because believers have strived to spread the Gospel (the Good News of Jesus' life and sacrifice) throughout the world since His death. Christians don't have to search hard to find God—He has found them through His love. This personal relationship has propelled Christianity to the top, numerically. [27]

A Possible Change

In the latter part of the 20th century and the 21st to date, there has been a movement to establish nondenominational, "free" churches, pressuring liturgical churches to modernize worship styles. Many liturgical churches have been struggling with low attendance and dwindling finances to maintain large buildings. I believe we are in the process of a major change in the way Christian worship will be conducted in the near future.

CHAPTER TWENTY-ONE

"And if anyone's name was not found written in the Book of Life, he was hurled into the lake of fire."
Revelation 20:15 AMPSB

God Is One God for All

The Old Testament records God's relationship with His chosen people, Israel. This historic connection is one of faith and has been open to "all, and those who share the faith of this family may be 'adopted' into it." [1]

Rabbi Donin outlines the Jewish relationship to God from the birth of the Hebrew nation:

> "This people, Israel, started life as one family tracing its antecedents back to Abraham, the Hebrew who lived approximately 3800 years ago.
>
> "Although the natural tendency for any family is to be exclusive and to look inward, this particular family was never exclusive. In times of persecution it was sometimes forced to be withdrawn in self-defense, but generally it looked outward and reached out to the world at large. When the central sanctuary in Jerusalem was built, Jews saw it as a 'House of Prayer for all peoples.' (Isaiah 56:7, see also Kings I 8:41-43) [2]
>
> "The history of the Jews has been a history of interactions with the rest of the world.
>
> "Though denied, despised, rejected, persecuted, confined, and restricted through history, Jews and Judaism, the people itself and its sacred books, have nonetheless often set in motion forces that marked major revolutionary changes and advances in Western religions, in the natural and medical sciences, and in social philosophies. The contributions by individual Jews in every field of creative endeavor, in the advancement of human knowledge, in the elimination of suffering, in the development of commerce, have filled volumes. Judaism's traditional emphasis on social justice through social action has had noticeable effect in contemporary times.
>
> "We believe that the nations and peoples of the world have their Divine purpose and their assigned roles to fulfill, too, for *God is the God of all the world*, {italics added for emphasis} not just of Jewry.

"And we see our divinely ordained assignment as involving a unique role, one to which history itself bears witness. It implies a special purpose in life, a reason for our existence. That purpose is not to make Jews of all the world, but to bring the peoples of the world, whatever their distinctive beliefs may be, to an acknowledgment of the sovereignty of God and acceptance of the basic values revealed to us by God. It is to serve as a means by which blessings will be brought to 'all the families of the earth.' (Genesis 12:3)

"It is this mission which underlies for Jews the coming of the day 'when the world shall be perfected under the reign of the Almighty, and all mankind will call upon Thy name.' " [3]

Jews and the Old Testament

Throughout the Old Testament the Jews were repeatedly punished by God for their failure to follow the first of the Ten Commandments: "worship only God."[4]

God set Jerusalem as the center of the surrounding nations with the expectation that the Jews would influence others' behavior toward God. Because the Jews failed to do as He expected, the city was destroyed and the Jews scattered worldwide.

Miller refers to Scripture to reiterate:

> "God had set them apart as a holy nation, as an example of how he wants everyone to live—devoted to Him. But not only do the Jews fail to live up to those higher standards, God says 'You have not even lived up to the standards of the nations around you. ... Because of your detestable idols, I will punish you like I have never punished anyone before or ever will again.' "
> (Ezekiel 5:7, 9) [5]

Despite their disobedience, God returns the land of Canaan (Israel) to them each time they repent from worshipping idols. He never revoked their selection as His chosen people as promised (Jeremiah 30:3 AMPSB). Even after 2,000 years, God returns the land of Israel to the Jews following the World War II Holocaust (6 million of them were killed) in 1946. It is clear that living a faithful life, repenting from our sins, and performing good works acceptable to God are what He expects of us.

The New Testament

The New Testament provides *good news* for God's creation—the gospel of His gift to save mankind It tells how we are to live in God's earthly kingdom, under Jesus' direction, so that all people through the ages can be saved, if they believe through God's grace. John's gospel explains his purpose in writing:

> "There are also many other signs (attesting miracles) that Jesus performed in the presence of the disciples, which are not written in this book; but these have been written so that you may believe [with deep, abiding trust] that Jesus is the Christ (the Messiah, the Anointed), the Son of God; and that by believing [and trusting in and relying on Him] you may have life in His name." [Psalm 2:7, 12] {Your name in the Book of Life at the end time}. 6 (John 20:30-31 AMPSB)

Jesus charged the disciples to begin the formation of Christian congregations as churches throughout the known world. 7 They first preached the good news to the Jews. The disciple Peter had a vision from God en route to the house of a Roman army officer who wanted to know if he could be saved, as he was not a Jew. During that encounter it was made known to Peter that Jesus' salvation was for all, not just the Jews, and there is no distinction between Jews and Gentiles in God's eyes. Jesus died for all mankind. Thereafter the term Christians was given to His followers 8

In the Acts of the Apostles, Luke records words Peter spoke to Cornelius in Caesarea:

> "Most certainly I understand now that God is not one to show partiality [to people as though Gentiles were excluded from God's blessing], but in every nation the person who fears God and does what is right [by seeking Him] is acceptable *and* welcomed by Him." (Acts 10:34-35 AMPSB)

The New Testament tells us how we are to live in this 'New Kingdom' as followers of our Savior, Jesus the Christ. The apostles' writings have provided the means for generations to believe and be saved.

The church remains the focus for spreading the gospel and their buildings provide a place for Christians to worship God. Thus Christianity was born more than 2,000 years ago.

Pastor Davis describes the church's development:

> "In Christianity, there are two prevailing and opposing schools of thought (Arminianism and Calvinism) on whether or not we have a choice in the matter of a personal relationship with God, as defined by being saved and forgiven of the sin and being able to approach God and communicate with Him personally.
>
> "In a nutshell, Arminianism teaches that man has a free will and a

choice in his relationship with God. Calvinism teaches that you are chosen by God, and as a result, even your desire to be in relationship with Him is a part of Him choosing you. [9]

"Some believe that God is infinitely aware but only involved with man as a distant, hands-off observer; others believe that nothing in this world happens outside of His will for mankind; still others believe that man plays an intricate role in how God's will is ultimately displayed on the earth, with even the relationship between God and man being our choice to relate to Him, while others insist that our relationship with Him is strictly His choice and limited by His choosing us individually and those who do not have a relationship with Him are simply not 'chosen' by Him."[10]

There is biblical evidence that both scenarios have occurred and both are acceptable, known and used by God. .

The Muslim Quran
Sharia Law (Quran) is considered the word of Allah [God] by Islam. Muslims believe Allah gave the Quran to Muhammad about A.D. 700. Pastor Qureshi points out, in "No God But One," the Muslim reasoning for why God give them the Quran:

> "Tragically, people did not faithfully follow the prophets that Allah sent them. So in His mercy, Allah sent Muhammad and gave him the Quran. Thus, Allah gave mankind the final, perfected religion (Quran 5:3). Islam is therefore the culmination of Judaism, Christianity and all other world religions, which started off in line with Islamic teaching. [11]

> "There's really no question that Islam and Christianity are close to one another on the broader religious spectrum. They are both monotheistic, the largest two faith communities in the world, and they share many similarities. Each teaches the doctrine of an eternal, all-powerful, all-knowing God who is sovereign over the universe. It is God who created mankind out of one man and one woman, yet mankind turns away from him. Each teaches that one day there will be a resurrection and final judgment. Before then, it is of paramount importance for us to seek God and follow him.

> "But the similarities between Islam and Christianity run even deeper, beyond the trappings of monotheism: Both lay claim to Abrahamic lineage; both teach that God has sent messengers, human and angelic, to steer people back to him; both teach that God has inspired divine scriptures to guide man; both teach that

Satan is a deceiver that misleads the unwary; and both teach that believers ought to sacrificially care for each other and proclaim the truth to nonbelievers.

"Perhaps the most surprising shared feature is reverence for Jesus. Both Islam and Christianity teach that Jesus was born of a virgin and that he was the most miraculous man who ever lived. Both the Bible and Quran teach that Jesus cleansed lepers, healed the blind, and even raised the dead. Indeed, both books teach that Jesus is the Messiah, and Muslims await his return, as do Christians.

"Where the difference matters most is in the ultimate message of each religion. According to Islam, the way to paradise is sharia, a code of laws to follow that will please Allah and earn his favor. *Sharia* is literally translated "the way." According to the Christian message, the gospel, the way to eternal life is Jesus. He said, "I am the Way, the Truth, and the Life; no one comes to the Father except through me." (John 14:6) In Islam, sharia is the way, and in Christianity Jesus is the way." [12]

If the Quran is the word of God, then Muslims may please God with their devotion.

Other Religions

There are other faiths, and atheists, agnostics and many others without any belief of a God at all. In Revelation, the apostle John recorded God's word that *all* people will be judged at the end time. Your name must be in the Book of Life for you to be saved. [13]

Therefore, since only God can create human life, all people are in His family, but all may not have the same ending unless they believe in Christ, the Son of God. I believe we are all children of God regardless of our religion, beliefs or nonbeliefs here on earth. Some theologians may argue that we are not all God's children, only those whom He calls. Some believe that salvation is our choice; Calvinists believe in unconditional election (man has no choice, he is selected by God). Regardless, choice or not, Revelation clearly states that each of us will have to answer God's judgment. God's plan tells us what we must do to be saved. It is up to us to listen, repent and do as He asks.

CHAPTER TWENTY-TWO

" 'I am the Alpha and the Omega [the Beginning and the End],'
Says the Lord God, 'Who is [existing forever] and Who was
[continually existing in the past] and Who is to come, the Almighty
[the Omnipotent, the Ruler of all].' "
Revelation 1:8 AMPSB

The Plan Is Fulfilled

God revealed His plan in Revelation to re-establish His kingdom in the end times, including all things He created as desired. Stephen Miller writes:

> "This is God's new plan: 'Both Gentiles and Jews who believe the Good News share equally in the riches inherited by God's children.' " (Ephesians 3:6) ₁

Paul's letter to the Ephesians reveals God's plan:

> "And he made known to us the mystery (secret) of his will (of his plan, of His purpose) according to his good pleasure (His merciful intention), which he purposed in Christ, to be put into effect when the times will have reached their fulfillment—to bring all things in heaven and on earth together under one head, even Christ." (Ephesians 1:9-10 NIV)

Christ died to atone for our (all human) sins, enabling us to spend eternity with God. But Jesus didn't come to earth to tell us what it will be like in heaven; He told us what it could and should be like in God's kingdom on earth.

Pastor Davis writes:

> "Jesus did not model a kingdom that was to come and would only be manifested after death in another dimension or existence 'somewhere out there' in heaven and eternity, while we strum a harp and sit on a cloud as a portly little angel. On the contrary, Jesus was the *present* model of what it looks like when God is the ruling force in a man's life and man uses his authority to establish God's rule, will and Word (kingdom) in his own life and

subsequently on the earth." [2]

Prayer is the most direct way to establish a relationship with God. Jesus illustrated how to pray (the Lord's Prayer). Pray, therefore, like this:

" 'Our Father who is in heaven, Hallowed (kept holy) be Your name. Your kingdom come, Your will be done on earth as it is in heaven. Give us this day our daily bread. And forgive us our debts, {trespasses}, as we have forgiven our debtors [letting go of both the wrong and any resentment] And do not lead us into temptation, but deliver us from evil. [For Yours is the kingdom and the power and glory forever.] Amen.' " (Matthew 6:9-13 AMPSB)

If we live only to prepare a place with God in eternity, we miss what He planned in His covenant with mankind and what Jesus told us during His human life. Jesus said He did not come to judge the world but to fulfill God's plan and to give us a more abundant life. Living in this world knowing and doing God's will makes life more abundant. Jesus changed the world forever and made possible an eternal life.

Davis writes:

> "Regardless of anyone's acceptance of these events (the good news), the accounts of His disciples and furthering of His message forever transformed world history, even dividing history's timeline by the life of this man Jesus with abbreviations BC (before Christ) and AD (anno Domini, which is Latin for in the year of our Lord).' " [3]

The plan will not be fulfilled until Jesus returns as told in Revelation. [4] He is coming to judge the world and will rule the universe. [5] God said:

> "He will build a new Jerusalem and live among His people... He will wipe away every tear, there will no longer be death, sorrow and anguish or crying or pain, for all these will pass away. He is making all things new. 'It is done... I am the Alpha and the Omega, the Beginning and the End.'... 'He who overcomes [the world by adhering faithfully to Christ Jesus as Lord and Savior] will inherit these things, and I will be his God and he will be My Son.' " (Revelation 21:1-7 AMPSB)

Filled Enough for Us

Though not yet fulfilled, the plan is complete enough for us and all our predecessors. This outline tells us the who, what and when of God's plan.

Inherent in the plan is the why. God provided a means for us to establish

His kingdom on earth and enjoy His pleasures, and save our spirits through Jesus Christ so that we can be with God for eternity, free of separation and suffering. All that is required is to believe with mind and heart in His Son Jesus, the resurrected Christ (our savior).

God loved His creation so much that He came to this earth, lived among His people and sacrificed Himself in the person of His Son so we can live with Him forever. God's plan does not stop here, but lives with all of us, each one contributing to keep the plan going, to continue the fight against evil until He comes again to defeat evil forever. We don't know exactly how we contribute, but we know we must believe, continue to worship, and spread the gospel. Maybe we don't need to know but simply have faith God does.

I am told you have a plan for me
But I really don't understand or see;
Yet I know I should have faith and pray
That you will work it out the best for me,
regardless what I say; because
Jesus died for me to wash my sins away.
I need not struggle to learn the plan,
I know that I should live my life the best I can
Knowing God will do the rest according to His plan.

Christs's Return

"Behold, He is coming with the clouds, and every eye will see Him, even those who pierced Him, and all the tribes (nations) of the earth will mourn over Him [realizing their sin and guilt, and anticipating the coming wrath]. So it is to be. Amen."
Revelation 1:7 AMPSB

Stephen   Miller summarizes God's plan as it appears in the Bible, excluding prehistoric time, and the predicted ending:

> " 'In the beginning God created the heavens and the earth.' (Genesis 1:1) Then in a paradise called Eden, God placed the first human (-spirit) beings: Adam and Eve. God nourished Eden with a river. And he offered Adam and Eve a future forever, provided by fruit from the tree of life. At least that's what some Bible experts say the tree was doing in Eden.
>
> "But the first humans broke the one and only rule God gave them. They ate (fruit) from a forbidden tree. This disobedience somehow contaminated God's creation, introducing sin and death into the cosmic equation. The rest of the Bible—from Genesis to Revelation—is the story of God working his plan to undo the

damage.

"John (the apostle), in his final vision, sees the end of that story. And it looks very much like the beginning. A pure river flows from the throne of God. Trees of life sprout up along both sides of the river.

"Paradise lost has now been found. It's better than ever. And it's forever and ever. Having seen the future, John has just one request: 'Come, Lord Jesus.' " (Revelation 22:20 NLB) [6]

What of the future? Jesus said there are many mansions in God's house' and a place has been reserved for all believers:

> " 'I am going there to prepare a place for you. And if I go and prepare a place for you, I will come back and take you to be with me that you also may be where I am.'
>
> "Jesus answered (His disciples who did not know where He meant): 'I am the way and the truth and life. No one comes to the Father except through me.' " (John 14:3, 5 NIV)

Revelation tells us that our Savior, Jesus, will come again at the end of time [7] as Christ—to separate believers from nonbelievers [8] and end the ongoing war with evil. God will prevail and conquer evil for all eternity. [9] All will be tested, but: for those who believe, God will save them at the trial. [10]

Pastor Kinley explains that the Rapture is Jesus' return, stressing the importance of being ready as the separation of the good and the evil ones will involve everyone. The question is whether the Rapture is true, and if judgment occurs before the period of harsh punishment and separation for all from God, or will only nonbelievers face punishment and separation. Either way, God's promise to those who persevered in their faith will spend eternity with Him

If there is no Rapture at or before the Great Tribulation depicted in Revelation 6-19, then all are in for seven years of harsh judgment and plagues. "So it is not a belief to be easily dismissed or taken lightly." [11]

Judgment

Based on the apostle Paul's writings in 2 Corinthians, Kinley warns believers that all will appear before the "judgment seat of Christ" in the end times, a process called *the bema.* [12]

> "For we [believers will be called to account and] must all appear before the judgment seat of Christ, so that each one may be

repaid for what has been done in the body, whether good or bad [that is, each will be held responsible for his actions, purposes, goals, motives—and the use or misuse of his time, opportunities and abilities]." (2 Corinthians 5:10 AMPSB)

If the judgment seat is in heaven and all go there to receive due punishment, it would be ironic only to be thrown out to the dark world. So, getting to heaven is not necessarily the problem—staying there is.

There is no free ride! But, Jesus has atoned for the believer's sins. The debt has been paid, if you accept His calling:

" 'Because you have kept the word of My endurance [My command to persevere], I will keep you [safe] from the hour of trial, that *hour* which is about to come on the whole [inhabited] world, to test those who live on the earth.' " {repeated here for emphasis} (Revelation 3:10 AMPSB)

Not to believe, however, means total disaster:

" 'But as for the cowards and unbelieving and abominable [who are devoid of character and personal integrity and practice or tolerate immorality], and murderers, and sorcerers [with intoxicating drugs], and idolaters *and* occultists [who practice and teach false religions], and all the liars [who knowingly deceive and twist truth], their part will be in the lake that blazes with fire and brimstone, which is the second (first one on earth) death.' " (Revelation 21:8 AMPSB)

Jesus told His disciples that the time of His second coming was only known to God. 13 While we wait for His return we must continue to carry out God's commandment to manage His creation, 14 and not consume it as if there is no tomorrow. The world must work together to preserve the planet for future generations until the Rapture occurs and God relieves mankind of that chore. 15

CHAPTER TWENTY-THREE

"Whoever believes in the Son has eternal life, but whoever rejects the Son will not see life, for God's wrath remains on him."
John 3:36 NIV

The Logic of Belief

Some people might agree that belief in a God we do not see, a God who allows so much tragedy—and trust in what the Bible clearly tells us—is not logical. The human experience includes tragedy and sorrow. The Bible records many horrid events in our history, things not caused by God but by mankind, the evil one or nature. The Bible does not promise good or bad times; mankind brings much of what happens on himself. God promises to be our help and strength, 1 to love and forgive, but does not control man's actions. He may orchestrate at times, but He does not control what each of us plays!

Jesus said that he who believes in Him shall not perish, but have eternal life. He told His disciples that he who sees Me has seen My Father [God].2 While we have not seen Jesus, He told His followers after the resurrection:

> "Because you have seen Me, you have believed; blessed are those who have not seen and yet have believed." (John 20:29 NIV)

TV evangelist Dr. Charles Stanley reminds us that of all the leaders of all religious faiths, God of Christianity is the only One who died and rose from the dead. All the others are dead, but Jesus, God as three persons in one, died, rose from the dead and promises eternal life to all who believe in Him.
3

Pastor Travis Zimmerman, in a "Family Guide to Joy," cites Paul's Letter to the Galatians:

> "Jesus, fully God and fully man, experienced the full range of human experiences and emotions throughout His earthly ministry. Jesus knew that He was born to die to fulfill God's plan to rescue man from his sin, according to the will of our God and Father," 4 (1:4)

Galatians continues:

"who gave (yielded) Himself up [to atone] for our sins [and to
save and sanctify us], in order to rescue and deliver us from this
present wicked age and world order, in accordance with the will
and purpose and plan of our God and Father."
(1:5 AMP)

Stephen Miller references Paul's First Letter to the Corinthians:

"Paul reminds the Corinthians about the witnesses who saw
Jesus—500-plus of them. Then Paul appeals to logic. For some
skeptics, this would have been the stronger argument. Witnesses—
even apostles—could lie. But logic makes perfect sense. Paul's
logic is this: Resurrection is the good news of Christianity. If you
don't believe in the resurrection, what's the point in calling yourself
a Christian?

" 'If Christ has not been raised,' Paul says, 'then your faith is
useless and you are still guilty of your sins. In that case, all who
have died believing in Christ are lost! And if our hope in Christ is
only for this life, we are more to be pitied than anyone in the
world.' " (1 Corinthians 15:17-19) 5

In light of a promised final testing, consider this: if you do not believe
(in Jesus' life, death, resurrection and substitution for your sins) and God
does not exist, you die and that's it; if you believe but God does not exist
you die and nothing else happens; if you do not believe and God *does* exist,
when you are tested your spirit will be separated from Him and tormented
forever; but *if you believe* and God *exists*, when you are tested, your name will
be in the Book of Life, and your spirit lives forever with God. (See Chart 3)
Which of these alternatives is the most logical choice?

Revelation states that all will be tested. Those who have received God's
grace through faith will be saved, but nonbelievers will be excluded in
God's kingdom and eternally separated from Him. 6

In the letters to the seven churches in Revelation, each was warned that
to survive judgment they must believe and those who do will sit beside
Jesus in heaven. The Bible reminds us that God wrote the knowledge in
our hearts.

The apostle Paul in Romans wrote that we lack any excuse for not knowing
God. The outcome of final judgment is based on our belief. All have been
warned and the outcome for each of us is justified. 7

CHAPTER TWENTY-FOUR

"God predestined and lovingly planned for us to be adopted to Himself as [His own] children through Jesus Christ, in accordance with the kind intention and good pleasure of His will..."
Ephesians 1:9-10 AMPSB

The Plan

In summary, God creates the earth and populates it with mankind (human-spirits) in His image. Man chooses evil over good and the war for mankind's love begins. Abram and his descendants become chosen people. God sends prophets and kings to help them do His will.

But they (and all mankind) continue to turn to evil. God sends His Son (Jesus the Christ) as a sacrifice (substitution), to atone for their sins and provide a way for them to be saved to live with God forever.

Jesus commissions His disciples to write the gospels so that succeeding generations can learn of His saving grace. Jesus promises He will come again in the end times to destroy evil forever. We have only to believe and receive God's grace to live eternally with Him. [1]

The letter to the Hebrews records the new covenant God made with Israel and Judah, which remains today for all believers. The covenant contains four provisions:

> "(1) God's law will be written on the believers' minds and hearts; (2) Believers will have a relationship with God fulfilling the promise of Leviticus 26:12 'I will walk among you and be your God, and you shall be My people'; (3) All will know God. No longer will Pharisees and scribes have to teach the intricacies of the law to the people; (4) God will forgive the sins of believers and remember them no more. The continual sacrifice of animals for the atonement of sin will cease." [2]

This book is based on what has been revealed biblically and scientifically to date, as the writer understands. While most of what appears in the original Bible text is more than 2,000 years old, it has been translated into many modern languages to remain current. While we have received no new evidence of God's dictated writing, we see His continued presence in the miracles that happen daily.

Ever since biblical times, God has interceded in our daily life. Disciples, apostles and historic figures such as Constantine, Martin Luther, John Wesley, George Washington, Abraham Lincoln, Martin Luther King Jr. and many others have influenced history for the better.

Each of us also has played a role in influencing God's creation. Our input is unknown to most of us, but all have been charged to work for good. God is alive and still in charge of the universe. Jesus came to save that which was lost by Adam. 3 Yes, evil still persists, and the fight will continue until the end times. Meanwhile, we must continue with God's grace to do our part to live as He dictates.

The Gospels of Matthew and Mark give us the Great Commission:

" 'Go then and make disciples of all the nations, baptizing them into the name of the Father and of the Son and of the Holy Spirit. Teaching them to observe everything, that I have commanded you, and behold, I am with you all the days (perpetually, uniformly and on every occasion) to the (very) close and consummation of the age. *Amen (so let it be).*' " (Matthew 28:19-20AMP)

" 'Go into all the world and preach and publish openly the good news (the gospel) to every creature [of the whole human race].

"He who believes [who adheres to and trusts in and relies on the Gospel and Him Whom it sets forth] and is baptized will be saved [from the penalty of eternal death]; but he who does not believe [who does not adhere to and trust in and rely on the Gospel and Him Whom it sets forth] will be condemned.' "
(Mark 16:15-16 AMP)

The Great Commission is reinserted here because of its relevance to today's mission for all believers.

The apostle Paul in his Letter to the Romans gives us the guidelines for Christian daily life:

"Love must be sincere. Hate what is evil; cling to what is good. Be devoted to one another in brotherly love. Honor one another above yourselves. Never be lacking in zeal, but keep your spiritual fervor, serving the Lord. Be joyful in hope, patient in affliction, faithful in prayer. Share with God's people who are in need. Practice hospitality.

"Bless those who persecute you; bless and do not curse. Rejoice with those who rejoice; mourn with those who mourn. Live in harmony with one another. Do not be proud, but be willing to associate with people of low position. Do not be conceited.

"Do not repay anyone evil for evil. Be careful to do what is right in the eyes of everybody. If it is possible, as far as it depends on you, live at peace with everyone. Do not take revenge, my friends, but leave room for God's wrath, for it is written: 'It is mine to avenge; I will repay,' says the Lord. On the contrary:

"If your enemy is hungry, feed him;

"If he is thirsty, give him something to drink.

"In doing this, you will heap burning coals on his head.

"Do not be overcome by evil, but overcome evil with good."
(Romans 12:9-21 NIV)

The First Letter of John commands:

"Do not love the world or anything in the world. If anyone loves the world, the love of the Father is not in him. For everything in the world—the cravings of sinful man, the lust of his eyes and the boasting or what he has and does—comes not from the Father, but from the world. The world and its desires pass away, but the man who does the will of God lives forever. Dear children, this is the last hour";.... (15-18 NIV)

Stephen Miller explains (the last hour):

"About 17 million hours ago John writes that the 'last hour' is here.

"By 'last hour' John isn't talking about the world's last few months or years. So say most Bible experts. He's talking about the last stage in God's plan to save human beings from sin—the era launched by the (second) coming of the Messiah.

"God starts His plan of salvation with one righteous man, Abraham. And from Abraham, God establishes a righteous nation, Israel. God entrusted Israel with guidelines for holy living and with a commission: 'You will be the light to guide the nations.' (Isaiah 42:6). But Israel fails its mission. So God sends his Son, Jesus, to complete this mission by showing people how to live as citizens of God's kingdom and by sending out disciples to 'go and make disciples of all the nations.' (Matthew 28:19)

"The 'last hour' begins and ends with Jesus—his coming and his coming again." 4

We are in the last hour as Jesus once lived on earth, and we await His return.

What about the immediate future, the period before He arrives? Each of us is part of God's plan. We don't know exactly how, but as we look back over our lives we may see evidence that in some small way we did God's work.

In my case…

> I am told You have a plan for me,
> I could only guess what it would be;
> yet, I trust in You to let me know
> when the hour is ripe to be told so.
> Now I pray for the patience, wait it out,
> till You reveal what it is all about—
> My hope is, much more than I deserve,
> while I take a knee and stay reserved.

The apostle Paul lays out how we are to live in his letter to the Romans., as recorded above. 5 Dr. Barclay advises that we should live as Paul outlines in Romans 12 with:

> "intensity…with no room for lethargy…, and we cannot take things in an easygoing way, for to him life is always a choice between life and death, the world is always a battleground between good and evil; the time is short; and life is a preparation ground for eternity." 6

The Proof is in the Believing

Nothing written here proves there is a God, that He created the heavens and earth, and that there is a plan. Rabbi Donin's summation:

> "Of course, one cannot offer scientific proof that God exists, or that it was through His will that the world was created, or that He is concerned with the perfection of that which He created. But neither can it be proven that He does not exist. The use of rational methods to 'prove' or 'disprove' God's existence, after the fashion of the medieval scholastics, may appeal to some. Since the dawn of modern philosophy, however, these proofs have been seriously questioned. Contemporary arguments pro and con are equally futile. That is why the acceptance of God's existence is a matter of faith (*emunah*). The one, indivisible, spiritual Supreme Being in whom Abraham and all his descendants expressed their *faith* and saw fit to worship defies proof. He is infinite and man is finite." 7

For Christians, Jesus is the proof there is a God. Jesus' birth, death and resurrection were prophesied hundreds of years beforehand. Only God could make that prediction and fulfill it. As you assess this plan you will realize it is about what God has done throughout history to lead us to salvation and show us the way to eternal life.

And if you believe, have faith, and come to recognize the Bible as God's word, you will know in your heart and mind there is a God, that He has a plan for His creation, and that His Son died for your sins so that you can live with Him here on earth, and He will spare you from eternal death. You are part of His plan. Live your life accordingly. God has shared His plan through His grace and eternal love for you and all mankind. Live the plan! Once you believe you will understand.

Part 2
CHAPTER TWENTY-FIVE

"For God so [greatly] loved and prized the world, that He [even] gave His [One and] only begotten Son, so that whoever believes and trusts in Him [as Savior] shall not perish, but have eternal life."
John 3:16 AMPSB

Life as We Know It

Why do I need God and His plan? Most of us have a plan for our life and really don't want someone else to tell us what they think it ought to be. For many of us, God is not necessarily a significant part of it. We balk at admitting our life is not our own, that it's part of God's creation. As the saying goes, if you want to make God laugh, tell Him your plan.

We are part of God's plan whether we want to be or not. But why should we believe in a God we cannot see, and if God exists why does He allow bad things to happen to good people? Does He really have a plan?
Answers to such questions would boost our understanding of God's role in our existence.

In "Quantum Christianity" Pastor Davis explores the possible reasons for disbelief in God in question format:.

> "Did I bring this (pain) upon myself? Why is this (bad thing) happening to me? Did I do something so wrong that God is mad at me and punishing me? Why did God allow this (evil) to happen? Why are things so different in this world than how the Bible says they should be? Why, when I prayed, did nothing happen? Why does it seem that such injustice takes place in the world when God is supposed to be a just God?
>
> "If God is love like the Bible says, then why does He allow hateful things to happen in the world? Either God is God or He is not. Either the Bible is His Word or it is not. But if the Bible is truth (as it and Christian leaders claim it to be), then it would seem consistent that our experiences should more closely line up with that truth than what they have. If they do not, then common-sense deduction would conclude one of three things:
>
> 1. There is either a problem with the truth;
> 2. There is a problem with our understanding of the truth; or

3.   There is possibly a problem with our experiences as it relates to the truth."1

"The problem with this entire line of thinking is that our faith becomes based upon ourselves rather than in God." 2

The problem arises when our experiences don't match what the Bible says, and based on our limited understanding we tend not to believe.

Pastor Zimmerman writes that he believes:

"God allows trials to enter our lives, and they often involve misery. Knowing this, when we enter into misery with Christ, we can be assured we will ultimately leave misery behind, because He does NOT remain in misery. Sure, God will extract from misery valuable attributes like patience and perseverance; and we can be confident that we will pass through misery *with* Him. God uses misery for His glory." (Romans 8:28 NIV) 3

The apostle James, writing to the 12 tribes of Israel, believes when your faith is placed under pressure it is strengthened.

"Consider it a sheer gift, friends, when tests and challenges come at you from all sides."(1:2 MSG)

Dealing with the stresses of life can be daunting, but as we address and work through them, we can grow stronger in faith and resolve to carry on.

Miller reminds us of what the apostle Paul wrote in Romans:

"Paul says that even Gentiles who were never taught religious laws such as the 10 Commandments "show that they know his law when they instinctively obey it, even without having heard it. They demonstrate that God's law is written in their hearts, for their own conscience and thoughts either accuse them or tell them they are doing right." (Romans 2:14-15) 4

Man's nature is to want a God that allows us to do what we want, a free will, but controls evil, keeps us safe, and makes life free of pain and suffering, allows us to lead a rich and full existence so that all can live happily ever after. Contrary to what man wants, life has been a battle between good and evil, which we know has existed since the very start.

If there is a God, and He is all powerful, why does He not control or eliminate evil? God is sovereign. He works through people. Things happen as man's action, from cause and effect and the laws of nature. God works through us to make the best of a strategic (life-changing) situation, but does not intercede or orchestrate life on earth. God has a plan for us and through His Son, who sacrificed His earthly life to atone for our sins, we can, if we believe, spend life eternal with God.

Pastor Hamilton believes God does not control mankind's every move, but rather picks up the pieces when we fail to make the best of the fallout. Our ability to do good or evil is free will. When bad things happen to us, we must remember that God is not necessarily the cause. Everything happens for a reason, but God is sometimes *not* the reason. Things happen due to cause and effect. God is not responsible for our actions, we are. God gives us the opportunity to do well, but we must accept that we are imperfect and will make mistakes. 5

We learn in 1 Thessalonians that God's will is for us to be holy—and we are to "live in a way that pleases God." (2:12 AMP) 6

Miller writes that Bible scholars offer several definitions of holiness:

> "Holiness is reaching a point of spiritual maturity that enables us to consistently refuse to do things we know are wrong. We'll make mistakes in judgment, but we won't choose sin over what we know God wants us to do.
>
> "Holiness is a goal. We should follow the example of Jesus as best we can—growing from spiritual infants to strong, spiritual adults. On those occasions when we slip up and sin, God offers grace and forgiveness to those who repent.
>
> "Holiness is a description of our one-of-a-kind God, who is superior to everything in creation. The Bible also uses this word to describe everything and everyone devoted to Him. Furnishings and utensils for the Jewish worship center were consecrated to 'make them holy.' (Exodus 40:9) We, too, become holy when we devote ourselves to God: 'You ...have been set apart as holy to the Lord.' (Ezra 8:28) We become a one-of-a-kind people serving a one-of-a-kind God." 7

The evil one encourages us to follow suit, but we must make the decision to avoid it. We may be impacted by the evil or accidents of others or our own. However, part of God's plan is to provide a way out of being tempted beyond our endurance. First Corinthians confirms:

> "No temptation [regardless of its source] has overtaken or enticed you that is not common to human experience [nor is any temptation unusual or beyond human resistance]; but God is

faithful [to His word—He is compassionate and trustworthy], and He will not let you be tempted beyond your ability [to resist], but along with the temptation He [has in the past, is now and] will [always] provide the way out as well, so that you will be able to endure it [without yielding, and will overcome temptation with joy]." (10:13 AMPSB)

In "A Family Guide to JOY," Pastor Zimmerman reminds us:

"The fact is: we can't really choose to *not* go through trouble! Jesus said so in John 16:33 (NIV): 'I have told you these things (troubled times), so that in me you may have peace. In this world you will have trouble. But take heart! I have overcome the world." 8

Zimmerman elaborates, citing this passage from NIV Life Application Study Bible:

"Many people believe that Christianity should offer a problem-free life. Consequently, as life gets tough, they draw back disappointed. Instead, they should determine to prevail with God through life's storms. Problems and difficulties are painful but inevitable; you might as well see them as opportunities for growth. You can't prevail with God unless you have troubles to prevail over." 9

C. S. Lewis wrote in his book "Mere Christianity" that God gave us free will for a purpose. While free will allows good or evil, it depends on how we use God's gift; otherwise we would not be human, but robots living as directed. God knew the risk of giving humans free will, but it was required for His plan. God knew that free will would cause mankind to fail to choose good only, but through His plan salvation is available when chosen.
10
James' letter (canonical book) tells us:

"Consider it nothing but joy, my brothers and sisters, whenever you fall into various trials. Be assured that the testing of your faith [through experience] produces endurance [leading to spiritual maturity and inner peace]. And let endurance have its perfect result and do a thorough work, so that you may be perfect and completely developed [in your faith], lacking in nothing."
(1:2 AMPSB)

God put man (Adam) in charge of His earthly kingdom and gave him the privilege to pray for His help. He told man that his prayers would be answered when aligned with His plan. God expected man to establish His kingdom on earth, but Satan interceded with evil and man failed. As a result, mankind has been in the battle of good vs. evil since the very start.

Mankind was created with a free will and thus must choose to do good or evil. The very nature of man's free will allows evil to exist. Good *and* evil have existed for every generation. Good does not control evil and evil does not control good. Either one can overcome the other, as circumstances allow.

Each generation has had its evil issues. Many of those issues have been around for eons. Each generation has had to battle with the evil that plagued it. Today's evil issues define our battlefield. Whether we want to or not, we must choose a side in the battle.

While selecting good does not guarantee we refrain from evil, it does give hope that, through grace, we will end up on the right side of the fight. Man has attributed good to God and evil to the devil. God gave us advice as how to prepare for battle, clothing us in the proper uniform to ward off evil's attack.

Paul's letter to the Ephesians tells us to wear a "wide band of truth," a breastplate [body armor] of righteousness, shoes of the "gospel of peace," a shield of faith, a helmet of salvation, and a sword of the word of God. [11]

Life, therefore, is not free of disappointment and tragedy. But there is help to make the way tolerable; the choice is ours.

CHAPTER TWENTY-SIX

"Trust in the Lord with all your heart and lean not on your own understanding."
Proverbs 3:5 NIV

How Do We Cope with This Life?

Why does evil exist? Why does God force mankind to choose between right and wrong, especially when serious consequences can result? Why does mankind have free will? Why does God care if we sin? How does your belief or faith influence what you are seeing or experiencing? How does your perception of life influence how you see Christianity and God?

These serious questions require answers so we can understand God and how He works in our life. We know from life's experiences that evil exists. We also know that things happen to us for no apparent reason.

The Bible tells us that God abhors sin. He dislikes it so much that at one point in the history of His creation, He caused a flood to destroy most of mankind. The flood served as a new start for us, a do-over. If God detests and just cannot countenance sin, why not another rerun?

Not everything that happens is God's fault. Pastor Davis agrees:

> "For instance, I agree that most everything happens for a reason, but not necessarily an unavoidable one or a divinely inspired one, as the tone or the cliché most often is quoted (God is the reason for everything; God's will.). I also agree that the Lord definitely does some things that I would consider mysterious at times (even from a biblical perspective), but this understanding doesn't necessarily imply that every time something happens and I don't understand why, that the only catalyst is the Lord and His mysterious ways." [1]

To Know God

Getting answers to our questions can best be accomplished by learning what has been written about God by those who have had direct contacts with Him. Human contacts with God began with the first human-spirit, Adam, and continued through the life of Jesus, God's Son, as recorded in *only one* source, the Holy Bible.

The Bible is one of God's means to communicate with mankind. He has provided a framework for establishing His kingdom on earth and foretells of His plan for man's salvation from evil's existence.

There have been many interpretations of what God expected mankind to derive from Scripture, but when all accounts are considered, it is clear that God created the earth and heavens, and man was placed here to manage this part of His kingdom.

In order to believe in God, we must start with the formation of the earth. Genesis 1 says God created the heavens and earth. It doesn't say how or when. We can believe that nature caused the universe to form (it just happened), or that some other force was responsible. As stated earlier, leading scientists and theologians agree that an intellectual being formed the universe. It just didn't happen, God created it.

Physicists agree that God, through mathematical exactness, formed all things using ratios of a single number, called the Golden Ratio Fye 1.6180339. [2]

Pastor Mason explains:

> "The Bible declares that 'In the beginning was the Word, and the Word was with God, and the Word was God.' (John 1:1 (NIV). The 'word of God' is not just a mere sound; it is a vehicle that conveys both simple and complex information, and this information is expressed through language. Whilst information can be communicated through any human language so that it can be clearly understood by those who understand code, it can also be expressed through the language of mathematics, as any trained physicist would be able to explain.
>
> "Mathematics is clearly part of the language of God. When we study this mathematical signature at the core of every aspect of creation it becomes increasingly difficult to avoid the conclusion that there is a God and that this intelligent and all-powerful being is an incomparably brilliant cosmic mathematician who has structured the universe on readily discernible patterns of precise mathematical formulas which enable scientists to describe the attributes and processes of the physical world." [3]

Mason's conclusion:

> "Biblical creation ... gives a solid explanation of the very cause and the means through which the universe came into existence, and it all points to a profoundly intelligent, omniscient and omnipotent being who crafted the cosmos in His mind before bringing it into existence through His power.

"As we explore this divine pattern (God's mathematical Golden ratio for creating all things) [explained earlier] in nature it strengthens the conviction that God is the author of nature and that His mathematical signature can be found everywhere in His creation."4

Paul's Letter to the Romans reveals man knew of God's great power but failed to glorify Him for their creation:

"For since the creation of the world God's invisible qualities—His eternal power and divine nature—have been clearly seen, being understood from what has been made, so that men are without excuse.

"For although they knew God, they neither glorified Him as God nor gave thanks to Him, but their thinking became futile and their foolish hearts were darkened. Although they claimed to by wise, they became fools and exchanged the glory of the immortal God for images made to look like mortal man and birds and animals and reptiles." (1:20-22 NIV)

God's Creation

God created the heavens and the earth from nothing, a "formless and void or a waste and emptiness." "Ex nihilo—out of nothing." Nothing existed—nothing! 5

Why was the earth formed so that it could support life? Why is there only one moon; water over more than half the earth; why is there only one sun, and why do the other planets in earth's solar system not yet support life or have water? 6

Scientists can explain **how** the earth and water were formed and why other planets do not support life as on earth. But, there is only one source that explains **why** the earth was formed, **why** mankind was created with a free will and **why** evil exists. The only source revealing why the earth was formed, why evil exists, why mankind has a free will, why man must choose sides in the battle between good and evil, and why God does not destroy the sinful earth, is the Holy Bible. It alone contains the plan for the outcome of the battle, and why it is important to end up on the winning side.

Genesis 1 records God's creation of the earth and creation of man in His image and likeness followed by breathing the breath of life into the nostrils of the first human-spirit being, Adam. 7 Imagine the power and love it took to create the earth and humans. Then consider the problems impacting human life caused by the introduction of sin:

First, from a spirit realm, God created a sinless and complete universe and everything in it from nothing but His spoken word.

Second, God created a sinless man in His image and likeness—including a free will—from His love. ₇ Pastor Qureshi emphasizes:

> "It was out of this (God's) selfless love that God created mankind. In other words, we were made in the image of a selfless, loving God, so in our very nature we are designed to be selfless and loving…. From the Christian perspective, people ought to be selfless loving toward others not just because it is a good idea, not just because it helps our species survive, not just because it earns us a reward, and not just because it pleases God. People ought to be selflessly loving because it is who we are. Humans are made in the image of a selfless God; loving others is what makes us truly human." ₈

Not only did God create us in human form, but He also gave us His spirit to enable us to join the spirit world after death.

Satan's Existence

Third, Satan came to earth and interrupted God's plan to create an earthly kingdom. ₉ God planned a "sin free" kingdom on earth, but Adam's sin, orchestrated by Satan, changed life on earth forever.

> "Adam became a sinner and as such he died. His spiritual death was immediate, the physical death progressive. Adam, who began the human race, then became the source of sin for the world. We are all sinners by nature because Adam sinned (Romans 5:12-14). We inherit sin from Adam in our nature in the same way we inherit many of our physical characteristics from our parents. Sin is a universal part of our spiritual inheritance."₁₁ (AMPSB footnote) 10

Ever since Satan's arrival man has been forced to opt between good and evil and to participate in the battle between them; having to choose became the human-spirit experience. Maybe Satan's presence on earth is part of God's plan for man to learn good and evil as known in Heaven and to understand eternal life.

Fourth, God does not orchestrate all that happens on earth. In fact, Satan (in Snake form) told man to sin by disobeying God's directive not to eat fruit from the Tree of Knowledge.

Fifth, all things happen for a reason, but God doesn't make all things happen. Sin causes guilt and shame, and we are helpless to avoid Satan's power by ourselves since God inscribed moral law on our hearts. However,

He does, as He did for Adam, make the best of a bad situation by planning the recovery from our sin and Satan's actions.

Sixth, Satan will continue to press man to disobey God, and God will steadfastly bear our guilt and punishment to make the best recovery from our disobedience *when we believe.*

God warns in 2 Peter:

> "But [in those days] false prophets arose among the people just as there will be false teachers among you, who will subtly introduce destructive heresies, even denying the Master who bought them, bringing swift destruction on themselves. Many will follow their shameful ways, and because of them the way of truth will be maligned." (2:1-2 AMPSB)

Seventh, God has had a plan since the beginning to triumph over evil.

> "There will no longer exist anything that is cursed [because sin and illness and death are gone]." (Revelation 22:3 AMPSB)

Seeing Is Evidence

Geology and other sciences, as we believe and understand today, explain how long it took to form our earth and identify the verity of life that has existed over the eons. Genesis describes how and why God made our universe and us. It explains how man was created in God's image and why man fell from grace as he exercised his free will and chose evil against His word. We know and see evidences of God's work in our lives.

Romans states it clearly:

> "For since the creation of the world God's invisible qualities—His eternal power and divine nature—have been clearly seen, being understood from what has been made, so that men are without excuse." (1:20 NIV)

Throughout history God has revealed His way so that man, having seen what He can do, will recognize Him as the author of all with unquestioned power and authority. We have no excuse for unbelief.

The rest of the Bible is God's story and the historical records of His, Satan's and man's relations.

Beginning in the Old Testament

All the books of the Old Testament of the Bible describe God's relationship with His creation. The conditions of the battlefield of each generation help depict man's struggle vs. evil. The story of Adam and Eve tells us that because they disobeyed God, choosing to eat from the Tree Of The Knowledge of good and evil rather than the Tree Of Life, they sinned, igniting a battle that continues today.

Cain kills his brother Abel because he believes his father and God favor Abel over him. God made a covenant with Abraham to choose him and his descendants as His people, and God as their God.

His chosen people are forced into slavery in Egypt for 400 years. Moses leads the Israelites to freedom and receives the Ten Commandments from God that provide the laws for mankind to live in harmony with God and one another.

However, man chose to disobey God's laws and thus has had to continue battling evil. God recognized that mankind is incapable of living without sin. So He made a new covenant with the people of Israel (and all of us) by placing His laws on the hearts and minds as their God forever.

But man ignored the covenant and continued to sin. So He sent His Son, as recorded in the New Testament, to atone for man's sin. If we believe that Jesus is God's Son (Christ) and was sacrificed (died on a cross) but rose to atone for man's sin, then believers may be acceptable in God's kingdom to fight evil and spend eternity with Him.

An explanation given by God is recorded in Hebrews:

> " 'This is the covenant I will make with the house of Israel after that time (Jesus' time),' declares the Lord. 'I will put my laws in their minds and write them on their hearts. I will be their God and they will be my people.' " (8:10 NIV)

Ending in the New Testament

Pastor John MacArthur in his book, "The Gospel According to Paul," reminds us that God placed His law in our hearts so we are without excuse for not knowing evil from good. 11

MacArthur further explains that God arbors sin, and since we know right from wrong deserve any punishment that He gives us. Yet rather than punish us, He sent His Son to atone for our sins on a cross. God's plan for substitution of His Son for our sins shows how much He loves us. In essence, "Christ's death on the cross was a penal substitution. He bore the guilt and punishment for His people's sins."12

The apostle Paul boils down the gospel message in 2 Corinthians:

> "But all *these* things (reborn and renewed by the Holy Spirit, spiritual awaking) are from God, who reconciled us to Himself through Christ [making us acceptable to Him] and gave us the ministry of reconciliation [so that by our example we might bring

others to Him]; that is, that God was in Christ reconciling the world to Himself, not counting people's sins against them, [but canceling them]. And He has committed to us the message of reconciliation [that is, restoration to favor with God].

"So we are ambassadors for Christ, as though God were making His appeal through us: we [as Christ's representatives] plead with you on behalf of Christ to be reconciled to God.

"He made Christ who knew no sin to [judicially] be sin on our behalf, so that in Him we become the righteousness of God [that is, we would be made acceptable to Him and placed in a right relationship with Him by His gracious loving kindness]."
(5:18-21 AMPSB)

God in 2 Corinthians is asking us to be saved through Him. Pastor Qureshi explains:

"Mankind seems incapable of saving itself. In our natural selves, we perpetuate cycles of destruction. Our hearts are broken, so we break other hearts. We were abused, so we abuse in return. Our families were fractured, so we leave fractured families in our wake. When loved ones are killed, we kill in revenge. This is the way of humanity, and we need an otherworldly solution—something radical to break these cycles. We need God to save us. The gospel is that radical solution. It teaches us that God gives us that otherworldly grace, forgiving us no matter what our sins. His love is extravagant: 'Neither death nor life, neither angels nor demons, neither the present nor the future, not any powers, neither height not depth, nor anything else in all creation, will be able to separate us from the love of God.' (Rom 8:38-39 NIV) He loves us, and we are forgiven. Our souls can rest in our loving Father and his all-embracing grace.

"The gospel is all about God and what God has done. God introduces life into the world, and when we rebel, God saves us. When we sin against God, God pays for our sins. When we sin against one another, God gives the grace of restoration. This message is all about him, not at all about what we can do or have earned for ourselves. ... The gospel is not just an answer that works; it is the only answer that will work."[13]

When God asks, we must answer.

CHAPTER TWENTY-SEVEN

"Jesus said, 'I am the Resurrection and the Life. Whoever believes in (adheres to, trusts in, relies on) Me [as Savior] will live even if he dies; and everyone who lives and believes in Me [as Savior] will never die. Do you believe this?' "
John 11:25-26 AMPSB

What Difference Does It Make Whether I Believe?

First, you must have faith that the Bible is God's word written so that we may know Him and the power He has over our lives. The apostle Paul noted that Scripture states unequivocally that the entire human race is evil and cannot on its own earn the grace of God.[1]

Paul continues in Romans to give the bottom line: "all have sinned and fall short of the glory of God," [2] warning that man is incapable of avoiding sin without God's intervention and without His grace would eventually be damned forever. [3]

The only valid hope we have is to believe, since that is God's only requirement. Life in this world is a constant battle with sin, and threatened with God's wrath we live in constant fear and guilt. But life in the next world will be infinitely worse without God's salvation through His grace. Unless we embrace God, we must deal with life's personal and individual battles alone and we will be forever damned. [4]

If we believe and ask, God's salvation is available to all. Only through God's grace can we be born again into a new relationship with Him to be saved. Although we are sinners, God alone can receive us into His kingdom because His Son, Jesus Christ, died on a cross to atone for the sins of all, but you must believe to receive salvation. [5]

The author of Hebrews: wrote:

> "And without faith it is impossible to please God, because anyone who comes to him must believe that he exists and that he rewards those who earnestly seek him." (11:6 NIV)

Second, you must believe that Jesus was and is God's Son. The apostle Paul's Letter to the Romans relates the historical facts proving that Jesus

Christ is the Son of God.

MacArthur writes that Jesus is God's Son; He was executed, (as predicted in Scripture by His ancestors), by Jewish leaders in front of many observers, so there is no question that He died, and in three days rose from death, leaving no question that Jesus was divine. And if there is a question for anyone, rising from death and appearing to His disciples and more than 500 of His followers leaves no doubt that He was, and is, the Messiah. These facts alone constitute irrefutable evidence that God provided a means for eternal life to all who believe through the sacrifice of His Son. 6

In Matthew, Jesus asks His disciples, who do the people say the Son of Man is?

> " 'And they answered, 'some say John the Baptist, others say Elijah; and others Jeremiah, or one of the prophets.' He said to them, 'but who do you [yourselves] say that I am?' Simon Peter answered:
> " 'You're the Christ, the Messiah, and the Son of the living God.' " (16:13-16 NIV)

Third, You must believe that Jesus was crucified, died and was raised from death to atone for our sins. Jesus' crucifixion is recorded in Mathew Chapters 27-28.

The apostle Paul's letter to the church in Corinth reiterated Jesus' death and resurrection:

> "Now, brothers, I want to remind you of the gospel I preached to you, which you received and on which you have taken your stand. By this gospel you are saved, if you hold firmly to the word I preached to you. Otherwise, you have believed in vain.
> "For what I received I passed on to you as of first importance for our sins according (as prophesied) to the Scriptures, that he was buried, that he was raised (from death) on the third day according to the Scriptures, and that he appeared to Peter, and then to the Twelve. After that, he appeared to more than five hundred of the brothers at the same time, most of whom are still living ...Then he appeared to James, then to all the apostles, and last of all he appeared to me also, as to one abnormally born (not a follower)." (1 Corinthians 15:1-8 NIV)

The apostle Mark recounts Jesus' encounter with a man possessed by an evil spirit. The man cried out:

> " 'What do you want with us, Jesus of Nazareth? I know who you are—the Holy One of God.'
>
> "Jesus quieted the man and ordered the evil spirit to leave him.
>
> "The evil spirit shook violently and came out of him with a shriek." (1:24-25 NIV)

This man was not a follower but an enemy (evil one) of God. Here is evil recognizing that Jesus is the Son of God. He knew that Jesus was of God. This event is one of many Jesus did to show that good triumphs over evil, and its recording is further proof that Jesus is the Holy One, the Son of God.

Fourth, you must believe there is life after death per God's promise as recorded in the Book of John:

> "For God so loved the world that he gave his one and only Son, that whoever believes in him shall not perish but have eternal life." (3:16 NIV)

After the death of Lazarus, Jesus told his sister:

> " 'Your brother will rise again.' Martha answered, 'I know he will be raised again in the resurrection at the last day (end of time).' Jesus replied: 'I am, resurrection and the life. He who believes in me will live, even though he dies; and whoever lives and believes in me will *never* die.' " (italics added) (John 11:23-25 NIV)

The apostle's writings in 1John serve as the New Testament bottom line:

> "Anyone who believes in the Son of God has this testimony in his heart. (Only he who believes that Jesus is the Son of God). Anyone who does not believe God has made him out to be a liar, because he has not believed the testimony God has given about his Son. And this is the testimony: God has given us eternal life, and this life is in his Son. He who has the Son has life; he who does not have the Son of God does not have life."(5:10-12 NIV)

Essentially, it makes a difference to believe in order to lead a full life with God in this kingdom and the hereafter. Jesus told His disciples:

> " 'Have faith in God. I tell you the truth, if anyone says to this mountain,' "Go throw yourself into the sea," and does not doubt in their heart but believes that what they say will happen, it will be

done for him. Therefore I tell you, whatever you ask for in prayer, believe that you have received, and it will be yours. And when you stand praying, if you hold anything against anyone, forgive him, so that your Father in heaven may forgive you your sins."
(Mark 11:22-26 NIV)

Again, the answer is to "have faith and belief" in God and it will make a difference in your life, here on earth and in the afterlife.

The Difference
When you believe is of great importance. In Matthew's epistle Jesus tells a crowd gathered to hear His preaching:

> " 'Ask and it will be given to you; seek and you will find; knock and the door will be opened to you.' " (7:7 NIV)

Pastor Mason observes:

> "Jesus imparts this glory realm (relational reality) to His brethren whenever they embrace the invitation to an intimate relationship with the Father. Jesus said, 'The glory which You [Father] gave Me I have given them.' (John 17:22 NIV) 'The manifestation of the sons of God' is really the manifestation of the Father's intimate love poured out upon the hearts of His sons and daughters. 'How great is the love the Father has lavished on us that we should be called children of God! And that is what we are.' (1John 3:1 NIV)…. {But} It only comes upon those who fall in love with the Father just as Jesus loved His Father." [7]

As we pray and ask God to answer our prayers (with love and pure motive) there must be an expectation that He will answer and hopefully grant our request. (As long as it takes you to where God wants you to be.)
Referring to "The Circle Maker"—in which author Mark Batterson points out the importance of expectancy when he writes, "King David waited on the Lord expectantly—Pastor Davis observes:

> "…There is possibly a significance hidden in the word *waited.*
> "Throughout the Old and New Testaments of the Bible, there are repetitive examples of displayed faith in which there was an expectancy revealed through the subsequent actions of the people who prayed or sought God about a situation and then waited for Him to respond. It was as if they understood God to be one who was in

covenant with them and they simply expected that He would fulfill His promises to them or fulfill His end of the deal (if you will). This example is mirrored throughout every book of the Bible.

"In fact, if you perform a search of the Amplified Bible, it reveals that the books of Psalms, Proverbs, Isaiah, Jeremiah, Lamentations, Daniel, Hosea, Luke, Romans, Hebrews, and James all have scriptures specifically outlining the importance of waiting expectantly on God (actually using those exact words), and it makes me wonder if there is something significant in the extension of faith demonstrated in *waiting* with *expectations.*" [8]

We also should wait with expectation. Biblical examples of people praying and God answering always require continuing communication with Him. God listens and answers prayers, not necessarily when and the way we want, but when and in the way that meets His plan—and what is best for us.

Jesus promised to come again in the end time to create a new heaven and new earth, void of evil. His followers waited expectantly and spread the message:

> "But (instead of a consuming fire) we look for new heavens and new earth according to His promise, in which righteousness (uprightness, freedom from sin, and right standing with God) is to abide." (2 Peter 3:13 AMP)

God comes to us daily through the Spirit if we are open to His visit. As Mason sees it:

> "The purpose of the Spirit coming upon us as believers is exactly the same as the purpose of the Spirit coming upon Jesus: it is to equip us for supernatural ministry." [9]

God emphatically tells the apostle John in Revelation there will be a final judgment (last unfilled prophecy) when Jesus returns to earth as He promised. [10]

Evil will not prevail forever. God will end it with His judgment as promised. Those who reject the Savior will pay the ultimate price. [11]

Revelation makes it imperative that we believe *now*:

> "Fear God and give him glory, because the hour of his judgment has come. Worship Him who made the heavens, the earth, the sea and the springs of water." (14:7 NIV) [12]

Man is instructed to fear God and give Him glory. Those who do will live eternally. Those who do not will be punished as God deems appropriate. ₁₂ Since we don't know the exact hour of judgment, it is critical that we give God glory and worship Him while we can.

Simply put, God said that you are either with Me or not. There is no fence to sit on. God offers His Holy Spirit to guide us and, upon death, to eternal life. Not believing ends in death eternal. " 'So, because you are lukewarm—neither hot nor cold—I am about to spit you out of my mouth.' " (Revelation 3:16 NIV)

Miller sees the main point of the Book of Malachi as emphasizing the importance of truly believing when worshipping God:

. "Don't expect to please God by going through the motions of worship. He expects sincerity and obedience." ₁₃

What difference does it make if I believe? The journey through life is much more meaningful, and it makes a huge impact in the end:. eternal life or eternal death.

CHAPTER TWENTY-EIGHT

"But no one knows the date and hour when the end will be—not even the angels. No, not even God's Son. Only the Father knows."
Matthew 24:36 TLB

Why Should I Believe Right Now?

Unless you know when you are going to die and/or when Jesus will return for the rapture, you can postpone the decision. Is that a chance you really want to take?

Looking back through God's plan, major events happened about every 1,000 years. (Adam to Noah to Abraham to Moses to Jesus to the crusades? to A.D. 2000?) We don't know if that interval will continue or what event God has in store for us today and in the immediate future. But we do know that Jesus was here on earth, died and rose from the dead, and said He will come again.

We are between His first coming and the second..

2 Timothy states:

> "BUT UNDERSTAND this, that in the last days dangerous times [of great stress and trouble] will come [difficult days that will be hard to bear].
>
> "For people will be lovers of self [narcissistic, self-focused], lovers of money [impelled by greed], boastful, arrogant, revilers, disobedient to parents, ungrateful, unholy *and* profane, [and they will be] unloving [devoid of natural human affection, calloused and inhumane], irreconcilable, malicious gossips, devoid of self-control [intemperate, immoral], brutal, haters of good, traitors, reckless, conceited, lovers of [sensual] pleasure rather than lovers of God, holding to a form of [outward] godliness (religion), although they have denied its power [for their conduct nullifies their claim of faith]." (3:1-5 AMPSB)

That sounds like a description of today's world! It would be a good idea to be ready just in case the last days are close.

Belief in a Religion

The world offers a religious smorgasbord. In, "To Be a Jew," Rabbi Donin describes the 'Cornerstone of Judaism':

> "We believe that the nations and peoples of the world have their Divine purposes and their assigned roles to fulfill, too, for God is the God of all the world, not just of Jewry. And we see our divinely ordained assignment as involving a unique role, one to which history itself bears witness. It implies a special purpose in life, a reason for our existence. That purpose is not to make Jews of all the world, but to bring the peoples of the world, whatever their distinctive beliefs may be, to an acknowledgment of the sovereignty of God and to an acceptance of the basic values revealed to us by that God. It is to serve as a means by which blessing will be brought to 'all the families of the earth.' "
> (Genesis 12:3)[1]

Christians, too, believe God rules the entire world. Because mankind is incapable of living a sin-free life, God sent His Son to take the repercussions of our sins for us.

In "No God But One, Allah or Jesus" Pastor Qureshi explains:

> "But in the Christian message, there is good news. In Greek, the word for good news is *euangelion,* which in English is translated "gospel." And the good news is this: Even though we cannot get to God, out of his great love, God has come to us and made a way for us. God himself has paid for our sins and will eternally restore our souls. All we have to do is repent of our rebellion, have faith in what he has done, and follow him.
>
> "To pay for our sins, God—specifically the second person [Christ] of the Trinity—entered into the world. Without changing his divine nature, God took upon himself a human nature. He was born as a human, but not of the broken lineage of Adam. He was born unbroken, the way mankind was intended to be, the way we will ultimately be when we are miraculously remade. He took the name *Jesus,* which means, "God saves." With respect to his human nature he grew as a human, ate food as a human, suffered alongside humans, and ultimately died [crucified on a cross] as a human. In all this he never sinned, so he was able to bear our sins. He lived the life we ought to have lived so he could die the death that we deserve to die. By dying on our behalf he took upon himself the sins of the world, so that whoever believes in him and accepts what he has done will have eternal life.
>
> "Those of us who wish to accept God's sacrifice on our behalf

must repent or our sins and yield ourselves to following him." [2]

Christianity, Islam and Judaism all claim Abraham as their ancestral beginning, and share belief in a monotheistic being (God) and the prophets recorded in the Bible, but only Christians believe in a Triune God: Father, Son (Christ, Jesus), and Holy Spirit.

Donin explains the Jewish belief re: a Triune God:

> "The Jewish conception of God also rejected any compromise with the spirituality of God. The notion of man becoming God or God assuming the form of man was equally repugnant to the Jewish religious spirit. The Jewish mind and faith cannot accept the notion of the infinite Divine reducing Himself to the finite mortal." [3]

Islam shares the belief with Christianity that Jesus was a Messiah, but they do not believe He was God. Qureshi relates:

> "Perhaps the most surprising shared feature is reverence for Jesus. Both Islam and Christianity teach that Jesus was born of a virgin and that he was the most miraculous man who ever lived. Both the Bible and the Quran teach that Jesus cleansed lepers, healed the blind, and even raised the dead. Indeed, both books teach Jesus is the Messiah and Muslims await his return, as do Christians.
>
> "Where the difference matters most is in the ultimate message of each religion. According to Islam, the way to paradise is sharia, a code of laws to follow that will please Allah and earn his favor. *Sharia* is literally translated "the way." According to the Christian message, the gospel, the way to eternal life is Jesus. He said 'I am the Way, the Truth, and the Life; no one comes to the Father except through me, (John 14:6 NIV). In Islam, sharia is the way, and in Christianity, Jesus is the way." [4]

Both teach that all will be held accountable to God for their sin:

> "The Quran (Islam's law) emphasizes that on that day, all people will be held accountable to Allah for their sins." [5]

But unlike Christianity, no one can take their place before God. Jesus died for the sins of all believers, so none must face God alone to account for his sins. [6]

You Don't Need a Religion

Nothing in the Bible directs us to select a religion or be religious. It does tell us to believe in God and His Son Jesus Christ. Religions are human organizations designed to help their members worship God, thank Him for what He has done for us, and show the way for treating one another.

Once you believe, you will desire to join a religious group to share in worshipping Him and strengthen your faith. All believers need to especially heed the most drastic failure of God's chosen people, the Jews, when they faltered in their continued relationship with Him. Frequently they chose to worship other gods. We may *think* we don't have that problem as we see no other gods in our daily life, or *do* we?

Considering what is taking place today, I think our society as a whole resembles the 2 Peter passage above—especially as it applies to worshipping the almighty dollar. It is not hard to fall from God's grace even though Jesus died for our sins. Jesus even said, after absolving sins, go in peace and sin no more. Repent! Even though Jesus died for our sins, He did not absolve us from obeying all of God's commandments.

Jesus said this is the most important commandment:

> "Love the Lord God (not other so-called gods or idols) with all your heart and with all your soul and with all your mind and with all your strength… and your neighbor as yourself."
> (Mark 12:30-31 NIV)

If Jesus died for our sins, why isn't it OK then to continue to sin? Miller insists the main point of the Book of Jude is the answer:

> "Don't believe false teachers in the church who say it's okay to sin. God punishes sinners. History is full of proof." [7]

Do You Believe This?"

If you believe these things, you must place your life before God [8] and become a child of God, a soldier in His army to fight evil.

In 2 Peter, the apostle writes that through God's divine power we have everything we need to live a dynamic spiritual life so that we can escape the world's immoral nature. [9]

In Paul's epistle to the Romans, he states:

> "But if Christ lives in you, [then although] your [natural] body is dead by reason of sin *and* guilt, the spirit is alive because of [the] righteousness [that He imputes to you]. And if the Spirit of Him Who raised up *Jesus* from the dead dwells in you [then] He Who raised up Christ Jesus from the dead will also restore to life

your mortal (short-lived,…perishable) bodies through His Spirit Who dwells in you." (8:10-12 AMP)

God has provided the written word to guide us to His help in a troubled world:

> "Trust in the Lord with all your heart and lean not on your own understanding; in all your ways acknowledge him, and he will make your paths straight." (Proverbs 3:5-6 NIV)

> "If any of you lacks wisdom, he should ask God (in faith), who gives generously to all and without finding fault, and it will be given to him." (James 1:5 NIV)

In faith, is essential when requesting God's gifts:

> "Only it must be in faith that he asks with no wavering (no hesitating, no doubting)." (James 1:6 AMP)

Faith is trusting in God:

> "Now faith is the confidence that what we hope for will actually happen; it gives us assurance about things we cannot see." (Hebrews 11:1 NIV)

Rabbi Donin teaches there is no middle ground in believing:

> "To accept the yoke of the Kingdom of Heaven is to throw off the yoke of human domination and dictatorship. 'You shall be servants unto Me,' said the Lord, 'and not servants unto My servants.' Man is given a choice. Some think they can pursue a middle road between these two forms of servitude, free of both. Such hopes have invariably proved illusory. If it is not the one, it will invariably be the other." 10

Why Do I Care If You believe?

I care as a believer because Jesus' commandment—as recorded in Matthew and Mark's gospels referenced in Chapter 24—commissioned all believers to spread the good news.

Paul's Letter to the Romans recommends believers also help others when they falter in the faith, or are in need:

> "We who are strong [able in the faith] ought to bear with the failings of the weak and not to please ourselves [not only do what is most convenient for us. Strength is for service, not status]. Each of us should please his neighbor for his good, to build him up."(15:1-2 NIV)

Peter's second letter stresses a holy life:

> "Since everything will be destroyed in this way (heavenly fire), what kind of people ought you to be? You ought to live holy and godly lives as you look forward to the day of God and speed its coming." (3:11-12 NIV)

John's first letter provides a simple means to receive God's forgiveness through His love and patience, and what love really is:

> "If we confess our sins, he (God) is faithful and just and will forgive us our sins and purify us from all unrighteousness."
> (1:9 NIV)
> "He (Jesus) is the atoning sacrifice for our sins, and not only ours but also for the sins of the whole world." (2:2 NIV)
> "Everyone who loves has been born of God and knows God (experiences a relationship with Him). Whoever does not love does not know God, because God is love. This is how God showed his love among us: He sent his one and only Son into the world that we might have life through him. This is love: not that we love God, but he loved us and sent his Son as an atoning sacrifice for our sins." (4:7-10 NIV)
> "We love because he first loved us. If anyone says, 'I love God,' yet hates his brother, he is a liar. For anyone who does not love his brother, whom he can see, cannot love God, whom he has not seen. And he has given us this command: Whoever loves God must also love his brother." (4:19-21 NIV)

The command we have from Christ is blunt: loving God includes loving people. Paul's second letter to the Corinthians states specifically why we should believe:

> "For we [believers will be called to account and] must all appear before the judgment seat of Christ, so that each one may be repaid for what has been done in the body, whether good or

bad [that is, each will be held responsible for his actions, purposes, goals, motives—the use or misuse of his time, opportunities and abilities]."(5:10 AMPSB)

Paul's letter to the Ephesians tells them (all people) of God's intent with every spiritual blessing in Christ before we were born:

"In Him also we have received an inheritance [a destiny—we were claimed by God as His own], having been predestined (chosen, appointed beforehand) according to the purpose of Him who works everything in agreement with the counsel and design of His will." (1:11 AMPSB)

Paul's letter to the Galatians answered the question of earning God's grace through following the Jewish laws. Obeying a set of rules does not justify you before God. Faith is the only way for the righteous. (3:11)

We live in a world seeking physical pleasures and goods. John's first letter says we need to seek the life God intended for us, as the world will "pass away." (2:15-17 NIV)

John assures us that although we may think we lack sin we deceive ourselves. But: "If we confess our sins to Him, He is faithful and just to forgive us our sins and to cleanse us form all wickedness." (1:8 NIV)

Finally, the Book of Ephesians tells us we cannot earn salvation, but most accept God's offer through His grace:

"For it is by free grace (God's unmerited favor) that you are saved (delivered from judgment *and* made partakers of Christ's salvation) through [your] faith. And this [salvation] is not of yourselves [of your own doing, it came not through your own striving], but it is the gift of God.

"Not because of works [not the fulfillment of the Law's demands], lest any man should boast. [It is not the result of what anyone can possibly do, so no one can pride himself in it or take glory to himself].

"For we are God's [own] handiwork (His workmanship), recreated in Christ Jesus, [born anew] that we may do those good works which God predestined (planned beforehand) for us [taking paths which He prepared ahead of time], that we should walk in them [living the good life which He prearranged and made ready for us to live]." (2:8-10 AMP)

These are among the most relevant passages of this book; each of us was predestined (before birth) to fulfill God's plan. But remember, Adam was also, and because he sinned, God's plan was interrupted. Because Adam sinned [creating original sin], we must now decide (free will) if we want to be part of His plan, and thereby spend eternal life with Him.

Jesus said, love God and your brother as yourself, and believe in Me to be saved. His command was not a request, a favor asked, or if you want to, or a directive. It was a command: just do it.

How Do I Know This Is True?

The passages and events written and described all involved real people who experienced God's love. The Bible is not just a single-author long ago fiction.

The Holy Bible consists of 66 books written by various authors spanning thousands of years recording events involving the Israelites, Jesus, His followers and many more. Roman historians have also recorded many of the events revealed in the Bible, thereby independently verifying the authenticity of biblical records.

Consider this history: Approximately 800 years *before* the birth of Jesus, from which time has been determined for us, the prophet Isaiah proclaimed:

> "A girl who is presently a virgin will get pregnant. Shall bear a son and name him Immanuel (God-with-Us). By the time the child is twelve years old, able to make moral decisions, the threat of war will be over." (7:14 MSG)

> "For unto us a child is born, unto us a son is given: and the government shall be upon his shoulder; and his name shall be called Wonderful, Counselor, The mighty God, The everlasting Father, The Prince of Peace." (9:6 KJV)

The first chapter of Matthew records the birth of Jesus describing it just as Isaiah had. Isaiah's prophecy came true *eight centuries* later. Isaiah also prophesied the punishment, trial, and death of God's Savior to the world; and His gift of salvation through His Son.[31] The book of Matthew *describes the actual events predicted* by Isaiah. That prophecy also came true. [11]

In 1 Corinthians, the apostle Paul writes:

> "The first thing I did was place before you what was placed so emphatically before me: that the Messiah died for our sins, exactly as Scripture tells it, that he was buried, that he was raised from death on the third day, again exactly as Scripture says, that he presented himself alive to Peter, then to his closest followers, and later to more than five hundred of his followers all at the same time, most of them still around (although a few have since

died), that he then spent time with James and the rest of those he commissioned to represent him, and that he finally presented himself alive to *me.*" (15:3-8 MSG)

The Bible records many of God's prophecies that came true, most of them many years after they were first recorded. God has given everyone on earth a prophecy in Revelation that we must help fulfill if we expect to live eternally. Simply put, we must believe and have faith in Him.

The Bible does not tell us we are to be religious; it tells us to believe and have faith. Abraham found favor with God because he had faith. We can do the same if we have faith as well. Paul makes it very clear. We are to live according to God's commandments, not the ways of the world.

"For all who are *allowing themselves* to be led by the Spirit of God are sons of God."(Romans 8:12-14 AMPSB)

"Do not be conformed to this world [any longer with superficial values and customs], but be transformed and progressively changed [as you mature spiritually] by the renewing of your mind [focusing on godly values and ethical attitudes], so that you may prove [for yourselves] what the will of God is, that which is good and acceptable and perfect [in His plan and purpose for you]." (Romans 12:2 AMPSB)

Time has been determined from Jesus' birth, thereby proving the importance of that event for mankind. The Holy Bible is far and away the most read book ever written. The Bible is God's true Scripture, telling mankind of His plan for winning the war of good vs. evil. God's word in the Bible is true: *Believe it.*

Being a good person is not the same as believing in God and His Son. Isaiah tells us that God's decree states:

"Seek God while he's here to be found, pray to him while he's close at hand.
"I don't think the way you think, the way you work isn't the way I work." (55:5, 8 MSG)

The question is not why should I believe, but rather why should I not believe? Why should I believe now? Unless you know when you are going to die or Jesus will return, you are taking a *huge* chance on not having life eternal. God's plan can also be viewed as developing in 2,000-year increments—Adam to Abraham to Jesus. It has been over 2,000 years since Jesus' death. What might happen in this 2,000-year period?

CHAPTER TWENTY-NINE

" 'I am the [only] Way [to God] and the [real] Truth and the [real] Life; no one comes to the Father but through Me.' "
John 14:6 AMPSB

What Should I Believe?

First and foremost, believe in the God who created the universe and made mankind in His image and likeness (combining human and spirit) with a free will, and that through His love and grace has provided a way to live eternally. Pastor Zimmerman writes:

> "The apostle Peter reminds us of God's promise in 1 Peter 1:8-9 NIV): 'Though you have not seen Him, you love him; and even though you do not see him now, you believe in him and are filled with the inexpressible and glorious joy, for you are receiving the end result of your faith, the salvation of your souls.' " [1]

As recorded in Proverbs:

> "Lean on, trust in, *and* be confident in the Lord with all your heart *and* mind and do not rely on your own insight or understanding. In all your ways know, recognize, *and* acknowledge Him, and He will direct *and* make straight *and* plan your paths. Be not wise in your own eyes; reverently fear *and* worship the Lord and turn [entirely] away from evil." (3:5-7 AMP)

The Book of Matthew bluntly describes God's omnipotence:

> "With men this (go through the eye of a needle) is impossible, but all things are possible with God." (19:26 AMP)

Pastor Davis thinks man's role working with God's omnipotence (making the impossible, possible for man) as a man-and-God equation: Man X God = Infinity. He calls this the physical-spiritual relativity equation, meaning: man working with God can achieve all things. [2]

Second, believe God created mankind to establish an earthly kingdom and gave them complete authority to rule over the creation, in accordance with His Ten Commandments and Jesus' rule of love God with all their heart and fellow mankind as their brothers, {" 'The kingdom of God is at hand.' "} Mark 1:15 AMP And as appears in Matthew:

> " 'For if you forgive men when they sin against you, your heavenly Father will also forgive you. But if you do not forgive men their sins, your Father will not forgive your sins.' "
> (6:14-15 NIV)

God's gift of complete authority over the earthly kingdom therefore made *us* responsible to live with the consequences of *our* actions without His interference, unless *we*, through prayer, ask His help and guidance. God therefore is not responsible for everything that happens on earth and certainly not for the evil caused by Satan.

Third, believe that Satan, a fallen angel who convinced man to sin and therefore stole the authority to rule the earth, continues to spread his evil through mankind. As recorded in the Book of Daniel, there is a dark kingdom on earth that Satan set up when he took the kingdom that Adam was charged to establish, and Satan and his followers work hard to convince man to sin.

How do we protect ourselves from Satan's attack? Paul's Letter to the Ephesians advises:

> " ...Be strong in the Lord ... Put on God's complete armor, *and* stand your ground on the evil day... having tightened the belt of truth around your loins ... and the breastplate of integrity *and* of moral rectitude *and* right standing ...shod your feet in preparation ... and (employ) the shield of saving faith ... take the helmet of salvation and the sword that the Spirit wields ... Pray at all times, keep alert and watch with strong purpose and perseverance."
> (6:10-18 AMP)

Fourth, believe that God has a contingency plan to save man from Satan's power and provide a way for *you* to live eternally with Him, through the birth and life of His Son, Jesus Christ.

Davis records in "Quantum Christianity" his belief that God's plan was always redemption. The description of his thoughts of God's sin-contingency plan is in Chapter 19, summarized here:

> "In essence, giving us the opportunity to choose for ourselves

what kingdom we would want to participate in establishing and ultimately be ruled by and freeing us from the default bondage that would otherwise by our reality." 3

Fifth, believe that Jesus was crucified and rose from death to atone for man's sin so that he would be acceptable to live eternally with God.

Sixth, believe that through belief and faith in the risen Jesus you can live in God's earthly kingdom on earth, and after death with God in heaven.

Seventh, believe that God has given believers the Holy Spirit to guide life through God's grace.

> "For it is by free grace (God's unmerited favor) that you are saved (delivered from judgment *and* made partakers of Christ's salvation) through [your] faith. And this [salvation] is not of yourselves [of your own doing, it came not through your own striving], but it is the gift of God." (Ephesians 2:8 AMP)

Unlike the Old Testament where God punished His people when they sinned and forgave them when they would repent, Jesus took the punishment for our sins and God forgives us unconditionally. However, in as much as we all will face judgment it behooves us to repent and sin no more (knowingly). 4

The downfall of the Israelites, time after time, was forgetting God and worshipping idols. That should be a heads-up for us, as there are lots of idols for us to worship: wealth, power, drugs and anything else that does not put God first. The wisest human ever to live (Solomon), after examining why humans live on earth came to the conclusion:

> "When all has been heard, the end of the matter is: fear God [worship] Him with awe-filled reverence, knowing that He is almighty God, and keep His commandments, for this applies to every person." (Ecclesiastes 12:13 AMPSB)

Ecclesiastes Chapter 3 tells us there is a season (a time to be born, a time to weep, a time for war, etc.) for everything. While we would like to set each of the seasons, the author is not saying that everything has an opportune time according to which one should choose one action or the other. Rather he teaches that all events are in the hand of God, who makes everything happen in the time He judges appropriate. 5

Eighth, believe that God has had an awesome plan since the creation of the earth, and through His grace He has a plan for you.

The Psalms tell us how to worship God, tell Him our problems, and offer a means to ask for His help through prayer.

177

The Book of Proverbs provides a practical guide to navigate through troubles.

God's plan includes the promise of eternal life if you believe and a more peaceful life on earth within His kingdom. Even though your life may not include God or follow Satan's ways, Jesus provides hope that you may still enter the kingdom on earth and Heaven if you are born again and live according to His ways. 6

God's kingdom is on earth now, and even though you may not know or feel that, He knows your status in His kingdom. Simply believing so that you might go to heaven falls short of what He expects. God wants you to feel His presence now, and through faith you can experience His love today, and live eternally. The psalmist tells us:

> "...People don't have to wait for an afterlife to receive God's glory. God has already honored human beings simply by giving them life and entrusting them the job of taking care of His creation— 'putting all things under their authority.' " (Psalm 8:6) 7

These beliefs are summarized in the Christian Creed in Appendix A.

Scottish Pastor William Barclay's "The Letter to the Romans" (12:9-13) sums up what life in God's earthly kingdom should be. In the section, "The Christian Life in Everyday Action," 8 he lists 12 traits that a Christian should possess through faith based on God's and Jesus' commandments. If we love God and our neighbors, the traits would naturally be manifested in actions. However, Christians are human and the evil one is constantly trying to interfere with our attributes and behavior.

Make no mistake: God asks a lot of believers. It is particularly difficult to do all these things when life is not going so well. Can't we question God in those times? Why me? Of course you can. Job did, and Jacob actually not only questioned God but even wrestled with Him.

In their book, "Kelly Tough," Erin with Jill Kelly answer the question based on their love of God:

> "Asking why is human, but it is rarely fruitful and oftentimes frustrating. God doesn't owe us an explanation. We were created by Him and for Him; therefore, we are called to surrender to Him without prejudice, conditions or ultimatums. He is Lord and we are not. His ways are not ours; they are higher, greater and beyond our finite comprehension. His perfect plans cannot be thwarted and He reasons from an eternal vantage point. Thankfully, however, He loves us without limit! So rather than pretend or go through the motions, hoping that whatever we're feeling will eventually go away, we can come boldly to God without

reservation or hesitation. His grace is sufficient for us and His mercies are ever present. As we learn to trust Him, we can still ask questions but also rest in not knowing because we know that He knows." 9

Jesus' parable of the servants investing their master's money, in the Gospel of Matthew, reveals what we really should understand—what God expects of us. In his book, "Legacy Now: Why Everything about You Matters," Pastor Phil Munsey captures it clearly:

> "Your actions confirm or deny what you believe. They determine how your beliefs make a difference in your life or how they don't readily affect it at all. Many people say they believe something, but lack the faith to live a life that expresses that belief." 10

The Book of Micah tells what God requires:

> "He has told you, O man, what is good: And what does the Lord require of you except to be just, and to love [and to diligently practice] kindness (compassion), and to walk humbly with your God [setting aside any overblown sense of importance or self-righteousness]." (6:8 AMPSB)

To do as God asks, you must first believe. God's love is one of forgiveness. The Kellys write:

> "We can't receive the forgiveness of God and not extend it to others. In fact, in receiving God's love and forgiveness, a direct result of this should be that the same pours out of our lives. It's all God. You can't forgive or be forgiven without Him.
>
> "Because in truly forgiving God also works in us the ability to forget." 11

The book of Colossians advises:

> "Bear with each other and forgive whatever grievances you may have against each other. Forgive as the Lord forgave you. And over all these virtues put on love, which binds them all together in perfect unity." (3:13-14 NIV)

Erin and Jill Kelly point out there is a clear path to salvation, which they call "The Romans Road: Walking the Path that Leads from Death to Life." That path is paved with passages from Paul's Letter to the Romans:

"For all have sinned and *continually* fall short of the glory of God." (3:23 AMPSB)

"The wages of sin is death, but the free gift of God [that is, His remarkable, overwhelming gift of grace to believers] is eternal life in Christ Jesus our Lord." (6:23 AMPSB)

"But God clearly shows and proves His own love for us, by the fact that while we were still sinners, Christ died for us."(5:8 AMPSB)

"For "WHOEVER CALLS ON THE NAME OF THE LORD [in prayer] WILL BE SAVED." (Romans 10:13 AMPSB) 12

The Bible is the greatest nonfiction book of all. It's not about religion, it's about God and His relationship with His creation. Of course there is a villain, one of God's own, Lucifer or Satan, who steals God's planned earthly kingdom and makes life difficult for His children on earth. It's about a power struggle between life and death leading to all-out war between good and evil.

Satan offers only earthly pleasures followed by pain, suffering and heartbreak.

God has provided a way for His children to join Him in eternal life. Besides eternal life, God makes 10 promises to support believers through this life. Dr. Charles Stanley cites the promises from biblical passages revealing God: walks with us (never leaves us), guides us (when we follow), listens to us (answers our prayers, when we ask, trust, wait and obey), encourages us (with His presence), empowers us (sealed as a child of God—assumes full responsibility to provide His help), provides for us (best for his children from whom He expects respect), protects us, forgives us, loves us unconditionally, and secures eternity for us.

God's children cannot win the war alone. They can fight off the temptations of the evil one, but need God to claim victory. His and our greatest weapon is love. The good news is that God provided a Savior to destroy sin and carry us to victory.

All will face death. By believing in God's Savior, Jesus Christ, we can be assured that Jesus on judgment day will intercede and save believers from the punishment they deserve, as He paid the price of our sins on the cross.

"Death has been swallowed up in victory." "O DEATH WHERE IS YOUR VICTORY?" [Hos 13:14] "O death where is your sting? The sting of death is sin, and the power of sin [by which it brings death] is the law; but thanks be to God, who gives us the victory [as conquerors] through our Lord Jesus Christ."
(1 Corinthians 15:55-57 AMPSB)

Jesus comforts us as He did His disciples:

> " 'DO NOT let your heart be troubled (afraid, cowardly). Believe [confidently] in God *and* trust in Him; [have faith, hold onto it, rely on it, keep going and] believe also in Me. In My Father's house are many dwelling places. If it were not so, I would have told you, because I am going there to prepare a place for you. And if I go and prepare a place for you, I will come back again and I will take you to Myself, so that where I am you may be also. And [to the place] where I going, you know the way.' Thomas (the disciple) said to Him, 'Lord, we do not know where You are going; so how can we know the way?' Jesus said to him, 'I am the [only] Way [to God] and the [real] Truth and the [real] Life; no one comes to the Father but through Me.' " (John 14:1-6 AMPSB)

Father Richard Rohr, in "The Universal Christ," notes that the apostle Paul provides the measure for determining the level of authentic faith.

> " 'Examine yourselves to make sure you are in the faith. Test yourselves. Do you acknowledge that Jesus Christ is really in you? If not, you have failed the test.' (2 Corinthians 13:5-6 NIV)
> "Paul's radical incarnationalism sets a standard for all later Christian saints, mystics and prophets. He knew that the Christ must first of all be acknowledged *within* before He can be recognized *without* as Lord and Master. God must reveal Himself *in you* before God can fully reveal himself *to you*. The proof that you are a Christian is that you can see Christ everywhere else." 13

The path is clear. We have only to recognize that we are sinners and speak it with our lips to God. He will hear and forgive.

CHAPTER THIRTY

"Nothing impure {evil} will enter it {the New Jerusalem}, nor will anyone who does what is shameful or deceitful, but only those whose names are written in the Lamb's {Jesus} book of life."
Revelation 21:27 NIV

The Book of Life

What appears in this book represents numerous people's comprehension of God's plan and what we are to believe. We are asked to seek understanding and believe in God. "He who has an ear, let him hear and heed what the Spirit says to the churches."[1]

Pastor Davis writes:

> "Let's be honest, from church to church what we have been taught is ultimately a leader's or organization's interpretation of scriptures that they have read in the Bible. And for every denomination represented in Christianity, there is an interpretation of a scripture, set of scriptures, or philosophy that differs. As a result, we have around 41,000 denominations of Christianity in existence in the world today based solely upon an individual or groups differing agreement with an interpretation of scriptures.... Although many people believe that they are right, not everyone can be 100 percent right, for if one is completely right, then the other with contrary view cannot be."[2]

This and many other books about God's love and His plan may provide overwhelming information. God said seek and you shall find. Only you can have your own understanding and personal relationship with God. Davis recommends learning about God to gain an understanding, and he believes:

> "As we learn who we are to God, how He feels about us, and embrace His love, we can then confidently pursue the establishment of God's kingdom in the earth, and we can begin to experience the fullness of the supernatural life that He always intended for us."[3]

The book of John contains a solemn promise:

> "I assure you, most solemnly I tell you, if anyone steadfastly believes in Me, he will himself be able to do the things that I do; and he will do even greater things than these, because I go to the Father."
> (14:12 AMP)

However, scripture is clear:

> "For it is by grace [God's remarkable compassion and favor drawing you to Christ] that you have been saved [actually delivered from judgment and given eternal life] through faith. And this [salvation] is not of yourselves [not through your own effort], but it is the [undeserved, gracious] gift of God; not as a result of [your] works [nor] your attempts to keep the Law], so that no one will [be able to] boast *or* take credit in any way [for his salvation]."
> (Ephesians 2:8 AMPSB)
> "Nor is there salvation in any other, for there is no other name under heaven given men by which we must be saved."
> (Acts 4:12 NKJV)

Part of the good news: There are no religious laws in Christianity that must be kept. There are celebrations of faith of the sacraments (baptism, confirmation, anointing the sick, marriage, Eucharist, penance and holy orders), believed to be ordained by Christ and observed in celebration of His life. Each denomination also has administrative procedures for operating its church. The Roman Catholic church has a system of regulations, called "cannon law," for operation within the church, but the procedures are not the judicial law of the land.

In the end times God's judgment is very clear in Revelation:

> "The lake of fire is the second death, and anyone whose name was not found recorded in the Book of Life was thrown into the lake of fire." (20:14-15 AMPSB)

Nonbelievers will perish in the lake of fire. There will be no second chance. [4]

If you believe, you can reside with God forever free of the evil of this life. In the end times, God will live among His people.

> "And I heard a loud voice (God's) from the throne saying, 'Now

the dwelling of God is with men, and he will live with them. They will be his people, and God himself will be with them and be their God. He will wipe every tear from their eyes. There will be no more death or mourning or crying or pain, for the old order of things has passed away.' " (Revelation 21:3-4 NIV)

The path to salvation for Christians [all believers in Jesus Christ] is clear. "If you declare with your mouth: 'Jesus is Lord,' believe in your heart that He was crucified to atone for your sins and that God raised Him from the dead, you will be saved."5

God is a God of love. He waits for us to call on His name through prayer. There are no rules to pray for God to hear you. Pray and listen. God will answer your prayer, maybe not granting what you want, but what best fits His plan for you. 6 Listen to the Holy Spirit that lives in you.

Jesus taught His disciples the Lord's Prayer.7 Knowing and relying on that prayer answers all our needs.

The judgment or *bema*, recorded in 2 Corinthians 5:10 sounds threatening, at least daunting, but Pastor Kinley points out that "Jesus paid for all our sin." He further explains the results of the *bema:*

> "The purpose of Christ's evaluation is *not* to determine destiny— heaven or hell. Sin is not the issue here. Our salvation is a gift from God, solely by 'grace through faith, not of works.' There is nothing we can do for God, either before or after our salvation, that has any bearing whatsoever on our righteous standing before Him. Your forgiveness was forever settled when you trusted in Jesus' payment for sin on the cross. Your salvation was sealed in Him and He declared you eternally righteous before Him. As a result, there is not an ounce of wrath or a drop of anger waiting for you in heaven. Not one sin will be brought up at the bema. To do so, Jesus would have to deny the efficacy of His own death and resurrection, not to mention contradicting His word and character. Salvation is complete. You are guilt–free." (Appendix B lists the rewards that await believers.) 8

Revelation paints a horrible picture of the end times. 9 There will be a gruesome war. Evil will be destroyed along with all who do not believe in God. The only way to live eternally is to believe in God, trust His promises, and through His grace be included in His kingdom. 10

God gave the apostle John a vision of being in heaven looking down on the earth. John recorded what he saw during the Tribulation. Kinley writes that he believes God gave John this vision for all believers and anyone who reads Revelation. Considering the world affairs today, he asks why we are not panicking:

> "Why do we despair? One. Simple. Reason: There is a *throne* in heaven. Therefore, to prepare His church [believers] and help her understand our planet's last days, Jesus takes John (and us) on a virtual tour of heaven. He knows, as we consider the cataclysmic events that 'must shortly take place' (4:1) here on earth, we (like our first century brothers and sisters), are likely to grow anxious, worried, insecure, or even become filled with panic. That's why Jesus paints a dramatic contrast between what *will* transpire on earth {and} what *is* taking place in heaven. Jesus wants His bride [believers] to know that even though all hell is about to break out on earth, heaven remains tranquil, secure, and filled with praise to a God who occupies a throne. And because of Him who reigns upon that throne, our hearts are filled not with anxiety but with awe. All is well in heaven because a Sovereign, Holy God is in charge.... No matter how bad things get in this present life, nothing threatens our guaranteed safe arrival in our eternal home." [11]

Many people may think that the great tribulation will not happen in their lifetime. That may be true, but all will die and all will face judgment. But there is hope if you believe. Miller explains:

> "Paul says a normal person wouldn't even die to save a good soul. 'But God showed his great love for us [believers] by sending Christ to die for us while we were still sinners. And since we have been made right in God's sight by the blood of Christ, he will certainly save us from God's condemnation.' " (Romans 5:8-7) [12]

Jesus told His disciples that the end time and His return are only known by God.

> " 'Heaven and earth [as now known] will pass away, but My words will not pass away. But of that [exact] day and hour no one knows, not even the angels of heaven, nor the Son [in His humanity], but the Father alone.' " (Matthew 24:35-36 AMPSB)
> "So Christ, having been offered once *and* once for all to bear [as a burden] the sins of many, will appear a second time [when he returns to earth], not to deal with sin, but to bring salvation to those who are eagerly *and* confidently waiting for Him."
> (Hebrews 9:28 AMPSB)

While the rapture and the consequences will be daunting, author Barbara Johnson reminds us: "Don't worry about tomorrow, God is already there."[13]

Remember the atheist talking to a Christian in Chapter 1? We can be foolish or blessed. God gave us the choice. Choose wisely. Read the Bible and decide for yourself. God has had a plan for you since *before* you were born, and you don't have to wait to learn what it is. When you believe you will understand that plan.

Now I know You had a plan for me,
I no longer have to wait to see what it could be;
considering all the lives You had me touch,
and what you had me do since I first believed,
I understand Your plan was, You leading me just as I am.

Live your life as though God is watching. Because *He is*!

BIBLIOGRAPHY

Bibles

The Amplified Bible, Zondervan Publishing House, copyright 1965
The Amplified Study Bible, Zondervan Publishing House, copyright 2017
The Living Bible, Tyndale House Publishers, copyright 1971
Life Application Study Bible, New International Version, published jointly by Tyndale Publishers Inc. and Zondervan Publishing House, copyright 1990
King James Version, set forth in 1611, American Bible Society, instituted 1816
The Message//Remix by Eugene H. Peterson, copyright 2003
Serendipity Bible, New International Version, 10th Anniversary Edition, Zondervan Publishing House, copyright 1988

Biblical Commentaries

Alexander, Pat and David, Zondervan Handbook to the Bible, published by Lion Publishing, plc, copyright 1999
Barclay, William, The Letter to the Romans, The Westminster Press, copyright 1955
Barton, Bruce B., [et al], Life Application Bible Commentary, Tyndale Publishers Inc., copyright 2000
Gangel, Kenneth O., and Bramer, Stephen J., Holman Old Testament Commentary, B&H Publishing Group, copyright 2002
Miller, Stephen M., The Complete Guide to the Bible, Barbour Publishing Inc., copyright 2007
Halley, Henry H., Halley's Bible Handbook, Zondervan Publishing House, 24th edition, copyright 1965
Nave, Orville J., Topical Bible, The Southwestern Company, copyright 1896
Richards, Lawrence O., The Teachers Commentary, Victor Books, copyright 1987

Authors

Brown, Dan, Origin, Anchor Books, copyright 2017
Bjornerud, Marcia, Timefulness, Princeton University Press, 2018
Buford, Bob, Half Time: Moving from Success to Significance, The Leadership Network Inc., copyright 2008

Davis, Aaron D., Quantum Christianity, copyright 2015

Donin, Rabbi Hayim Halevy, To Be A Jew, Basic Books, copyright 1972

Eldredge, John, Waking the Dead, Thomas Nelson Publishers, copyright 2003

Hamilton, Adam, Creed, Abingdon Press, copyright 2016

Hamilton, Adam, Half Truths, Abingdon Press, copyright 2016

Johnson, Barbara, We Brake for Joy, Women of Faith, Zondervan Publishing House, copyright 1998

Jones, Dan, The Templars, Viking, copyright 2017

Kelly, Erin with Jill, Kelly Tough, Broad Street Publishing Group, LLC, copyright 2015

Kinley, Jeff, Wake the Bride, Harvest House Publishers, copyright 2015

Krusen, Christobal, They Were Christians, Published by Baker Books, copyright 2016

Lewis, C.S., Mere Christianity, Touchstone, published by Simon and Schuster, copyright 1943

MacArthur, John, The Gospel According to Paul, Nelson Books, copyright 2017

Mason, Phil, Quantum Glory, Published by XP Publishing, copyright 2010

Munsey, Phil, Legacy Now: Why Everything about You Matters, Published by Charisma House, copyright 2008

Nordgren, J. Vincent, The Heart of the Bible, Fortress Press, copyright 1953

Qureshi, Nabeel, No God But One, Zondervan, copyright 2016

Rohr, Richard, The Universal Christ, copyright 2019 by Center for Action and Contemplation Inc.

Ross, Hugh, The Creator and the Cosmos, Reasons to Believe Press, fourth edition, copyright 2018

Willimon, William H., Why I Am a United Methodist, Abingdon Press, 1990

Zimmerman, Travis, A Family Guide to Joy, copyright 2018

Reference Materials

The Big Bang, TV sitcom 2018

Dr. Charles Stanley, TV evangelist

Google search

The New Book of Knowledge, first edition, copyright 1966 by Grolier Inc.

Reckless Love Song, written by Cory Asbury, Caleb Culver, and Ron Jackson, Bethel Music Publishing

The Register, Google search

Smithsonian.com, Smart News on Google Search

Time Life Books, The Emergence of Man Series, published in New York, 1973

Chart 1

ERA	PERIOD	EPOCH	A	B
			C	
CENOZOIC	QUATERNARY	RECENT		
		PLEISTOCENE		
		PLIOCENE		
	TERTIARY	MIOCENE		
		OLIGOCENE	69	70
		EOCENE		
		PALEOCENE		
MESOZOIC	CRETACEOUS		65	135
	JURASSIC		45	180
	TRIASSIC		50	230
PALEOZOIC	PERMIAN		50	280
	CARBONIFEROUS			
	PENNSYLVANIAN		65	345
	MISSISSIPPIAN			
	DEVONIAN		60	405
	SILURIAN		20	425
	ORDOVICIAN		75	500
	CAMBRIAN		100	600

GEOLOGICAL TIME SCALE

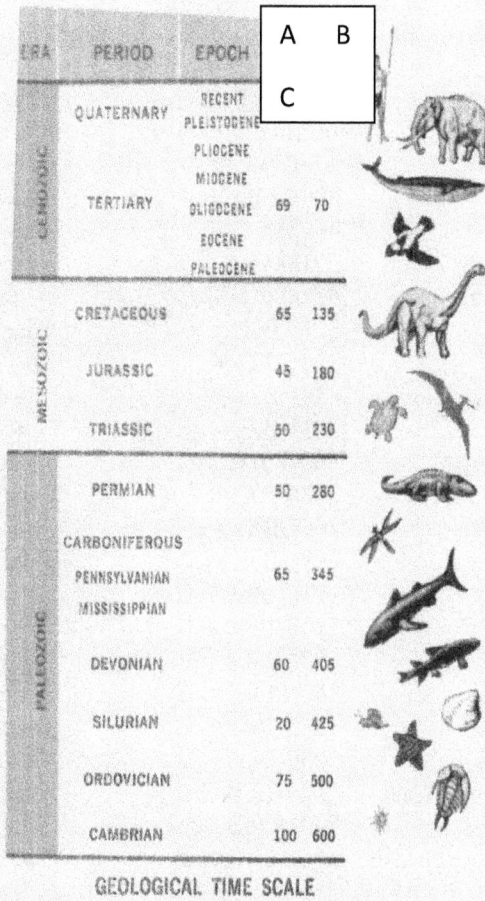

The Book of Knowledge 7G Page 113

A - Beginning of Period

B - End of Period

C - Millions of Years

Chart 2

Biblical Timeline of God's Plan

The Plan	Time Period	Earthly Event
God's Existence	Infinite 1	The beginning
God's Creation	4.5 B B.C. 2.	Earth is formed
Prehistoric life	600 M B.C. 3	Sea & land life
First Human	400,000 B.C. 4	Homo erectus
Ice Age	20,000 B.C. 5	Homo sapiens
Adam is created	6,000 B.C. 6	1ST Human-Spirit
Adam's death	5070 B.C. 7	Adam's descendants
Noah born	4941 B.C. 8	Noah's era
World flood	4341 B.C. 9	Life destroyed
Noah dies	4211 B.C. 10	Land repopulated
Tower of Babel	3000? B.C. 11	Separate languages
Abraham	2166 B.C. 12	Faithful servant
1st Covenant	2067 B.C. 13	Chosen people
Abraham dies	1991 B.C. 14	Canaan land given
Joseph's life	1916-1805 B.C. 15	Egypt authority
Land of Slavery	1805-1440 B.C. 16	Slavery, Exodus
Life of Moses	1526-1406 B.C. 17	Ten Commandments
Promised Land	1406-1375 B.C. 18	Conquer and settle
Time of Judges	1375-1050 B.C. 19	Othniel-Samuel
Time of Kings	1050-740 B.C. 20	Saul-Hoshea
Assyria conquers Israel	722-612 B.C. 21	Israelites captive
Time of Prophets	740-430 B.C. 22	Isaiah-Malachi
Babylon conquers Judah	586-539 B.C. 23	Captivity again
Persia conquers Babylon	539-333 B.C. 24	Judah province
Greeks take Israel	333-198 B.C. 25	Ruled by Greece
Syria takes control	198-44 B.C. 26	Palestine province
Maccabeus revolt	191-160 B.C. 27	Preserves Judaism
Roman invasion	44 B.C.-356 A.D. 28	Roman occupation
A Savior is born	0-33 A.D. 29	God's Son
Gospels written	60s-90s A.D. 30	Record of Jesus
First churches	90s-312 A.D. 31	The Way
Catholic Church	312-present 32	Constantine
Crusades	1095-1271 33	Defend Holy Land
Holy Lands lost	1453 34	Turkish invasion
Reformation	1517-1648 35	Protestant Church
Israel nationhood	1948	Land returned

Chart 3

The Logic of Belief

Believe	God Exists	Result*
No	No	No afterlife
Yes	No	No afterlife
No	Yes	Afterlife of torment
Yes	Yes	Eternal Life with God

* The fact that we have a spiritual soul confirms there is a spiritual realm beyond earth our souls travel to after death. We don't know if the spiritual realm is a single realm broken in two parts—heaven and hell—or two separate realms. According to Revelation, when we die our soul raises to God's spiritual realm. There Jesus determines where your spirit will spend eternity. While on earth Jesus tells us we must believe to remain in heaven. Without belief in Him our soul is cast from heaven to hell.

Appendix A

The Christian Creed

I believe in God, the Father Almighty, creator of heaven and earth.
I believe in Jesus Christ, His only Son, our Lord,
Who was conceived by the Holy Spirit,
born of the Virgin Mary, 1
suffered under Pontius Pilate,
was crucified, 2 died, and was buried;
He descended to the dead,
On the third day He rose again;
He ascended into heaven,
Is seated at the right hand of the Father,
And will come again to judge the living and the dead.
I believe in the Holy Spirit,

> the holy catholic (universal) church,
> the communion of saints,
> the forgiveness of sins,
> the resurrection of the body,
> and the life everlasting. Amen.

1 Father Richard Rohr calls the comma at the end of this phrase [born of the virgin Mary] the "Great Comma." He believes that the authors left out a very important part of the creed. As written, the creed goes from Jesus' birth to His death, leaving out His 33 years of sin-free life on earth. Without His life on earth, we would not know of Jesus' example as how we are to live in God's kingdom on earth as God desires until we die.

We were born as a gift from God, [we had nothing to do with our birth] we live life as we want, [a free will] and we die, [at God's time, unless we take our own life] and God determines our afterlife destiny. The only time we have control of our life is from our birth until we die. During that time God expects us to live without sin, worship Him, and maintain His kingdom.

Jesus the Christ was sent to earth not only to teach us how to achieve eternal life, but to show us how to treat and love one another, to look out for each other and to respect and thank God for all He has done for us. Jesus promised believers eternal life, but besides focusing on that promise, He also wants us to continue His kingdom as He did during His earthly life. We are to act as He did while on earth; He will tell us how to live life eternal when the time comes.

God sent His Son to show us how God expects us to live. He knows we will sin, but He forgives us if we believe in Him and that His Son [died to atone for the sins of all mankind.

2 Inherent in the term crucified is the act of atonement for man's sins (yours and mine). Jesus took the punishment we deserve. Without atonement the crucifixion would have been another punishment for wrongdoing by the authorities.

192

Appendix B

The Judgment Crowns

Many Bible passages promise deserving followers of Christ a crown after judgment. In his book "Wake the Bride," Pastor Jeff Kinley summarizes such passages by describing the various crowns referred to in the Bible. Here is his summary:

1. *The Imperishable Crown (1 Corinthians 9:24-27)* Given to those who exercise self-control as they run the race of service set before them.
2. *The Crown of Righteousness (2 Timothy 4:6-8)* Worn by those who look forward to and love the appearing of Jesus.
3. *The Crown of Life (James 1:12; Revelation 2:10)* Presented to those who persevere under trials and persecution, and who are faithful to Jesus until death.
4. *The Crown of Exultation / Rejoicing (1 Thessalonians 2:19-20)* Received by those who win others to Christ.
5. *The Crown of Glory (1 Peter 5:1-4)* Awaits those obedient pastors/elders who faithfully shepherd the flock of God.

Appendix C
The Genealogy of Jesus Christ

6000 B.C.   **Adam** 1

Cain	Seth	Abel
Enoch	Enosh	
Irad	Kenan	
Mehujael	Mahalalel	
Methushael	Jared	
Lamoch	Enoch	
Adah Zillah	Methuselah	
Jabal Jubal Tubal Cain Naamah	Lamech	

4941 B.C.   **Noah** 2

Ham	Shem	Japheth
Elam Asshur	Arpachshad Lud Aram	
	Shelah	
	Eber	
	Peleg 3 Joktan	
	Reu	
	Serug	
	Nahor	
	Terah	

2166 B.C.   **Abram** 4   Nahor Haran

Lot

Isaac

Judah

Perez

Hezron

Ram

Aminadab

Nahshon

Salmon

Boaz

Obed

Jesse

1000 B.C.	**David***	
	Solomon	Nathan
900s B.C.	Rehoboam*	Mattaha
	Abijah	Menna
	Asa*	Melea
800s B.C.	Jehoshaphat*	Eliakim
	Joram	Jonam
	Uzziah	Judah
	Jotham*	Simeon
700s B.C.	Ahaz*	Levi
	Hezekiah*	Matthat
600s B.C.	Manasseh*	Jorim
	Amon*	Eliezer
	Josiah*	Joshua
500s B.C.	Jeconiah*	Er
	Shealtiel	Elmadam
	Zerubbabel	Cosam
	Abihud	Addi
	Eliakim	Melchi
	Azor	Neri
	Zadok	Shealtiel
	Achim	Zerubbabel
	Eliud	Rhesa
	Eleazar	Joanan
	Matthan	Joda
	Jacob	Josech
	Joseph-Husband of Mary	Semein
	Jesus 5	Mattathias
		Maath
		Naggi
		Hesli
		Nahum
		Amos
		Mattahias
		Joseph
		Jannai
		Melchi
		Levi
		Matthat
0 A.D.		*Eli-Father of Mary* 6

1 Genesis 5 AMPSB
2 Genesis 10 AMPSB
3 Genesis 11 AMPSB
4 Matthew 1 AMPSB
5 Matthew 1:16 AMPSB
6 Luke 3:23-38 AMPSB
* Kings of Judah

Study Guide

Introduction

1. The introduction claims God exists and has a plan. Do you believe this is true? Either way, why?
2. Do you believe there are two spiritual realms, and why or why not?
3. The world in which we now live is filled with many terrible things. Is God really in control?
4. What role does science play or how does it fit into God's plan?
5. Which theory do you believe best explains the word "day" as used in Genesis and throughout the Bible?

Chapter One   God's Existence

1. How would you explain the factors that lead you to believe there is a God?
2. Explain why you think the Bible is the word of God.
3. Do you think geological evidence supports human life in prehistoric time? What evidence is there?
4. How many religions exist in the world? How many have more than a million believers and which three have the most? How many of the world's people practice one of the five most influential religions, and, what are the five? What two religions do half the population of the world practice? Which religion has the most members?
5. What credibility to God's existence do famous scientists and other people lend by expressing belief in Him?

Chapter Two   God and His Word

1. What is the Torah and who is credited as its writer? Whom was he writing about, and what led to the conclusion that he was the author?
2. What is the purpose for the Bible? Do you think it is the word of God or just a story concocted by religious people? Does it really reveal God's plan?
3. What role do biblical prophecies play in God's plan?
4. What effect does Satan have in God's plan?
5. Explain the analogy of Professor Mouw's idea of the Bible as "God's manufacturer's instructions."

Chapter Three   The Spiritual Realm

1. Do spiritual realms exist? Explain!
2. What proof is there that spiritual realms do or do not exist?
3. Many people say they don't believe in or need a God. Do we need a God and if so, why?
4. Do we have a spiritual component and why?
5. Do you agree with Father Rohr's description of a true Christian?

Chapter Four   A Plan and God's Prophecies

1. What role do prophecies play in the Bible?
2. Why do you think God revealed the prophecies He did?
3. How extensively have prophecies been included in the Bible?

4. If God knew that Satan would hijack His earthly kingdom, why do you think He continued to create it?
5. Why do you think God revealed His plan to us?

Chapter Five   God's Creation

1. Close your eyes. Imagine a loud bang. As you open your eyes, see the light and the earth. Can you fathom God creating the heavens and the earth from nothing?
2. What has quantum physics contributed to our understanding of God's creation in this realm?
3. What do you think would be God's explanation for creating the universe and human life?
4. What is your understanding of how God created the universe?
5. As you read the first chapter of Genesis do you believe it could refer to prehistoric times?
6. Based on your answer to question 5 in the introduction, how long do you think it took God to create the universe? Why?
7. Does it really matter whether there was a prehistoric time, and why do you think God only hinted of a prehistoric time in Genesis 1?
8. Genesis 1 states that the triune God (Father, Son and Holy Spirit) were present at the creation. Do you think all three were active in the Old Testament? Give examples to support your answer.

Chapter Six   Creation or Happenstance?

1. Why does Pastor Mason say even if a big bang did coincide with the creation of earth, it was not a random act?
2. How did God create the universe?
3. What is the evidence of creation?
4. What was the source of light on the first day of creation?
5. Earth has a moon, but is it needed?

Chapter Seven   Life is Created

1. When God created life on earth, what evidence do we have of what it looked like?
2. Do you think the humans created in Chapter 1 of Genesis are exactly like Adam as created in Chapter 2?
3. What was God's first commandment to His creation?
4. Do you believe in evolution of animal and/or human life?
5. What is your understanding of creation in "Our image and likeness"?
6. Read Chapter 1 of Genesis and close the Bible. Where was Adam at this point?
7. Do you think Lucifer possibly was the guardian angel of prehistoric earth, fell into sin, and as a result prehistoric life was destroyed by God and life started over with Adam? Does it matter or is it just speculation?
8. What do we know about God?
9. Do you think it is possible for man to create life without God? Why?
10. Do you agree the geological evidence, as explained by Professor Bjornerud, proves there was life on earth before Adam?

Chapter Eight   God's Day

1. What is your understanding of the length of a "day" as written in the Bible?
2. Why do you think Moses did not include any reference to prehistoric time when he wrote the first five books (Torah) of the Bible?
3. Do you agree the substitution of the term "period" for the word "day" would clarify the understanding of the biblical text?

Chapter Nine   God's Love

1. Why do you think God created the universe?
2. Why do you think God created human-spirits, differing from just human?
3. How would you explain that God is love?

Chapter Ten   Adam Is Created

1. Explain why you think Adam was the same or different than the humans created in Genesis Chapter 1 on the sixth day?
2. Why do you think God gave Adam and all mankind a free will?
3. Since God made man on the sixth day of creation, why does Genesis 2:5 state "there was no man to cultivate the ground," indicating a need for Adam?
4. What is your belief concerning the creation of man in Genesis 1 and 2?
5. If Adam and Eve had eaten only from the Tree of Life instead of the Tree of Good and Evil do you think the eventual outcome would have been different?
6. How would you describe the term, created in His image and likeness?

7. Do you believe everything that happens is
God's will?

Chapter Eleven   Woman Is Created

1. How did Eve receive God's spirit?
2. How would you explain the concept of original
sin?
3. God told Adam and Eve that if they ate from
the Tree of Good and Evil they would die.
Although they did die, they obeyed the first
commandment God made in Genesis. What is
that commandment and what very important
effect did their obedience have?
4. What is the importance of Abraham in God's
plan?
5. While the bloodline of Jesus is traced through
the male members, were they really needed to
implement God's plan?

Chapter Twelve   Conflicting Spiritual Kingdoms

1. All indications are that Lucifer rebelled against God
before Adam was created. Why do you think God
created Adam with the same image and likeness as
Lucifer must have had? Were Lucifer and Adam the
same?

2. Satan has great powers. What is one thing he
cannot do?

3. Pastor Davis cites passages from the book of
Daniel wherein God was delayed in answering
Daniel's prayers because He was busy in
another kingdom. Do you think it is possible

that sometimes God may be delayed in answering our prayers?

4. God said His ways and thinking are not like ours. Do you believe everything that happens on earth is God's will? Can you explain?

5. Do you believe in "spiritual realms" as explained by Pastor Mason?

6. If God is responsible for all that happens, why would His plan to destroy evil, as recorded in Revelation, not be possible?

7. Since God is all-powerful, why do you think He has not destroyed Satan to date?

8. Why do you think the book of Job, even though he was not a prophet, was included in the Bible?

Chapter Thirteen   God's Kingdom

1. Why would an omnipotent, omnipresent, omniscient God create a kingdom on earth, knowing another spiritual realm existed?

2. Do you think God is still here, and if so, is He around as much as He was in biblical times?

3. Do you think following the passages in 1 Peter 2:13-17 is sufficient to maintain God's kingdom on earth?

4. Why are we, or why or we not, living life to the fullness God intended?

5. Did you ever consider that the Revolutionary War was fought to restore God's kingdom in America?

Chapter Fourteen   The War with Evil Begins

1. Do you consider your life to have been a fight since birth, and that each individual has a personal battleground in waging this war?

2. Do you see the Bible as a covenant document from God?

3. The Bible records many instances when God spoke directly to man. Do you believe He still speaks directly with us today?

4. There are several different concepts of the flood's expanse that Noah and his family experienced. Do you think the entire earth was flooded or just that part known at the time? Does it really matter?

5. What was the most significant outcome of the flood?

Chapter Fifteen   God's Chosen People and His Covenants

1. Why do you think God chose Abraham to make a lasting covenant with him and his descendants?

2. Ishmael, Abraham's son to Hagar his maid, is regarded as a prophet and ancestor of Muhammad, founder of Islam (according to Google). Do you think it was God's idea or just Abraham's to father Ishmael?

3. Why was it necessary for God to have a chosen people?

4. Why couldn't God send His Son as a savior if He broke the covenant He made with Abraham?

5. What does the new covenant made with God's Son contain that was not in the one with Abraham?

6. In the covenant with Abraham, God gave the land of Canaan to Abraham and his descendants as their home. Why *that* land?

Chapter Sixteen   Land of Slavery

1. When a famine occurs in Canaan, Jacob moves his entire family to Egypt. He is received by his son Joseph and remains in Egypt. Because His offspring were so numerous they were enslaved. Why do you think God allowed that to happen to His chosen people? (See Genesis 15:13-16, 46:27, Ex 12:37.)
2. Describe God's plan in Moses' life.
3. How does wandering the desert for 40 years after the exodus from Egypt fit into God's plan?
4. Why did God select the land of Canaan for His chosen people? After all, the land was occupied by other tribes.
5. Considering the obstacles encountered in the land of Canaan, what does God's selection of it reveal?

Chapter Seventeen   Israelites and God and the Promised Land

1. Why do you think God wanted to live among His chosen people?
2. What makes the Israelites and us right with God?
3. What was the function of a judge?
4. Are we any different from the Israelites and their propensity to sin, repent and sin again, going through life in a circle of worship of God?
5. Are we like the Israelites—wanting God's favor but not His guidance?
6. Do you agree with Solomon's assessment of the life of a human?
7. Why was the temple such an important place for the Israelites, and the church for us?
8. What is this chapter's main point?

Chapter Eighteen   Time of Prophets

1. How does this period reveal part of God's plan?
2. What is the significance and why does God insist on building a temple in the Old Testament?
3. What does God require to make man acceptable to Him?
4. How is the present-day church similar to the Old Testament temple?
5. Why do you think God was so specific in His directions for making sacrifices?
6. What is the importance of atonement to God?
7. Do you think most Christians employ the lessons of the wisdom books in their daily life?
8. What is the key point of Jonah's story?
9. What is the significance of the division of the House of David in God's plan?
10. Why is it important to read the Old Testament before becoming a Christian?

Chapter Nineteen   A Savior Is Given

1. What role does Jesus play in the battle between good and evil?
2. Do you see God, Himself, in the person of Jesus, coming to this earth to live as a human to save mankind, as Pastor Kinley writes?
3. Why did God have to impregnate a virgin for Jesus to be born?
4. Why do you think God chose the time He did for His life on earth?
5. How would you explain the triune God to a nonbeliever?

6.   What is the most important effect of the Crucifixion for us today?
7.   Were Pilate and the Jewish leaders who had Jesus crucified evil or unknowingly just carrying out God's plan?
8.   What is the importance of Jesus' resurrection?
9.   What was the divine revelation given to Paul, and how does it impact us?
10. Why do Christians worship Jesus and continue to wait for His second coming?

Chapter Twenty   The Battle for God's Kingdom:
                  The Spread of   Christianity

1.   With more than a billion nonbelievers, do you think the church (body of believers) spread the gospel as Christ commanded?
2.   Why would you agree, or not, with Pastor Qureshi's point that the apostle Paul's epistles may have been very instrumental in separating Christianity from Judaism and Islam?
3.   When and why did religious freedom start in the Roman empire?
4.   Matthew 10:34 records Jesus' statement that "He did not come to bring peace to the world but to divide it." What did He mean?
5.   What was a major dilemma for early Christians, especially the Crusaders? How do we deal with it today?
6.   Why do you think the Crusaders were necessary?
7.   How does the spread of Christianity fit into God's plan?

Chapter Twenty-One   God is One God for All

1.   Are you surprised by Rabbi Donin's outline of the Jewish belief that God is a God of all and is

not out to make Jews of all the world as
written in this chapter?
2. In spite of all their disobedience God leads the
Jews back to the promised land in 1946. What
do you make of that?
3. Why do you think God included the gentiles in
His kingdom and made them part of His
chosen people?
4. Considering the similarities between
Christianity and Islam, what makes us so
different?
5. God has plainly told us what we must do to be
saved at judgment time. What is *that*?

Chapter Twenty-Two   The Plan Is Fulfilled

1. What is the plan?
2. What makes it possible for sinners to spend
eternity with God?
3. When will the plan be completed?
4. Hopefully this book has clearly detailed the
who, what and when of God's plan. Can you
explain the why?
5. Can we escape judgment and punishment for
our sins?

Chapter Twenty-Three   The Logic of Belief

1. Is it logical to believe in a God we cannot see in
a world filled with evil?
2. What if anything would you add to the logic
statements made in this chapter and in Chart
3?
3. The apostle Paul in Romans tells us we have no
excuse for not knowing God. Why?

Chapter Twenty-Four   The Plan

1. What do you believe the major steps are in God's plan?
2. What do you think God's plan is for you?
3. What evidence can you cite for believing?

Part 2

Chapter Twenty-Five   Life as We Know It

1. Often we hear, "Why do I need God and His plan?" Do we?
2. When life is not going well for you, do you ask the same questions Pastor Davis posed in "Quantum Christianity," and if so how do you answer them?
3. Looking back over your life, what major trials have you had to deal with, and how were they solved?
4. Do you agree with Pastor Hamilton that God does not control our every action? Why?
5. With so many suicides, do you believe that God will not let us be tempted beyond our ability to resist?
6. Do you agree with Pastor Zimmerman's perception of trials bringing joy to a Christian's life?

Chapter Twenty-Six   How Do We Cope with This Life?

1. Knowing evil exists, why do we tend to blame God when troubles arise?
2. How does knowing God help us to understand our life?
3. Pastor Mason states that God created everything using a mathematical number called the Golden Ratio. Have you ever considered math as part of understanding

God? Do you see a connection with Paul's letter to the Romans 1:20-22?

4. Why does Pastor Qureshi say "loving others is what makes us truly human"?
5. Why is evil such a large part of life?
6. How does learning from science help us understand God?
7. Do you see your life as a daily battle with evil and, if so, how do you explain it?

Chapter Twenty-Seven   What Difference Does It Make Whether I Believe?

1. What do you say when asked, "What difference does believing make?"
2. How do we avoid the consequences of our sins and eternal death?
3. What is the significance of Jesus' encounter with a man harboring an evil spirit as described in Mark's gospel?
4. Do you see any importance in "waiting" for the Lord to answer prayers as Pastor Davis outlined? What experience did you have while waiting? Do you think that often we don't expect God will answer our prayer?
5. Do you think God always answers your prayers?

Chapter Twenty-Eight   Why Should I Believe Right Now?

1. Is it critical to become a believer right this moment?
2. Does 2 Timothy 3:1-5 describe life today or life throughout history?
3. If we have religion, doesn't that make us acceptable to God?
4. Islam and Christianity share many similar beliefs. What is their main difference?
5. Do you really need a religion?

6. What is the bottom line to find favor with God?

7. Do you think we practice Jesus' command to spread the gospel or was that command just to His apostles?

8. In what way do you consider yourself part of God's plan?

9. Why are the prophecies that came true sufficient to convince anyone that the Bible is the true word of God?

10. Major events in the Bible happened about every 2,000 years. Should we be concerned we are in the final hour?

Chapter Twenty-Nine   What Should I Believe?

1. Is a belief in a God enough to live without fear of judgment day?

2. Why do you think you should believe the eight things listed in this chapter?

3. What does Pastor Davis' physical=spiritual relativity equation mean?

4. Do you see Satan at work in your life?

5. Does God ask a lot of believers?

6. Where does the Roman road in Paul's letter to the Romans end?

7. How do we make our faith authentic?

Chapter Thirty   The Book of Life

1. What characterizes a personal relationship with Jesus?

2. Do you think your name appears in the Book of Life?

3. Why should God's judgment scare you?

4. Considering your life to date, do you know what God's plan is for you?

5. Can you make any changes that would alter
    God's plan for you?

Notes

A Personal Note
1. Pastor Aaron Davis, Quantum Christianity, pg. 169

Introduction
1. Dr. Lawrence Richards, The Teacher's Commentary, pg. 23-24

Chapter One   God's Existence
1.   The following is from Holman Old Testament Commentary, Genesis, Vol. 1, pg. 8 God created the world in six days, speaking everything into existence. The creation account in Genesis shows us that God existed before all, God has made all, and therefore God deserves all our obedience and adoration. This creation account is foundational for our understanding of who God is and what place we as humans occupy in His plan.
"A house testifies that there was a builder, a dress that there was a weaver, a door that there was a carpenter; so our world by its existence proclaims its Creator, God."   Rabbi Akiba Ben Joseph
2. Rabbi Hayim Halevy Donin, To be a Jew, pg. 18
3. Pastor Jeff Kinley, Wake the Bride, pg. 114
4. Kenneth O. Gangel and Stephen J. Bramer; Max Anders, and general editor, Holman Old Testament Commentary, Genesis, pg. 10: Ps 19:1-4
5. The Amplified Study Bible, footnote, pg. 1
6. Pastor Phil Mason, Quantum Glory, pg. 110, 119, 120
7. Holman Old Testament Commentary, Genesis, Vol. 1, pg. 17
8. Genesis 1:27 AMPSB
9. Father Richard Rohr, The Universal Christ, pg. 49-50
10. Adherents, an independent, nonreligiously affiliated organization that monitors the number and size of the world's religions—The Register
11 Pastor Adam Hamilton, The Creed, What Christians Believe and Why, pg. 22-23
12. Davis, Quantum Christianity, pg. 3
13. ibid., pg. 106
14. Stephen Miller, The Complete Guide to the Bible, pg. 379
15. Mason, Quantum Glory, pg. 98-99
16. Cristobal Krusen, They Were Christians, pg. 7

Chapter Two   God and His Word
1. Halley's Bible Handbook (1965, 24th edition), pg. 58

2. Miller, The Complete Guide to the Bible, pg. 9
(See Miller's book for the entire report)
3. Mason, Quantum Glory, pg. 152
4. Davis, Quantum Christianity, pg.16
5. ibid., pg. 32
6. ibid., pg. 178
7. Mason, Quantum Glory, pg. 36, 152
8. Pastor J. Vincent Nordgren, The Heart of the Bible, pg. 13
9. Public Broadcasting System, Fires of Faith, aired April 5, 2020

Chapter Three   Spiritual Realm
1. Davis, Quantum Christianity, pg. 71 (See Davis' note 20)
2. Mason, Quantum Glory, pg. 120
3. ibid., pg. **93**
4. AMPSB Topical Index, pg. 2,100
5. Davis, Quantum Christianity, pg. 183
6. John 18:36 NIV
7. Mason, Quantum Glory, pg. 93
8. ibid., pg. 356-7
9. Rohr, The Universal Christ, pg. 30
10. John 1:4 AMPSB
11. Rohr, The Universal Christ, pg. 30
12. Revelation 20:11-15 NIV

Chapter Four A Plan and God's Prophecies
1. Genesis 3:17 AMPSB
2. ibid., 6:17 AMP
3. ibid., 13:16 AMPSB
4. Micah 5:2-5 AMPSB
5. Isaiah 7:14 AMPSB
6. Jeremiah 29:11 AMPSB
7. ibid., 31:31-34
8. Daniel 7 AMPSB
9. Life Application Bible Commentary, Revelation, pg. 4
10. Kinley, Wake the Bride, pg. 64-65
11. Chaplain Orville J. Nave, A.M., D.D., LL.D., Nave's Topical Bible, copyright 1897, pg. 1,009 (Work based on the King James Version)
12. Kinley, Wake the Bride, pg. 25
13. ibid., pg. 11
14. Davis, Quantum Christianity, pg. 141
15. Mason, Quantum Glory, pg. 58-59
16. Davis, Quantum Christianity, pg. 173-174
17. ibid., pg. 239

18. Kinley, Wake the Bride, pg. 25- 26
19. Hebrews 1:3 NLT
20. Ephesians 1:9-10: "God has now revealed to us His mysterious plan regarding Christ, a plan to fulfill His own good pleasure. And this is the plan: At the right time He will bring everything together under the authority of Christ—everything in Heaven and earth."
21. Kinley, Wake the Bride, pg. 30
22. Jeremiah 18:6-8 AMPSB
23. Zechariah 14:9 AMPSB

Chapter Five   God's Creation
1. Mason, Quantum Glory, pg. 209-210
2. ibid., pg. 230
3. ibid., pg. 120
4. ibid., pg. 124
5. Davis, Quantum Christianity, pg. 71
6. Mason, Quantum Glory, pg. 236
7. Davis, Quantum Christianity, pg. 84
8. Miller, The Complete Guide to the Bible, pg. 379
9. Davis, Quantum Christianity, pg. 143
10. Holman Old Testament Commentary, Genesis, Vol. 1, pg. 3
11. Davis, Quantum Christianity, pg. 148-149
12. ibid., pg. 151
13. Halley's Bible Handbook, 13th edition, pg. 60
14. Zondervan Handbook to the Bible, third edition, pg. 116
15. TV sitcom, Big Bang Theory, 2007-18
16. Davis, Quantum Christianity, pg. 141, 142
17. Holman Old Testament Commentary, Genesis, Vol. 1, pg. 18
18. Davis, Quantum Christianity, pg. 149
19. Holman Old Testament Commentary, Genesis, Vol. 1, pg. 19
20. Rohr, The Universal Christ, pg. 12

Chapter Six   Creation or Happenstance?
1. Holman Old Testament Commentary, Genesis, Vol. 1, pg 16
"The creation story refutes atheism because it declares the existence of God; it refutes macroevolution because it states that God created all things; it refutes pantheism because it shows that God is separate from creation; it refutes eternality of matter because there was a beginning to creation; it refutes fatalism because there is purpose to creation. ...Genesis gives us the 'what' of creation. The 'how' is assumed [established] by the concept of 'God said... and it was so.'

"This demonstrates the sovereignty of and the fact that we as finite creatures will never know everything. Sometimes
we experience delays in the fulfillment of God's promises, but this only reflects our finite understanding of the divine plan."

2. Mason, Quantum Glory, pg. 201-202
3. ibid., pg. 28, 54
4. Davis, Quantum Christianity, pg. 211
5. Genesis 1:3 AMPSB
6. Holman Old Testament Commentary, Genesis, Vol. 1, pg. 11-12
7. Hamilton, Creed, pg. 25
8. Genesis 1:6-13 AMPSB
9. ibid., 1:14, 19 AMPSB
10. Google search
11. Davis, Quantum Christianity, pg. 255-256
12. Miller, The Complete Guide to the Bible, pg. 379

Chapter Seven   Life is Created
1. Davis, Quantum Christianity, pg. 149
2. Hugh Ross, The Creator and the Cosmos, pg. 168-169
3. Genesis 1:1-14 AMPSB
4. Holman Old Testament Commentary, Genesis, Vol. 1, pg. 11
5. Genesis 1:20-22 AMPSB
6. The New Book of Knowledge 7/G, pg. 113
7. Probe.Org, July 17, 2015, Ann Gauger, Science and Human Origins
8. Time Life Books, The Emergence of Man series, published in New York, 1973
9. Genesis 1:1 AMPSB, footnote, pg. 1
10. Dr. William Barclay, Letter to the Romans, pg.18, 21
11. Dan Brown, Origin, pg. 527-528
12. ibid., pg. 547, 550
13. ibid., pg. 581
14. ibid., pg. 541
15. Professor Marcia Bjornerud, Timelessness, pg. 9

Chapter Eight   God's Day
1. Genesis 1:14-19 NIV
2. Genesis 1: 26-31 AMPSB

Chapter Nine   God's Love
1. Davis, Quantum Christianity, pg. 156
2. Pastor Nabeel Qureshi, No God But One, pg. 35
3. Erin with Jill Kelly, Kelly Tough, pg. 74-76
4. Reckless Love, written by Cory Asbury, Caleb Culver, Ron

Jackson. Bethel Music Publishing
5. John Eldredge, Waking the Dead, pg. 40-41

Chapter Ten   Adam Is Created
1. Genesis 2:7 AMPSB
2. Davis, Quantum Christianity, pg.153-154
3. Mason, Quantum Glory, pg. 132-133, 135
4. Davis, Quantum Christianity, pg. 41
5. Even though Adam was created in God's image and likeness as a spirit-being, man cannot create physical beings by simply saying the words as God did.
6. John 20:22; Acts 3:6-8 AMP
7. But man is not merely of this earth. He is a combination of dust and divinity. Genesis 2:7 records that the Lord God **breathed into his nostrils the breath of life, and man became a living being.** It was God who gave man a unique life. Animals had life, too, but man had a portion of deity within him because he was made "in the image of God."
8. Mason, Quantum Glory, pg. 271
9. Davis, Quantum Christianity, pg. 98   From Ralph Allan Smith, The Covenantal Structure of the Bible (revised edition) copyright 2006, Ralph Allan Smith covenant Worldview Institute Tokyo, Japan http://berith.org/pdf/ The Covenantal Structure of the Bible, pdf, pg. 23
10. Davis, Quantum Christianity, pg. 157
11. Hamilton, Half Truths, pg. 42, 43, 133

Chapter Eleven   Woman Is Created
1. Davis, Quantum Christianity, pg. 155
2. Genesis 2:17 AMP
3. ibid., 3:4 AMP
4. ibid., 3:16-17 AMP
5. ibid., 5:1-32 AMP
6. ibid., 6:8; 9:29 AMPSB
7. ibid., 11:32 AMPSB
8. ibid., 9:19 AMPSB
9. ibid., 12:12-20; 12:5 AMPSB
10. ibid., 16:2 AMPSB
11. ibid., 17:2-9 AMPSB
12. 2 Samuel 5:14 AMPSB
13. ibid., 11:4-17 AMPSB
14. Matthew 1:18 AMPSB

Chapter Twelve   Conflicting Spiritual Kingdoms
1. Mason, Quantum Glory, pg. 240-241
2. Davis, Quantum Christianity, pg. 143
3. ibid., pg. 203
4. Mason, Quantum Glory, pg. 242-244
5. Davis, Quantum Christianity, pg. 87
6. Kinley, Wake the Bride, pg. 160
7. Mason, Quantum Glory, pg. 106
8. Davis, Quantum Christianity, pg. 201
9. ibid., pg 206 Cited from Pastor Jurgen Mathesius, PUSH, pg. 146
10. Hamilton, Half Truths, pg. 17, 19
11. Davis, Quantum Christianity, pg. 206-207
12. ibid., pg. 221
13. Mason, Quantum Glory, pg. 93
14. Francis A. Schaeffer, A Christian Manifesto, pg. 27-28
15. Revelation 20:14 LAB
16. Life Application Bible Commentary, Revelation, pg. 250
17. Genesis 3:1 AMPSB
18. Matthew 4:2 AMPSB
19. AMPSB, pg. 790
20. Job 1:1 NIV
21. ibid., 42:12 NIV
22. ibid., 38:4 AMPSB
23. Miller, The Complete Guide to the Bible, pg. 148
24. Davis, Quantum Christianity, pg. 175
25. Job 42:10-17 AMPSB

Chapter Thirteen God's Kingdom
1. Davis, Quantum Christianity, pg. 171
2. Qureshi, No God But One, pg. 81
3. Acts 2:39 AMPSB
4. Davis, Quantum Christianity, pg. 155
5. John 3:16-17 AMPSB
6. Davis, Quantum Christianity, pg. 88
7. Schaeffer, A Christian Manifesto, pg. 91

Chapter Fourteen   The War with Evil Begins
1. Davis, Quantum Christianity, pg. 62 Paraphrased from Bill
   Johnson, When Heaven Invades Earth, (Expanded Edition) A Practical
   Guide to a Life of Miracles, pg. 30-31 digital edition
2. Davis, Quantum Christianity, pg. 88
3. Genesis 3: 16-19 AMPSB
4. Hamilton, Half Truths, pg. 45

5. Davis, Quantum Christianity, pg. 64
6. Hamilton, Half Truths, pg. 19-20, 22, 33
7. Genesis 5:24; 2 Kings 2:11-12 AMPSB
8. Genesis 6:14 AMPSB
9. Genesis 9:16 NIV
10. Miller, The Complete Guide to the Bible, pg. 15
11. Genesis 10:1-32 NIV
12. Miller, The Complete Guide to the Bible, pg. 120
13. Holman Old Testament Commentary, Genesis, Vol. 1, pg. 56, 59, 63

Chapter Fifteen   God's Chosen People and His Covenants
1. Mason, Quantum Glory, pg. 104
2. Rabbi Donin, To Be a Jew, pg. 19
3. Genesis 17:4, 25:17 AMPSB
4. ibid., 17:7 AMPSB
5. ibid. 17:8
6. Davis, Quantum Christianity, pg. 60
7. ibid., pg. 61
8. Hebrews 6:13-18 NIV
9. Genesis 19:24-26 AMPSB
10. ibid., 22:12
11. ibid., 27:33; 29:30; 32:28
12. ibid., 36:8
13. ibid., 35:1

Chapter Sixteen   Land of Slavery
1. Genesis 35:23-26 AMPSB
2. ibid., 37:36
3. ibid., 38:2
4. ibid., 41:40
5. ibid., 46:7
6. Exodus 1:13 AMPSB
7. ibid., 1:32
8. ibid., 2:2-6
9. ibid., 2:11-12
10. ibid., 12:32
11. ibid., 20:1-17
12. ibid., 16:35
13. Miller, The Complete Guide to the Bible, pg. 28
14. ibid., pg. 58
15. Deuteronomy 34:4 AMPSB
16. ibid., 34:10-12   Moses dies (Joshua 1:2), but nothing is recorded

about an afterlife until the New Testament. Jesus is on a high mountain with the disciples Peter, James and John. As Jesus' appearance changed to "white as light" Moses appears with Elijah from heaven, (Matthew 17:3 AMPSB). Although the Old Testament did not say Moses died and went to heaven, the New Testament reveals he did at some point. Even though Moses was not in the bloodline of God's Son Jesus, God gave Moses a very high tribute: "Since that time no prophet has risen in Israel like Moses, whom the Lord knew face to face, [none equal to him] in all the signs and wonders which the Lord sent him to perform in the land of Egypt against Pharaoh, all his servants, and all his land, and in all the mighty power and all the great and terrible deeds which Moses performed in the sight of all Israel."

17. Genesis 10:6,19 AMPSB   Canaan was a son of Ham, Noah's son. Canaan settled in the territory extending from Sidon as one goes to Gerar; as far as Gaza; and as one goes to Sodom and Gomorrah [southern shore of the Dead Sea] and Admah and Zeboiim and as far [probably north] as Lasha; or Genesis 15:18 On the same day the Lord made a covenant (promise, pledge) with Abram, saying "To your descendants I have given this Land, From the river in Egypt to the great river Euphrates…."
18. Miller, The Complete Guide to the Bible, pg. 17
19. Genesis 3:24 AMPSB
20. Zondervan Handbook to the Bible, pg. 36
21. ibid., pg. 214
22. Genesis 12:9-10 AMPSB
23. ibid., 13:1 AMPSB
24. ibid., 46:7 AMPSB
25. Deuteronomy 34:1 AMPSB
26. Joshua 1:2 AMPSB
27. Miller, The Complete Guide to the Bible, pg. 95
28. Judges 3-10 AMPSB
29. Miller, The Complete Guide to the Bible, pg. 239-240
30. Google search
31. ibid

Chapter Seventeen   Israelites and God in the Promised Land
1. Exodus 25:8-9 NLT
2. Leviticus 19:18 AMPSB
3. ibid., 26:11, 33 AMPSB
4. Judges 2:10-11 AMPSB
5. ibid., 2:16-19
6. Nordgren, The Heart of the Bible, pg. 61

7. Miller, The Complete Guide to the Bible, pg. 73
8. ibid., pg. 71
9. Esther 9:26-28, AMPSB note, pg. 789
10. Ruth 4:17 AMPSB
11. 1 Samuel 8:5 AMPSB
12. ibid., 13:1
13. ibid., 31:6
14. AMPSB, pg. 843
15. Proverbs 1:1-7 AMPSB
16. 2 Samuel 11:15 AMPSB
17. 1 Kings 3:12 AMPSB
18. Miller, The Complete Guide to the Bible, pg. 170
19. ibid., pg.101
20. ibid., pg 131
21. Esther 8:3 AMPSB
22. Miller, The Complete Guide to the Bible, pg .131
23. ibid., pg. 283
24. Ezra 10:10-11 AMPSB
25. Miller, The Complete Guide to the Bible, pg .130

Chapter Eighteen   Time of Prophets
1. Miller, The Complete Guide to the Bible, pg. 261-292
2. Leviticus 1:3 AMPSB
3. Malachi 1:13 NLB
4. Miller, The Complete Guide to the Bible, pg. 283
5. ibid., pg. 293
6. Leviticus 27:30, 32 AMPSB
7. Miller, The Complete Guide to the Bible, pg. 464
8. AMPSB, pg. 843, 994
9. Miller, The Complete Guide to the Bible, pg. 254
10. Jonah 1:2 AMPSB
11. Miller, The Complete Guide to the Bible, pg. 258
12. 2 Chronicles 10:16 AMPSB
13. Nordgren, The Heart of the Bible, pg. 77, 83
14. ibid., pg. 83
15. Davis, Quantum Christianity, pg. 69
16. Miller, The Complete Guide to the Bible, pg. 301

Chapter Nineteen   A Savior Is Given
1. Miller, The Complete Guide to the Bible, pg. 335
2. Matthew 4:17 AMPSB

3. Leviticus 19:18 AMPSB

4. Davis, Quantum Christianity, pg. 173-174

5. Miller, The Complete Guide to the Bible, pg. 460

6. Kinley, Wake the Bride, pg. 29

7. Davis, Quantum Christianity, pg. 204-205

8. ibid., pg. 174

9. Mason, Quantum Glory, pg. 307

10. Miller, The Complete Guide to the Bible, pg. 381

11. Matthew 28:6 AMPSB

12. ibid., 3:17

13. John 1:1 AMPSB

14. Qureshi, No God But One, pg. 56

15. ibid., pg. 62-163

16. ibid., pg. 169

17. ibid., pg. 188-189

18. ibid., pg. 153

19. Mark 9:31 AMPSB

20. Qureshi, No God But One, pg. 214-215

21. Isaiah 63:11-13 AMPSB

22. Luke 1:35 AMPSB

23. Acts 9:17 AMPSB

24. The apostle Paul wrote: "God has now revealed to us His mysterious plan regarding Christ, a plan to fulfill His own good pleasure. And this is the plan: At the right time He will bring everything together under the authority of Christ—everything in Heaven and earth." (Ephesians 1:9-10 NLT)

25. John 14:26 AMPSB

26. Matthew 4:23; 8:32; 20:34; Mark 10:52 AMPSB; John 11:17-45 AMPSB

27. John 11:43 AMPSB

28. Barclay, Letter to the Romans, pg. 63-64

29. Matthew 28:19 AMPSB

30. Mason, Quantum Glory, pg. 169

31. Matthew 26:26-28 AMPSB

32. Mason, Quantum Glory, pg. 300-301

33. Barclay, Letter to the Romans, pg.49

34. Miller, The Complete Guide to the Bible, pg. 433

35. ibid., pg. 462-3

36. Life Application Bible Commentary, Revelation 7:4-8 NIV, pg. 85

37. Genesis 1:1 AMPSB

38. Matthew 1:18-23 AMPSB

39. Rohr, The Universal Christ, pg. 19

40. ibid., pg. 20-21

41. ibid., pg. 27

Chapter Twenty   The Battle for God's Kingdom: The Spread of
            Christianity
1. AMPSB, Topical Index, pg. 2,103
2. In the New Testament, churches meant a local congregation or
   the body of Christ, the universal church—a called-out-group.
   AMPSB, pg. 1,777
3. Miller, The Complete Guide to the Bible, pg. 370
4. The New Book of Knowledge, pg. 159 This reference is from a
   set of encyclopedias published in the 1960s and sold door to
   door to build a home reference library.
5. Qureshi, No God But One, pg. 198, 205
6. ibid., pg. 75
7. New Book of Knowledge, 3 C, pg. 489
8. ibid., pg. 489
9. ibid., 2B, pg. 483
10. ibid., 3C, pg. 289
11. ibid., 3C, pg. 538
12. Qureshi, No God But One, pg. 131
13. New Book of Knowledge, 3 C, pg. 538-539
14. Matthew 26:52 AMPSB
15. Exodus 20:13 AMPSB
16. Qureshi, No God But One, pg. 139
17. Dan Jones, The Templars, pg. 45-46
18. Qureshi, No God But One, pg. 139
19. New Book of Knowledge, 3 C, pg. 540
20. ibid., 3 C, pg. 288-298
21. ibid., 16 Q-R, pg. 294
22. ibid., 11 C, pg. 378
23. ibid., 2 B, pg. 156
24. William Willimon, Why I Am a United Methodist, pg. 12, 16- 17
25. Bible Gateway APP/Google search
26. The Register/Google
27. Kinley, Wake the Bride, pg. 152

Chapter Twenty-One God Is One God for All
1. Donin, To Be a Jew, pg. 8
2. ibid., pg. 8
3. ibid., pg 10-12
4. Exodus 20:2-4 AMPSB
5. Miller, The Complete Guide to the Bible, pg. 216
6. Revelation 20:15 AMPSB
7. Matthew 28:19 AMPSB

8. Nordgren, The Heart of the Bible, pg. 189
9. Davis, Quantum Christianity, pg. 166-167
10. ibid., pg. 166
11. Qureshi, No God But One, pg. 33
12. ibid., pg. 30-31
13. Revelation 20:15 Only the names of those who have accepted Jesus Christ as their Savior will be found in the Book of Life. The rejection of the eternal gospel results in eternal condemnation. AMPSB, pg. 2,080

Chapter Twenty-Two The Plan Is Fulfilled
1. Miller, The Complete Guide to the Bible, pg. 411
2. Pastor Davis, Quantum Christianity, pg. 89-90
3. ibid., pg. 114
4. Revelation 1:7 AMPSB
5. ibid., 14:7
6. Miller, The Complete Guide to the Bible, pg. 510
7. Revelation 1:7 AMPSB
8. Jude 14-15 AMPSB
9. Revelation 20:12-15 AMPSB
10. ibid., 3:10 AMPSB
11. Kinley, Wake the Bride, pg. 57
12. ibid., pg. 83
13. Mark 13:32 AMPSB
14. Genesis 1:28 AMPSB
15. Bjornerud, Timefulness, pg. 11

Chapter Twenty-Three   The Logic of Belief
1. Hamilton, Half Truths. pg. 93
2. John 12:45 AMPSB
3. Dr. Charles Stanley, TV evangelist
4. Zimmerman, A Family Guide to Joy, pg. 10
5. Miller, The Complete Guide to the Bible, pg. 393
6. Life Application Bible Commentary, Revelation, pg. 43, 272 These passages from Revelation are fundamental to understanding God's plan: "Because you have patiently obeyed Me despite the persecution, I will protect you from the Great Tribulation and temptation, which will come upon the world to test everyone alive." (TLB 3:10).
"Behold, I am coming soon, and I shall bring My wages *and* rewards with Me to repay *and* render to each one just what his own actions *and* his own work merit." (AMP 22:12) The Book of Revelation clearly tells the reader of God's plan to judge all and to reward those who believe in Him with eternal life in His kingdom.

7. Romans 1:20 AMP

Chapter Twenty-Four The Plan
1. Ephesians 1:5 AMPSB
2. Hebrews 8:10-12, footnote, pg. 1,994-95 AMPSB
3. Matthew 18:11 AMP
4. Miller, The Complete Guide to the Bible, pg. 489
5. Romans 12:9-13 NIV
6. Barclay, The Letter to the Romans, pg. 178
7. Donin, To Be A Jew, pg.19-20

Part 2
Chapter Twenty-Five   Life as We Know It
1. Davis, Quantum Christianity, pg. 25-26, 29-30
2. ibid., pg. .30
3. Zimmerman, A Family Guide to Joy, pg. 126
4. Miller, The Complete Guide to the Bible, pg. 379
5. Hamilton, Half Truths, pg. 42-43
6. 1 Thessalonians 2:12 AMP
7. Miller, The Complete Guide to the Bible, pg. 434
8. Zimmerman, A Family Guide to Joy, pg. 7
9. ibid., pg. 8
10. C.S. Lewis, Mere Christianity, pg. 53
11. Ephesians 6:13-17 AMPSB

Chapter Twenty-Six   How do We Cope with This Life?
1. Davis, Quantum Christianity, pg. 125
2. ibid., pg. 150
3. Mason, Quantum Glory, pg 185, 188
4. ibid., pg. 230, 211
5. Genesis 1:1-2 AMP
6. Genesis 1:5-16 AMPSB
7. ibid., 1:26 AMPSB
8. Qureshi, No God But One, pg. 71
9. Genesis 3:1 AMPSB footnote, pg. 6 Without introduction, Satan appears in the Garden of Eden. This is the first clue in Scripture of creation outside the one Adam and Eve experience. Note that Eve expressed no surprise at the serpent speaking to her in intelligible language.
10. Genesis 3: 17-24 AMPSB
11. John MacArthur, The Gospel according to Paul, pg. 28
12. ibid., pg. 80
13. Qureshi, No God But One, pg. 45-46

Chapter Twenty-Seven What Difference Does It Make Whether I
Believe?
1. Romans 3:10-18 AMPSB
2. Romans 3:23 NIV
3. MacArthur, The Gospel According to Paul, pg. 29
4. ibid., pg. 28
5. ibid., pg. 83
6. ibid., pg. 9-22
7. Mason, Quantum Glory, pg. 313
8. Davis, Quantum Christianity, pg. 126
9. Mason, Quantum Glory, pg. 308
10. Revelation Chapter 6 AMPSB
11. Life Application Bible Commentary, Revelation, pg. xxiv
12. ibid., pg. 167
13. Miller, The Complete Guide to the Bible, pg. 292

Chapter Twenty-Eight   Why Should I Believe Right Now?
1. Donin, To Be a Jew, pg. 11-12
2. Qureshi, No God But One, pg. 36
3. Donin, To Be a Jew, pg. 22
4. Qureshi, No God But One, pg. 30-31
5. ibid., pg. 33
6. 1 John 2:1 NIV
7. Miller, The Complete Guide to the Bible, pg. 497
8. Romans 12:7 AMP
9. 2 Peter 1:3-4 NIV
10. Donin, To Be a Jew, pg. 23-24
11. Matthew 26-28 KJV

Chapter Twenty-Nine What Should I Believe?
1. Zimmerman, A Family Guide to Joy, pg. 156
2. Davis, Quantum Christianity, pg. 209-210
3. ibid., pg. 173-174
4. Revelation 2:5 AMP
5. AMPSB, footnote, Ecclesiastes 3:1-15, pg. 1,054
6. John 3:3 AMP
7. Miller, The Complete Guide to the Bible, pg.156
8. Barclay, The Letter to the Romans, pg.176
9. Kellys, Kelly Tough, pg. 17

10. Pastor Phil Munsey, Legacy Now, pg. 52
   11. Kellys, Kelly Tough, pg. 86,88
    12. ibid., pg. 209-213
    13. Rohr, The Universal Christ, pg. 42, 51

    Chapter Thirty The Book of Life
    1. Revelation 3:6 AMPSB
    2. Davis, Quantum Christianity, pg. 123-124
    3. ibid., pg. 224
    4. Life Application Bible Commentary, Revelation, pg. 250
    5. Romans 10:9 AMPSB
    6. 1 John 5:14 NIV
    7. Matthew 6:9-13 NIV
    8. Kinley, Wake the Bride, pg.83- 87
    9. Revelation 9:18 AMPSB
   10. ibid., 21:7
   11. Kinley, Wake the Bride, pg. 116-117
   12. Miller, The Complete Guide to the Bible, pg. 380
   13. Barbara Johnson, We Break For Joy, pg. 39

    Appendix A
    1. Rohr, The Universal Christ, pg. 103

    Chart 2 Notes

    1. Note 1.1
    2. Note 5.16
    3. Chart 1
    4. The First Man, Time-life Books, Time Inc., copyright 1973
    5. Google search
    6. There have been many computations for the birth of Adam. 6000
       B.C. is used by most scholars as a baseline.   Based solely on the
       genealogies in Genesis, Holman Old Testament, Genesis records
       the earth's formation at 6,176 years ago. There is no indication
       that Adam was created at the exact time as the earth... . In Genesis
       5:5 Adam is recorded to live 930 years.
    7. Genesis 5:4
    8. ibid., 5:3-32 (Adam's death to Noah's birth)
    9. ibid., 8:13
   10. ibid., 9:28
   11. Exact date not recorded
   12. Genesis 17:1

13. ibid., 17:7
14. ibid., 25:7
15. Life Application Study Bible, NIV 1997, Chronology pg. xv
16. ibid., pg. xvi
17. Deuteronomy 34:5-7
18. Books of Joshua-Judges 3:9
19. LASB, pg. xvi
20. 1 Kings
21. LASB, pg. xvi-xvii
22. ibid., pg. xviii
23. Miller, Complete Guide to the Bible, pg. 206
24. Zondervan Handbook Timeline, pg. 29
25. ibid., pg. 29
26. LASB, pg. xxi
27. ibid., pg. xxi
28. ibid., pg. xxi
29. ibid., pg. xxii
30. ibid., pg. xxiii
31. See Note 20:10
32. Matthew 1:25
33. See Note 20:8
34. See Note 20:9
35. See Note 20:24

About the Author

A graduate of the United States Naval Academy and the University of Colorado with a Masters in Civil Engineering and a Minor in Geology, Don Sheaffer served as a commissioned officer in the United States Navy Civil Engineer Corps for 24 and a half years. Don and his wife, Belva, and all of their married children and grandchildren live in Derry Township, PA.

" 'O Lord, You have examined my heart and know everything about me…. Every moment, You know where I am….You know what I am going to say before I even say it…. I can *never* be lost to Your Spirit. I can *never* get away from my [yours and the *only*] God.' "

Excerpt from Psalm 139:1-6 TLB

Your life matters to God.

www.ingramcontent.com/pod-product-compliance
Lightning Source LLC
Chambersburg PA
CBHW060920040426
42445CB00011B/712